Beyond the Learning Curve

Beyond the Learning Curve
The construction of mind

Craig P. Speelman
School of Psychology
Edith Cowan University
Perth, Australia

Kim Kirsner
School of Psychology
University of Western Australia
Perth, Australia

OXFORD
UNIVERSITY PRESS

OXFORD
UNIVERSITY PRESS

Great Clarendon Street, Oxford OX2 6DP

Oxford University Press is a department of the University of Oxford.
It furthers the University's objective of excellence in research, scholarship,
and education by publishing worldwide in

Oxford New York

Auckland Cape Town Dar es Salaam Hong Kong Karachi
Kuala Lumpur Madrid Melbourne Mexico City Nairobi
New Delhi Shanghai Taipei Toronto

With offices in

Argentina Austria Brazil Chile Czech Republic France Greece
Guatemala Hungary Italy Japan Poland Portugal Singapore
South Korea Switzerland Thailand Turkey Ukraine Vietnam

Oxford is a registered trade mark of Oxford University Press
in the UK and in certain other countries

Published in the United States
by Oxford University Press Inc., New York

British Library Cataloguing in Publication Data

Data available

Library of Congress Cataloging in Publication Data

Speelman, Craig P.
  Beyond the learning curve / Craig P. Speelman, Kim Kirsner. — 1st ed.
    p. cm.
  Includes bibliographical references and index.
  1. Cognitive psychology. I. Kirsner, Kim. II. Title.
  BF201.S64 2005
  153—dc22

                                          2005019361

Typeset by Newgen Imaging Systems (P) Ltd., Chennai, India
Printed in Great Britain
on acid-free paper by
Biddles Ltd., King's Lynn

ISBN 0–19–850885–9 (Hbk.: alk.paper) 978–0–19–850885–4 (Hbk.)
ISBN 0–19–857041–4 (Pbk.: alk.paper) 978–0–19–857041–7 (Pbk.)

10 9 8 7 6 5 4 3 2 1

This book is dedicated to our children
Maggie and Stella
Mark, Sarah, and Tyko
May they acquire much as they journey along
life's learning curves

Preface

This book was originally planned as a review of research and theories in skill acquisition. Several years ago we began discussing the book in the Dome café in Claremont, Western Australia. Every second Friday we would meet and discuss what should go in the book, how it should be structured, and chat about many other topics such as university politics, football, the progress of our children, and other projects we were undertaking unrelated to the book. All the while, the dome in the ceiling of the café, which portrayed a concave impression of the world, held court over our discussions. At the beginning of this project we had no idea how far our review of skill acquisition research would go, but as ideas bounced between us and the ceiling dome, we began to see the universality of many of the concepts and phenomena we were considering for our review. We were struck by how easily the connections we once noted between skill acquisition and repetition priming could be extended to other domains. We wondered if such easily drawn parallels were indicative of something fundamental. Of course, the ease with which we talked about these matters was not matched by the translation of these arguments onto the page. The time to complete this book is a testament to the difficulty of conceptualizing our argument in a form we considered digestible by not only our colleagues in Cognitive Psychology, but also by those from outside this domain, both within and beyond Psychology. We hope we have succeeded at least to the extent of exciting the reader to the prospect that the theory we present here, or something like it, may provide the key to understanding many Psychological phenomena.

We would like to express our gratitude to some people who have been involved in the creation of this book to varying extents. First, our graduate students have provided inspiration and challenges for many of our ideas, and two, in particular (John Forbes and Kris Giesen), gave generously of their time to return the 'red-pen' treatment on several drafts. Second, John Dunn provided insightful comments and suggestions to an earlier version of the book. Third, Stephan Halloy patiently explained the mysteries and elegance of the relationship between complex systems and log-normal distributions.

Finally, this book could never have happened without the unwavering support of our wives, Nicky and Kathryn. Thanks must go to them for putting up with our late nights and furrowed brows during the difficult times and indulgence during moments of excitement. Thank you for your patience and love.

C.P.S.

K.K.

Contents

Chapter 1

Introduction

Force has no place where there is need of skill.

Herodotus (484 BC–430 BC)

If practice did not make perfect, nor habit economize the expense of nervous and muscular energy, (we) would be in a very sorry plight.

William James

If an act became no easier after being done several times, if the careful direction of consciousness were necessary to its accomplishment on each occasion, it is evident that the whole activity of a lifetime might be confined to one or two deeds...A man might be occupied all day in dressing and undressing himself; the attitude of his body would absorb all his attention and energy; the washing of his hands or the fastening of a button would be as difficult to him on each occasion as to the child on its first trial; and he would, furthermore, be completely exhausted by his exertions.

Henry Maudsley

Have you ever marvelled at the performance skills of accomplished musicians? The way they can execute incredibly complicated sequences of movement over their instrument with perfect accuracy, and yet, seem to do so with ease. The intricacies of their movements seem not to concern them as they appear focussed more on conveying an emotional message. Have you ever wondered about the dedication possessed by a musician to undertake the many years of practice necessary to acquire such skill? Have you ever observed with the same level of fascination someone engaged in the act of speaking? The movement sequences necessary to utter particular sounds are intricate and complicated— slight changes to the relative positioning of the various components of the vocal apparatus can alter the sounds dramatically. And yet the speaker seems quite unaware of the complexity of their physical task, and indeed appears unconcerned with directing or monitoring that aspect of the task. Instead, they seem more concerned with conveying a particular message to someone else rather than worrying about the details of how to execute the act of speaking. Have you ever wondered about the amount of practice that is necessary to achieve this level of skilled performance? How long does it take for someone to be able to perform a task without having to think about the act? Certainly, in the case of a musician, to have acquired sufficient skill with an instrument such that one's primary concern is with the emotionality of the performance rather than the accuracy is extremely rare for someone without at least 10 years dedicated practice. But in the case of speaking, many fluent and emotional speech acts are possible in someone as young as 3 years. Arguably the two forms of performance are at least as complicated as each other and yet one is acquired much earlier and with seemingly far less effort. Furthermore, many more people acquire the skill of speaking compared to the skill of playing a musical instrument. Do these differences indicate that the two domains of performance constitute qualitatively different types of behaviour, that they are acquired according to different principles, that they are mentally represented in different ways? Or is it possible that quantitative differences associated with the acquisition of these skills can account for the observed differences in these skills but that both types of skill are acquired according to the same principles?

These questions drive the arguments presented in this book. The overall aim of the book is to propose that the vast majority of cognitive performance, and hence behaviour, can be explained by recourse to a small set of learning principles. We identify and discuss these principles in the context of empirical and theoretical work involving skill acquisition and transfer effects. We then demonstrate how these principles operate in other domains of Psychology, where learning is not usually treated as the central theoretical platform. Our conclusion is that learning is a universal feature of all human activity and is a powerful influence on the behavioural repertoire acquired by each individual. We also suggest that this observation holds an important lesson for Psychology as a science and indeed, for how human behaviour is related to other natural phenomena.

Ever since the dominating influence of behaviourism was overturned with the onset of the cognitive revolution in the 1960s, learning has been neglected as an explanation for psychological phenomena. In our view, this represents a classic case of the baby being thrown out with the bathwater. Not that we are rabid neo-behaviourists intent on reinstating conditioning as the only explanation of everything. On the contrary, our feet are firmly grounded in cognitive science. For many years, though, we have observed how repetition can transform perception and behaviour, and we believe that this reflects transformations of mental representations associated with learning.

Our aim, then, is to refine the notion of learning, because we are using this term in ways that would not be obvious to the learning scientists of an earlier generation, and to move the concept to a pivotal position in cognitive thought.

Many current theories are full of genetic explanations for the way behaviour develops. In addition, there are many explanations for the way particular cognitive systems work without any concern for the practice functions and representational trajectories responsible for quantitative and qualitative change. There are several reasons why we should review the role of learning. Since the cognitive revolution, a further 40 years of empirical and theoretical development involving skill acquisition and transfer has accumulated. This body of research reveals a number of general principles that characterize the changes in behaviour that result from practice. These principles suggest that the scope of learning influences on behaviour is much broader than may have been believed decades ago. In this book we will describe these principles, present a new theory of skill acquisition, and discuss the pervasiveness of these principles with a view to demonstrating how the theory in particular and learning in general, can inform explanations of many psychological phenomena.

1.1 **Learning curves**

'It was a great game. A pity that we lost, but it was a big learning curve'. This sort of statement is heard increasingly in sport these days. But what does it mean? It would appear to be an oblique reference to the fact that the tough game provided a useful learning experience. But what is this 'learning curve' that is bandied about so frequently these days in sport and other areas, such as business? Why do people not just use the more obvious phrase 'learning experience'?

It would seem that the increasingly popular use of 'learning curve' reflects the influence of psychologists as they have spread their wares into the fields of sport and business, providing motivational tips and methods for achieving improved performance. Unfortunately, something has been lost in the translation from academic psychology to the sporting grounds and boardrooms of the world.

Learning curves are used in Psychology to represent the relationship between practice and associated changes in behaviour. One obvious property of learning curves is that they possess a characteristic shape. Typically, early in the practice of a task, performance gains are quite dramatic, but as practice proceeds, gains in performance are harder to come by—a case of diminishing returns. Indeed there is a vast literature suggesting that the speed of performance is a power function of practice (i.e. $Time = bPractice^{-c}$—see Chapter 2 for details).

Learning curves have been used to describe improvements in human performance in a wide range of domains, from simple arithmetic, to cigar rolling, to the writing of books, and even to the production of cars in a factory. It is not surprising then, that they have been used to represent the benefits of practice to sports and business people. One would be hard pressed to find two groups keener to seek improvements in order to get the jump on the opposition. But how could people in these domains get the concept of a learning curve so wrong? Are they so obsessed with the quick fix that they see one learning experience as providing them with all the experience necessary to make great gains? If there is one thing that real learning curves tell us, it is that great leaps in performance typically require massive amounts of practice. Highly skilled means highly practiced. So, one big game, or one tough financial year does not make a learning curve. In a successful career it usually only represents one point on a learning curve.

This is not to suggest that the concept of a learning curve has been misinterpreted by all that use it. A number of years ago, one of us spent several weeks on a submarine and was struck by the frequent use of the phrase 'The navy is a learning curve'. Invariably this phrase was invoked at times when something unexpected occurred related to the running of the ship and the speaker wanted to convey the idea that no matter how long someone is in the navy, learning experiences are always encountered.

So, what of the more enlightened souls who use such phrases as 'He's on a steep learning curve'? At least this suggests some appreciation that a learning curve represents more than one experience. But what does the slope of the learning curve have to do with anything? Often this phrase is heard in reference to a sportsperson who is relatively inexperienced, but shows promise. It would appear, then, that the speaker is trying to suggest that the person in question has a long way to go to achieve top performance, but they seem to be heading in the right direction. Again, though, this represents a misunderstanding of learning curves.

Certainly, psychologists are interested in the slopes of learning curves. This is not, however, because the slope indicates how much someone needs to improve before reaching an elite level. Instead, the slope indicates how quickly improvement is proceeding. The steeper the slope, the faster the learning. Being on a steep learning curve, then, is actually better than seems to be implied by those using this phrase, but it does usually imply that someone is at an early stage of skill acquisition.

In Chapter 2, we show how learning curves have been an important tool in the study of skill acquisition and transfer, and in Chapter 3, we discuss the many factors that influence the shape of learning curves. We also demonstrate how learning curves can be viewed as reflections of the operation of the many component processes that contribute to task performance. As such, learning curves form not only the bulk of the data upon which our theory of skill acquisition is based but also an important metaphor for the way behaviours are acquired throughout a person's life.

1.2 **The problem**

This book can be viewed as an attempt to provide a solution to what we see is a problem with Psychology. In particular, our focus is on Cognitive Psychology but we believe the problem pervades much of modern Psychology. Cognitive Psychologists are interested in how we come to have and use knowledge. Theorizing in this field usually proceeds by proposing that particular behaviours occur because we have in our heads systems that have certain characteristics. Research then becomes a matter of generating predictions from such hypotheses to match against measurements of behaviour. As would be expected, hypotheses that match data survive, while those that are inconsistent with data are either rejected or modified. The problem we see in this process, however, relates to the types of systems that are proposed as explanations of behaviour. It is more often than not the case that there is little consideration for how these systems got into our heads in the first place. In some cases it is assumed that the systems are part of our biological make up. Sometimes it is assumed that such systems develop along with normal maturation. In relatively few cases, it is tacitly assumed that these systems result from learning, but invariably the process of acquisition of such systems is not considered. Well, we think this lack of consideration for the role played by learning in system acquisition is a problem, for three related reasons: First, we think that learning is in fact responsible for many of the systems posited by Cognitive Psychologists. Second, we think that consideration of the learning origins of a system can explain many of the workings of that system. Third, it might even be the case that there are no systems *per se*, just many adaptations to the many problems faced by humans learning to deal with the world. Thus, the Problem of interest to us in this book is that we think Cognitive Psychology is missing an important ingredient in its attempts to explain the workings of the human mind. For too long Cognitive Psychology has merely *described* systems that might be responsible for mental phenomena, whereas we think that the field should also be concerned with trying to *explain* why such systems exist in the first place. Achieving this would provide more complete explanations of phenomena. It is thus our aim in this book to demonstrate how it is possible to explain a vast range of cognitive behaviours with only a small number of principles. These principles all relate to the way in which we acquire skills.

What then do we mean when we talk about skills and their acquisition, and how is this likely to be relevant to explanations of cognitive phenomena other than those traditionally considered in skill acquisition research? In the following section, we consider a range of different types of skills and give a brief overview of some of the characteristics of skill acquisition. This will provide a context for the final section of the chapter in which we provide an overview of how the rest of the book will offer a solution to the Problem just identified.

1.3 **What is skill?**

What is 'skill', and what is 'skill acquisition'? In this book we are going to entertain and exploit broad definitions of these terms. According to the Oxford Dictionary, the term 'skill' refers to 'expertness, practiced ability, facility in doing something, dexterity (*and intriguingly*) tact'. We have no quarrel with this definition. But we suspect that it places, perhaps implicitly, an unwanted barrier around the psychological questions and processes involved in skill.

Regardless of the definition, however, people acquire an extraordinary portfolio of skills during their lives. If skill is defined so as to include not only the traditional examples of riding a bicycle, playing the violin and swimming, but talking, reading, socializing, and all forms of clinical and corporate decision-making, the actual number might reach into the hundreds. How many skills does a person actually acquire in the course of one lifetime? It is difficult to estimate the size of this portfolio because it is difficult to draw a sharp line between 'skills'. For example, to what extent does learning the violin involve a new and distinct skill for four more or less hypothetical children, Stella, Maggie, Tyko, and Sara? Let us assume that Tyko has no musical experience whatsoever, and that Maggie, Stella, and Sara have already mastered the clarinet, cello, and viola, respectively. From the point of view of the first violin in a philharmonic orchestra, each of these instruments involves a more or less unique skill. But from the point of view of a cognitive psychologist, the challenges posed for the first and fourth of these children are quite different. Tyko will have few if any component skills to draw on, whereas the other three children can exploit successively more component processes for mastery of the new instrument. In Sara's case indeed, she may have acquired virtually all of the component processes from her experience with the viola.

This issue is by no means confined to music. It also applies to that most universal of skills, language. The languages of the world can be divided into a dozen or more superfamilies, where each superfamily can be divided into many families and subfamilies (e.g. Greenberg and Ruhlen, 1992). At the bottom of the relevant genealogical chart the orthographic differences at least can be relatively small, involving contrasts between words, such as PUBLICITY (English) and PUBLICIDAD (Spanish), TIGER (English) and TIGRE (French), and TABLE (English), TABLE (French), and TAVOLA (Italian). It can be shown, furthermore, that these differences influence performance when people are tested on second-language words that have first-language cognates

(Cristoffanini, Milech, and Kirsner, 1986). Thus, a person who has mastered two 'close' languages, such as English and German, might have to master only 90,000 distinct words to be regarded as a true bilingual (assuming that fluency in each language requires a vocabulary of 50,000 words), whereas a person who has mastered two 'distant' languages, such as English and Chinese might have to master 100,000 distinct words, the assumption being that there are no English–Chinese cognates. The precise definition of a new skill is beside the point in this case. The question of psychological interest concerns the extent to which mastery of one skill enables the user to master another skill. But the critical point in our argument is that this problem is more or less universal. Once a child has passed say 10 years of age, she or he will face very few skills where there is absolutely no transfer from an existing portfolio of component processes.

Thus, when the problem is posed in cognitive terms, the boundaries between skills are inherently fuzzy. This analysis is, furthermore, the rule rather than the exception; every time we try to acquire a new skill, the starting point and the rate of progress on that skill will be influenced by the extent to which our background has provided us with component processes that are required for that skill. It may also be the case that individuals adopt different strategies under these conditions. Some people might, for example, routinely adopt strategies that discover and exploit component processes while others assume that the new problem is unique, and resist recognition of component elements in the new task or language system.

The topics covered by the term 'skill' are very broad. The definition clearly includes literacy and numeracy, and the host of more specific tasks that fall under these general headings. Tasks, such as lexical decision, naming, and word identification for example, have been specifically developed to explore component processes in reading, while virtually all of the specific tasks involved in arithmetic have been used to explore the acquisition of numeracy skills. There is also a broad body of research involving human performance, in both the cultural and sporting domains. The term is also used to refer to performance on a wide variety of professional tasks. Surgery and medical and paramedical decision-making are obvious examples. Psychiatric and psychological diagnoses have also been treated as research topics. Additional domains of interest include financial decision-making, in the stock market for example, firefighting, and various forms of combat. An exhaustive list would or should eventually include virtually every form of employment that humans undertake.

Where should we draw the line or lines? The basic answer is that each and every type of human activity eventually involves a measure of skill, and therefore skill acquisition. But there are many territorial questions. One of these concerns team and corporate performance. Should we treat these topics as skills, or should we restrict skill acquisition to processes that operate strictly within the individual? What about team performance in sport? Is team performance anything more than the sum of a number of intraindividual skills, some of which involve anticipation about the future movements of other players? Or does team performance involve collaborative processes that stand apart from the skills of the individual team members? Are there aspects of team performance that are not simply the sum of the skills possessed by the individual players and, if so, can we measure them, and refer to this shared capacity or knowledge as a skill? What about tacit communication between players, for example? Does the 'instinctive' ability of individual players to put themselves in the right position at the right time involve a skill? For some aspects of team and corporate performance, the answer is easy. Skill is obviously a factor where we are concerned with the ability of an individual to react to, communicate with, or predict the performance of another person or a group of people. But what about corporate knowledge and corporate performance? Should we treat information or knowledge that a team has acquired about its competitors as a form of skill?

What about industrial performance? Does our definition include the cooperative processes that emerge with practice in industrial organizations? The answer is probably 'yes' where communication is concerned. But what about organizational knowledge, involving management, market segmentation, and the operation of an industrial assembly line, for example? And, should we include case-knowledge that is latent except when a particular type of case is encountered? And what about tacit knowledge, where there is no transaction between partners or colleagues, but they nevertheless share an understanding about how they will respond to particular types of corporate challenges. Can we treat industrial performance measures in the same way as we treat individual performance measures? Do they honour the same principles or laws?

Questions about the relevance of team and corporate performance involve a possible restriction on the range of problems that should be considered as skills. But there are other types of boundaries that merit consideration. How do we draw a line between developmental change and skill acquisition for instance? A vast proportion of skill acquisition actually involves children, and it is possible therefore that changes in their performance are moderated by developmental processes rather than or as well as skill acquisition. There is evidence, moreover that particular skills are shaped by early childhood experience, and these changes produce more or less permanent effects. If you are born to English-speaking parents, for example, the distinction between /r/ and /l/ is acquired in the first few months of life, well before any form of speech can be detected. But if you are born to Japanese-speaking parents, and you remain in a Japanese-speaking environment for the early years, this distinction might never be mastered, even after years in an English-speaking environment. In this case therefore, very early experience places constraints on skill acquisition, and these constraints influence the subsequent acquisition of related skills for better or worse, depending on the fit.

So where do we draw the line between developmental processes and skill acquisition? Let us consider a straw person. Is it possible that the entire pattern of developmental changes in performance is driven solely by practice effects, without a genuine developmental contribution? Developmental changes in short-term memory are of course well established in empirical terms. But is it possible that these changes simply reflect changing proficiency with objects and words, so that the empirically observed changes in the capacity of short-term memory actually stem from the increased processing time associated with relatively unpractised items (e.g. Case, 1978, 1985). This proposal should not of course be confused with the idea that speed of processing *per se* is the critical factor. Rather, it is that unavoidable age-related differences in practice and familiarity are responsible for performance differences in memory tasks.

1.4 **What is skill acquisition?**

So how are skills acquired? Typically, they can only be acquired as a result of practicing a particular task for some extended period of time. But how do we know when a skill has been acquired? As the term is conventionally used in experimental psychology, 'skill acquisition' usually involves reference to improvement in the speed of performance. Let us consider a task, such as syllogistic reasoning. In a typical experiment, a subject might be asked to study 300 premises where each trial takes the general form depicted in Figure 1.1.

Figure 1.1 is a summary of the structure of a single trial in an experiment involving syllogistic reasoning. The participant is exposed to two premises for a period that is terminated when he or she presses the space bar. Then, after an interval of about one second, a test stimulus is presented for classification, as valid or invalid. Thus, if the premises are ALL OF THE ACROBATS ARE BUTCHERS and ALL OF THE BUTCHERS ARE CRICKETERS, and the conclusion is ALL OF THE ACROBATS ARE CRICKETERS, the correct classification would be 'valid', meaning that the conclusion follows from the premises. By contrast, the conclusion ALL OF THE CRICKETERS ARE ACROBATS would not follow from the premises and should be classified as 'invalid'. This measure can be used to collect information about several variables. The first of these involves the accuracy of the response. Over a 300 trial

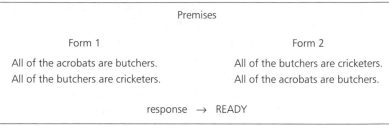

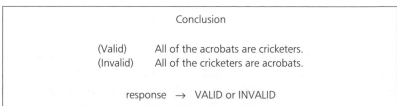

Fig. 1.1 Sample syllogism illustrating two forms of premise pairs, two forms of conclusions (VALID and INVALID), and the appropriate responses to each part of the syllogism.

experiment a subject might receive 150 valid and 150 invalid trials (trials where the conclusion does and does not follow from the premises, respectively), and per cent correct is a simple calculation. The procedure also supports collection of two reaction time measures. The first and more obvious measure involves the time from the onset of the conclusion to the response. The less obvious but no less interesting measure involves the time from the onset of the premises to the response that instructs the computer to terminate presentation of the premises and present the conclusion. This measure is of particular interest because, while the reaction time or RT to the conclusions usually occurs under an expectation of speeded responding, the RT to the premises is incidental, and subjects may perform this part of the task without speeded instructions.

Figure 1.2 depicts the results of a typical experiment involving this paradigm. The figure shows inspection time, for the premises, and decision time, for the test stimuli. RTs for the inspection and decision times decrease systematically as a function of practice, from around 5s to about 2.5s in the case of inspection time, and from 2s to less than 1s in the case of decision time. The data shown in Figure 1.2 is shown on linear–linear axes. The data are re-plotted in Figure 1.3 with log–log axes, and the result is at least superficially consistent with the hypothesis that the practice effects involve the power law or one of its close relatives (e.g. Speelman, 1991).

The RT picture depicted in Figures 1.2 and 1.3 is more or less ubiquitous, a point that has been emphasized by Anderson (1982) and Newell and Rosenbloom (1981). Qualitatively comparable functions have been observed

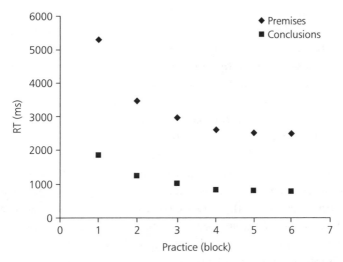

Fig. 1.2 Reaction times to inspect premises and judge the validity of conclusions in a syllogism task as a function of practice. Axes are linear–linear.

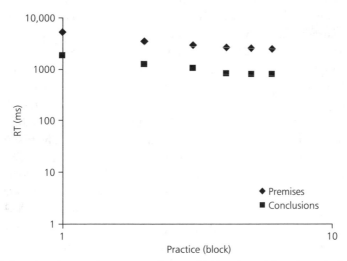

Fig. 1.3 Reaction times to inspect premises and judge the validity of conclusions in a syllogism task as a function of practice. Axes are log–log.

for cigar-making (Crossman, 1959), counting (Lassaline and Logan, 1993), lexical decision (Logan, 1990), authorship of science fiction books (Ohlsson, 1992), and many other tasks. The change in accuracy varies dramatically from task to task, however, and may or may not reflect a similar function. In lexical decision for example, where subjects simply classify letter strings, such as

BONUS and BONSU as 'genuine' or 'false' English words, accuracy usually commences at 95% correct or better, and changes only slightly if at all with practice. It might be possible to detect power function improvement in accuracy in tasks, such as this, but it is equally possible that in the absence of feedback there is no improvement. But there are other tasks where the anticipated improvement in RT is evident, but there is no improvement in accuracy even though performance is barely above chance. We (Midford and Kirsner, 2005) have found such a relationship in a task designed by Reber (1967). In brief, Reber's subjects were required to learn and then apply complex grammatical rules to patterns involving arcs and nodes. Our subjects were given several hundred trials and showed the expected improvement in RT, but this occurred in the absence of any improvement in accuracy. No doubt, this was due to the absence of feedback. But it provides a useful caveat for research involving practice; that it cannot be assumed that accuracy and RT are simply two measures of a single underlying process.

Skill acquisition is usually concerned with speed as distinct from accuracy in task performance, and data that follows the same general pattern can be derived from hundreds of experiments. But the main focus of this work is generally on speed, and accuracy is often treated as a peripheral issue. In many cases, accuracy is actually treated as a precondition for data acquisition and modelling. In lexical decision and many other tasks, subjects are omitted if they do not reach accuracy levels of 90% or more. Is this omission critical? It is our contention that the disciplinary focus on RT data has tended to draw our attention away from task mastery, and, therefore, failure. Has research into skill acquisition been unduly constrained by pragmatic considerations? Three factors probably influence laboratory practice in this area. The first of these involves the development of information processing models. When consideration is restricted to accuracy, a simple binary classification of each response—as right or wrong—provides little basis for inferences about specific processes, and it is therefore necessary to accumulate hundreds of responses before even simple questions can be considered. RT data on the other hand provides a graded response to each trial or each trial type, and it therefore provides a richer platform for process and model differentiation.

A second factor involves the role of guessing. The value of RT data becomes less clear as accuracy falls away from the ceiling. If we choose a word frequency band for lexical decision that enables all of our subjects to get 98% or more of their trials correct, for example, we can use all of the data for analysis. But if we choose a word frequency band that places most of our participants at or near chance on lexical decision, the RT data is of little or no value because it really reflects 'guessing time' rather than decision time or classification time.

At 50%, in fact, it must be assumed that the participant is guessing, and the RT data cannot be used to model anything other than guessing strategies.

The third factor involves the problems that arise when we give human subjects tasks that they simply cannot master. The outcome could involve an ethical challenge or, more probably in practice, a lack of interest on the part of potential participants ('Who wants to be a subject in that laboratory; they always use tasks that no one can do!'). But, unlike the laboratory, 'life' is not and cannot be shaped so that everyone masters a particular task. On the contrary, 'life' for most people is rich in tasks that they cannot master. For some people this might be as basic as reading, where failure all but removes the individual concerned from the workplace. For others it might be differential equations, where failure could be masked entirely by judicious career choices. Failure is of course relative rather than absolute. Even illiteracy might not be a problem if the individual concerned has aspirations that do not require reading skills. And, by the same token, individuals who establish extreme criteria for themselves may experience failure even while they are producing world-class performances in a sporting arena.

Figure 1.4 was designed to highlight the transition that arguably occurs as accuracy approaches the ceiling, and the door opens for RT or 'fluency' analyses. Figure 1.4 includes two ordinates and two functions. The 'mastery' function depicts changes in accuracy as a function of practice *for individuals who master the task*. The 'fluency' function depicts changes in RT as a function of practice from the point where accuracy is high enough for meaningful analysis of the RT data. The figure highlights several problems. The most obvious of these involves the point of transition. There is of course no such point, and the

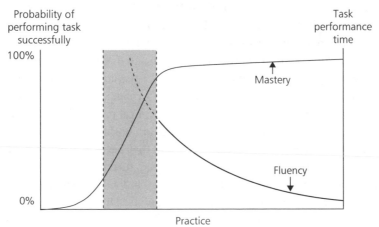

Fig. 1.4 Performance curves underlying skill development.

way in which individual experimenters handle data in the grey region arguably depends on convention as much as anything else.

Let us consider the problem in a 'real' task, a task with life or death outcomes. The twentieth century has seen dramatic changes to our attitudes towards training and industrial safety, and 'failure'. But these changes are surprisingly recent. If we look back to the challenge posed by pilot training during the First World War, the apparent disregard for the cost of 'failure' in skill acquisition comes as a shock. These were of course the early years of aviation. But consider the following. The official figures for the Royal Air Force for the period 1914–1918 showed that 14,166 pilots died overall, *and that 8000 of these deaths occurred during training in the UK* (Winter, 1982). Furthermore, this percentage actually conceals a dramatic change associated with the introduction of a new training regime, in 1917, a change that reduced the fatal accident rate from 1 per 92 training hours to 1 per 192 training hours.

Failure might therefore reflect a variety of processes. One process involves the mastery function. A trainee pilot might not be able to reach the second or third step in a training program and, depending on the attitudes and technology of the day, he or she would be killed or discarded. The surviving cohort has then been selected for the processes or skills that were required for that step, and, assuming that these processes are useful for subsequent steps, the survival rate for the new cohort might be correspondingly higher. Another process might be operating, however. It is possible that a pilot will master all of the technical requirements for flight, and combat, but that he or she will not be far enough down the fluency function for survival. She can do it, but she cannot do it fast enough, and she too is removed from the cohort. Thus mastery and fluency are both critical in this instance.

Combat and flight during the First World War offered crisp criteria for survival. But this is not the case in all walks of life. It is probably valid for most domains where public performance is an issue, however. Dancers, actors, and musicians who cannot meet the criteria associated with a given role will be identified and discarded, from the professional ranks at least. But in professions where performance unfolds in private, and performance data is unavailable, the situation might be very different. Consider clinical psychology, for example. The published research suggests that experts do not show much improvement in diagnostic and predictive performance after they have received their training (Camerer & Johnson, 1991). It may be inferred, furthermore, that the group data behind these conclusions actually included individuals who perform at or below chance level in their professional capacity. Thus, in situations where there are no external and independent criteria, people may 'succeed' or fail for reasons that have little or nothing to do with skill.

Mastery of milk extraction from the breast

According to University research (one of our wives), one of our infants required approximately 2 days to master milk extraction, where practice accumulated at the rate of 600 sucks/sitting and 12 sittings/day; that is, 14,400 sucks from novice to expert. Infants have to master nipple stretching techniques among other things to ensure adequate flow, and if they fail to do this, the bottle provides an appropriate alternative because the natural flow rates for bottles are generally higher. Furthermore, if the infant has been indirectly affected by substances delivered during birth, his or her arousal levels may be low, and skill acquisition retarded accordingly. In earlier times, failure to master the relevant skills would have created situations where particular infants would have failed to reach the top of the mastery function (see Figure 1.4), and therefore sustained life.

1.5 **Transfer**

Thus far, we have considered the boundaries between different types of skill, the general character of skill acquisition, and the contribution of various cognitive processes to skill acquisition. It is our contention that transfer or, to use an archaic term, 'transfer of training', stands at the heart of all discussions about skill and skill acquisition. However, our use of the term does not conform exactly to the traditional treatment.

Traditionally the term transfer of training has been used with reference to a specific and narrow range of situations. In a typical study, a group of subjects is exposed to a particular training regime. The objective of that exposure is to prepare them for a particular set of operational conditions (Group T1). Subsequently, their performance is compared with that of other groups who have received either no training (Group C) or a different form of training (Group T2).

In its simplest form, transfer of training might be measured by reference to the performance of T1 relative to Groups C and E, where E is a group of Experts. If performance levels for the expert, transfer, and control groups are 100, 60, and 20, respectively, it might be inferred that the transfer effect is 50% (i.e. $(60-20)/(100-20)$). The training program produced an improvement but the benefit fell far short of the performance levels achieved by experts.

In our approach, however, performance on a particular task is seen as a product of performance levels on a large or even infinite number of practice functions, where each function involves a particular information-processing component of the overall task. Consider lexical decision, for example. There will be a practice function for the task itself. A person who has already completed 10,000 trials on this task will have benefited from that practice, and there will not be much room for further improvement on the component that is directly concerned with the task. There will be another practice function for the words used in the actual experiment, and, possibly, for the word frequency bands occupied by those words. If that individual has had extensive experience with the particular words being used in the experiment, RT for those words is likely to be short, although it is also likely that their future performance on those words will show little improvement because they are already on or at least near the asymptote. But we can still move down to another level of granularity, for early readers in particular. Practice effects at the level of letters are usually overlooked, and rightly so, because the practice levels on letters are so high that performance on letter analysis is asymptotic; there is no room for further improvement on the component processes involved in the analysis of letters and letter combinations. Even for a 6-year-old, practice on the individual letters might exceed 10,000 trials or observations per letter, on average. This would be the case if, for example, he or she had 'read' 1000 words per day for 365 days. The actual values for some of the individual letters and letter pairs might be as low as 1000, however, a figure that might still leave much room for improvement.

One of the implications of this approach is that rapid rates of improvement will actually co-occur with low levels of transfer from preceding or neighbouring tasks. It is the child or adult with no practice on related tasks that should show rapid early progress. Consider Figure 1.5, for example. Both graphs in this figure reflect the assumption that performance on some tasks is a composite based on three components, a, b, and c, and that the practice functions for these components are identical. Where they differ is in their assumptions about the amount of prior practice on the component tasks. In Figure 1.5(a), it is assumed that the subject has had 1000 practice trials that involved each component. In Figure 1.5(b), however, it is assumed that only components a and b had received 1000 practice trials, and that component c had received only 100 practice trials. Performance on the overall task in this situation involves an apparently higher asymptote but exhibits a significantly faster rate of learning. This approach also raises interesting questions where individual differences in learning are concerned. Ackerman (1988), for example, has argued that individual differences in working memory dominate the slope of the learning curve during the early phases of skill acquisition. He attributes this relationship to the role of working memory as it works with declarative

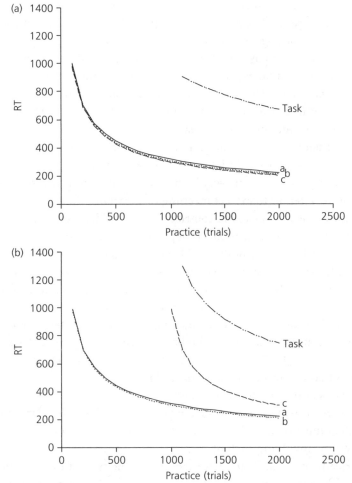

Fig. 1.5 Learning curves for a task that comprises three component processes, a, b, and c.

knowledge during this stage. According to our analysis, however, rapid learning during the early phase of learning reflects low practice levels on one or more component processes rather than working memory. These ideas are not of course mutually exclusive.

Lexical decision is of course an artificial task. It involves static displays and de-contextualized processes. And, it was designed to facilitate the analysis of questions associated with just one aspect of reading, lexical access. When consideration is expanded to reading, a plethora of additional and more complex components come into play, and they are all subject to practice. One relatively low level component process involves visual scanning. We know that readers do not usually read all of the words on a page. Rather, they adopt tracks or patterns across the page that tend to focus on key words or groups of words. The tracks are affected by the reader's experience with a domain, and they are sensitive to a host of other variables including, for example, the difficulty and word frequency characteristics of the text, the reader's aims and objectives, and the amount of time the reader can allocate to the task. The scanning process also includes provision for substantial movement, to points beyond the current sentence or even paragraph. (For a review of the influence of these factors on eye movements during reading see Rayner (1998).)

But reading involves some very high-level component processes too. The reader must attempt to extract meaning or meanings that fit and enhance the theme of the discourse, and contribute to the reader's appreciation of the writer's intentions. And the products of processes must, furthermore, conform to the reader's knowledge of the world and, more narrowly, the world created by the author; tasks that pose significant challenges for various aspects of memory. And, finally, as we return to the lexical level, readers routinely use the local context to facilitate word and even sentence recognition and interpretation as well. If these processes could be measured separately, the relevant measures for most of them would probably be asymptotic. But this would not be the case with 4-, 5-, 6-, or even 7-, and 8-year-olds. The component processes that we are associating with reading arguably take years of practice and millions of practice trials to master.

When we consider reading as a 'process' therefore, the relevant skill acquisition function must be a composite, involving dozens or even hundreds of functions involving each of its many component processes. In recent work, Heathcote *et al.* (2000) have shown that the type of function that fits learning data depends on the origin of that data. When consideration is restricted to individual data, exponential functions provide the best fit. But when consideration is expanded to include groups of participants, power functions provide a better fit. Our argument is similar but takes the problem of averaging one step or level further. Thus, where individual performance on lexical decision might in practice involve the finest available level of analysis, that function is itself a compound involving a number of component processes, not all of which can be measured directly and independently. The shapes of the skill acquisition functions for these finer component processes is unknown. But the component processes that we can hint at may not represent the end of the road. It may also be necessary to explore and measure practice effects at even finer levels, involving groups of cells or even individual cells.

S for Stella in learning

Stella (4) was learning about the relationship between letters and their sounds. Predictably, one of the first letters she learned was 'S', with the mnemonic 'S for Stella'. Driving with her family one day she announced that 'There's an S-for-Stella in that shop' and 'There's another S-for-Stella over there', and so on. Stella had learned to associate the shape of the S with a sound in her name, but at this stage, the egocentrism of childhood had not allowed her to appreciate that S played a role in many other words. This egocentrism is further illustrated by the remainder of the episode. After several announcements in the space of a minute or two about the various locations of 'S-for-Stella', she then announced, 'There are lots of S-for-Stellas. They must really like me'. She then turned to her sister, and said, with a glint in her eye, 'There aren't many M-for-Maggie's!'

Transfer of training—swimming

Maggie (7) had been learning to swim since she was 3 years old. All of her lessons had been in swimming pools, either from qualified instructors, or her parents. In the summer following her sixth birthday, she was able to keep afloat and move around for the first time in water deeper than her height. Finally, in the following summer she began to get the hang of swimming freestyle, and in particular, being able to breathe without stopping the stroke. While learning to swim, Maggie also visited the ocean on many occasions, and could dog-paddle there at the same time as she was able to dog-paddle in a pool. However, despite a summer of surf life-saving training, her freestyle feats in the pool could not be matched in the ocean. For some reason, she was reluctant to put her face in the water. She would not even attempt freestyle with her face out of the water, persisting with a form of dog-paddle. It appears that whatever fear she had of the ocean prevented her from exhibiting a skill she clearly possessed and was able to execute in other contexts.

Our argument about component processes in skill acquisition can be illustrated in the industrial performance arena. In this case, of course, no one would question the claim that overall performance, for a company, depends on the performance of many component individuals and processes in the organization. Figure 1.6 shows performance in truck production for one company (from Epple *et al.* 1991). The spike in the figure was associated by the authors with the addition of a second production shift. Although workers in this second shift had received training, the overall level of expertise in this shift did not match that of the first shift. The spike therefore represents an overall loss of knowledge or expertise per worker from the company, and the subsequent slope of the production function is presumably dominated by the learning performance of the second shift. The subsequent slope is also influenced by the performance levels of the first shift of course, but since most of that shift's improvements have already occurred, most of the subsequent improvements will be due to the second shift refining their skills. The impact of different types of skill insertion is interesting. Insertion of a skilled shift would have little or no impact on the performance function at all, whereas insertion of an unskilled shift will produce a sudden reduction in performance followed by rapid learning, as suggested by Figure 1.6. One implication is surely that the significance of intercepts and slopes in learning functions can only be determined by reference to their overall context.

A critical issue in transfer then involves the balance between 'old' and 'new' processes. Psychologists generally adopt an operational approach to the distinction between 'old' and 'new' treatments and items in memory, and skill acquisition research. If a particular item or problem has not been presented before, it is classified as 'new'. But if the item or problem has been presented before it is classified as 'old'. The distinction that we wish to advance is in some respects similar to this concept. But it involves a different level of granularity, and that change has dramatic implications for the relative balance of old and

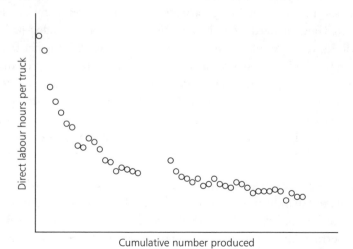

Fig. 1.6 Relation between direct labour hours per truck and cumulative number produced (from Epple *et al.*, 1991).

new elements. It is our contention that the critical level of granularity involves component processes rather than items or problems, and that, at this level, new problems are routinely solved by reference to component processes that are familiar or 'old'. Thus, unlike the experimental paradigms, where old and new items are usually balanced, under our definition, the proportion of component processes that qualify as 'old' might be of a far higher, although unknown and perhaps unknowable, value. In reading, for example, the proportion of genuinely new problems faced by an 8-year-old reader might be a vanishingly small number. The vast majority of reading processes stand outside lexical access, and most of these processes will be well established and practiced by this age. From time to time this reader will face a new string of letters, but this will occur in a context where the rich panoply of pragmatic, thematic, and semantic processes are in place, and the new item requires only grapheme–phoneme conversion and a little prediction. One implication of our argument is, then, that we should re-contextualize skill acquisition.

1.6 Overview of the book

One of our aims in writing this book is to present an argument for a broader perspective on performance than is currently provided by modern Psychology. In our view, traditional approaches to studying behaviour have been too narrowly focussed. That is, researchers have typically examined performance on highly specific tasks, and often only consider performance in such situations in isolation. This approach, particularly in the study of perceptual and cognitive behaviours, has certainly been productive in terms of producing generalizations about specific mechanisms. However, this approach is only a first step in terms of understanding the principles that underlie the origins, nature, and limits of all performance. In this book we present a case for skill acquisition to be considered one of the underlying factors that regulate behaviour.

Other attempts to foster a similar change in approach to Psychology have been made before. Probably the most famous was by Newell (1973) in a presentation, and later an article, entitled 'You can't play 20 questions with nature and win'. Newell's entreaty may not have sparked a revolution in the way the mind is studied, however, he did follow his own advice and began developing a unified theory of cognition, a veritable 'theory of everything'. Two decades later Newell (1990) proposed his SOAR theory as an exemplar of what a unified theory of cognition should be. Apparently also inspired by Newell's 1973 address, Anderson (1976, 1983a, 1993; Anderson and Lebiere, 1998) developed another candidate unified theory of cognition—the ACT family of theories. SOAR and ACT are theories that are designed to account for a large range of cognitive phenomena with only a small number of principles. These theories are considered in greater detail in Chapter 2.

This book is not designed to present a fully realized unified theory of cognition, as advocated by Newell (1990). We do, however, propose a theory that has pretensions to some day taking on this mantle. More importantly, though, the theory embodies a new way of approaching psychological theorizing. Thus, the book aims to present a new perspective on Psychology, and in particular Cognitive Psychology, that we propose be adopted by researchers whenever they consider the wider implications of their data. That is, how do the conclusions of a body of research relate to other areas of research? Are there similar themes? Could one area inform another area in terms of the origins of particular mechanisms? Several examples of how this approach has been fruitful in a number of areas in Cognitive Psychology are presented in the book. The specific view presented is that when human behaviour is considered in the context of learning curves, which represent prior learning history, likely performance trajectories, and the interaction of myriad influences on behaviour, then some insight is gained into the large number of mechanisms that are responsible for any one behaviour. And yet, many of these mechanisms appear to operate according to the same small number of principles: performance on a task improves as a negatively accelerated function of amount of practice; skills developed in the context of one task can be transferred to performance of another task (although conditions apply); a learning curve describing improvement on a task is a summary of many learning curves that represent improvement on a vast array of component processes.

In essence, we will be focussing on the role skill acquisition plays in many different forms of behaviour. In this sense, what we are setting out to do does not differ substantially from Newell's aim with SOAR and Anderson's aim with ACT. Both of those theories have learning mechanisms as central elements, and indeed explicitly claim that these mechanisms underlie behaviour in many domains of cognition, ranging from memory to problem solving and language. We accept this position and aim to extend it by applying it to domains and in ways beyond those considered by either Newell or Anderson.

1.7 **The solution**

The Problem we introduced earlier in this chapter was that Psychology has neglected an important ingredient in its explanations of behaviour, and that ingredient is learning. The Solution to this Problem is therefore straightforward—include learning principles in explanations of behaviour. If we are to make the claim, however, that learning principles underlie a much broader range of cognitive phenomena than has been traditionally considered, there are a number of things that need to be established about such a claim. In particular, we propose that there are several conditions that should be satisfied by this claim that would establish whether or not the claim was a worthy solution to the Problem. Furthermore, we consider these conditions to represent a hierarchy of importance criteria. In other words, we suggest that a theory of skill acquisition that is proposed as a theory of more than just skill acquisition should be subject to several levels of test.

Skill acquisition phenomena criterion. Typically, when cognitive phenomena are explained, data are considered and theories are tested against the data. In our view, the ability of a theory to account for data represents the basic criterion for establishing whether the theory is acceptable. So, in the current context, it is necessary to establish the basic phenomena associated with skill acquisition, and then consider current theories of skill acquisition in terms of whether or not they can account for all of the data.

We feel also that it is necessary to evaluate any theory of skill acquisition that purports to account for more than just skill acquisition phenomena against more advanced criteria. Below we describe several such criteria.

Behaviour Phenomena Criterion. Essentially the Behaviour Phenomena Criterion is a test of whether or not a theory can account for phenomena in areas outside the domain of its origins. In the current context, this is a test of whether a skill acquisition theory can account for a set of behaviours that are not traditionally considered in skill acquisition terms.

Biology and Evolution Criteria. The Biology and Evolution Criteria represent more advanced tests of the scope of a theory of skill acquisition in that they concern areas of science not traditionally considered relevant to the target domain. In the current context, this refers to whether or not a skill acquisition theory fits with non-psychological data. So, for example, is the theory compatible with known principles of brain function and evolution?

Explanation Criterion. The final criterion concerns description versus explanation. In particular, can a theory of skill acquisition provide an account for why a system produces particular phenomena without resorting to a re-description of the phenomena? For instance, does the skill acquisition theory account for principles of learning without building those principles into the theory?

1.8 **Chapter outline**

We distribute our presentation of the Solution to the Problem across several chapters. In Chapters 2 and 3, we review basic skill acquisition phenomena, and focus on the shape of learning curves, the issue of transfer, and how transfer impacts on the shape of learning curves. We also review existing theories of skill acquisition, and their ability to account for the basic phenomena. We demonstrate that most theories can only account for some of these phenomena. Our most generous conclusion regarding these theories is that most of them almost satisfy the Skill Acquisition Phenomena Criterion.

In Chapter 4, we present five Principles of learning. The principles represent a distillation of the basic phenomena presented in Chapters 2 and 3 which must therefore be accounted for by any theory of skill acquisition. We then present a theory that accounts for the Principles. The theory is presented only as a sketch at this stage because we postpone consideration of the mechanisms underlying the theory (i.e. the Explanation Criterion) until after consideration of whether the theory satisfies the Behaviour Phenomenon Criterion.

In Chapter 5, we test our theory against the Behaviour Phenomenon Criterion by considering research on the Mental Lexicon—a cognitive system that is traditionally studied without consideration of its development and/or learning origins. We highlight how a skill acquisition approach fits with existing data, particularly, with respect to transfer and the effects of experience (practice) on performance speed. We conclude that our theory satisfies the Behaviour Phenomenon Criterion, at least with respect to this area of research. The analysis in this chapter results in a pointer to further development of our theory, particularly, with respect to underlying mechanisms and hence its ability to satisfy the Biology, Evolution, and Explanation Criteria.

Chapter 6 describes a further development of the theory in which the brain/mind is presented as a complex adaptive system. We then demonstrate how the theory satisfies the Biology, Evolution, and Explanation Criteria. Finally, we consider a number of implications that follow from the conclusion that a theory of skill acquisition can provide explanations of seemingly nonskill acquisition phenomena. We note that many features of skill acquisition in particular, and behaviour in general, are similar to many other areas of nature. Indeed, we make the claim that this is because the mind reflects universal laws of nature. A number of areas of Psychology are examined to consider the extent to which the theory can provide a unifying and parsimonious explanation of phenomena that have traditionally provoked explanations that are highly specific to the particular domain. We finish the book with a call to arms—we propose that when Psychologists consider explanations of cognitive phenomena, they should begin to consider explanations that can potentially apply to other domains within Psychology. In other words, Psychologists should resist working in isolated domains. They should try to understand the mind as a whole rather than focussing on many tiny bits with a hope that they will all fit together somehow in the future. Our suggestion is that by considering the origins of the phenomena (i.e. could they result from learning?), a theory, such as our skill acquisition theory may provide an explanation that cuts across domains and relies on the same principles regardless of domain.

Chapter 2

Skill acquisition: History, questions, and theories

Only those who have the patience to do simple things perfectly ever acquire the skill to do difficult things easily.

Author Unknown

2.1 What is skill acquisition?

Skill acquisition is a specific form of learning. For our purposes, it will be sufficient to define learning as the representation of information in memory concerning some environmental or cognitive event. Thus, learning refers to an organism storing something about its past in memory. Skill acquisition refers to a form of prolonged learning about a family of events. Through many pairings of similar stimuli with particular responses, a person can begin to develop knowledge representations of how to respond in certain situations. These representations have some form of privileged status in memory because they can be retrieved more easily and reliably than memories of single events. Thus, skilled behaviours can become routinized and even automatic under some conditions.

The range of behaviours that can be considered to involve skill acquisition could potentially include all responses that are not innate. That is, any response that can be learned can potentially be refined with practice, given the right conditions. Furthermore, these responses are not restricted to overt behaviours. For instance, consider learning to recognize a symbol such as 'f' as the letter F, or 'dog' as something that denotes 'a four legged mammal, sometimes referred to as man's best friend'. In both cases, a mental representation has been developed that evokes some response (in this case the appreciation of meaning) upon encountering a particular stimulus. Furthermore, such recognition is normally not accompanied by any conscious deliberation over meaning. The meaning just pops into our heads. Clearly the same sort of process is operating when experienced chess players know the most appropriate next move, when expert radiologists spot abnormalities in an X-ray slide, and when we recognize others as friends or family. Of course, skilled behaviour also includes overt behaviour. Writing, playing a musical instrument, driving a car, and laying bricks are all examples of behaviours that could not be performed well without a great deal of practice. Thus skilled behaviour and the acquisition of skills is potentially involved in the full range of human behaviour. This is certainly the point of view we have adopted, although it appears to us that it is not an opinion that is held universally. Certainly it is clear that many behaviours, and in particular cognitions, are studied without any consideration of their history. That is, has there been any form of skill acquisition, and if so, how much, and under what conditions? We demonstrate in this book why such questions are important, even in areas where learning seemingly plays no role. In this chapter, we consider some of the history of research in skill acquisition, some of the issues that have been of concern to researchers in this area, and some of the theories that have been proposed as accounts of the major phenomena associated with skill acquisition. In particular, we begin to evaluate the theories with respect to how well they meet the Skill Acquisition Phenomena Criterion introduced in the previous chapter. That is, how well do the theories account for skill acquisition phenomena?

2.2 **Great questions and issues**

From the late 1800s to the early 1960s, research into skilled performance and skill acquisition was largely devoid of any clear direction, theory, or results. The research was mainly applied in nature and concerned motor skills almost exclusively. The focus was typically on discovering the best methods for training motor skills, where the best methods were those that enabled the fastest learning and the greatest transfer to different situations and tasks. The major areas of research during this period are summarized below. A more comprehensive treatment of this research can be found in Adams (1987).

2.2.1 **Plateaus**

Research on complex skills really began with the work of Bryan and Harter (1899). They trained subjects in the sending and receiving of Morse code signals and examined the learning curves of these two tasks. The most interesting result of this research was the observation of plateaus in the learning curves of the receiving task. These plateaus represented periods during training where subjects' performance did not improve. However, further training usually resulted in further improvement. Similar plateaus were also reported during the training of typewriting (Book, 1925). The observation of plateaus led Bryan and Harter (1899) to propose that skill learning involved the acquisition of a hierarchy of habits. In a statement that has no doubt influenced some of today's theories of skill acquisition, Bryan and Harter described plateaus as periods where 'lower-order habits are approaching their maximum development, but are not yet sufficiently automatic to leave the attention free to attack the higher-order habits' (p.357).

The concept of plateaus in learning curves has not enjoyed wide support. Since Book's research, there has been little replication of the original findings (Adams, 1987; McGeoch, 1931, 1942). In addition, the extent to which plateaus can constrain theories of skill acquisition is questionable, since any variable that retards learning will produce them (Hunter, 1929). Still, as indicated above, the hierarchical view of skilled behaviour is fundamental to many modern theories of skill acquisition. Moreover, evidence of plateaus in learning curves does appear regularly in the literature, particularly where the tasks being performed involve the acquisition of many skill components that may be acquired at different rates (e.g. Thomas, 1998).

2.2.2 Part–whole training

One of the aims of early research in skill acquisition was to determine whether training on parts of a task and then combining these parts could be more efficient than training on the whole task. The benefits of such a training strategy are obvious, especially where the criterion task involves a large degree of cost or danger. For example, there is obvious value in a training method that would allow a substantial portion of pilot training to be achieved on the ground. Unfortunately, generalizations are not easy to arrive at in this area (McGeoch and Irion, 1952). The best approximation to a definitive answer to this research issue is that the relative benefits of part versus whole training are dependent on the task. Welford (1968) suggests that whole task training is the most efficient means of learning to perform tasks that involve highly interrelated activities, such as flying an aircraft. In contrast, those tasks that involve components which are performed in a fixed order and are largely independent of each other appear to benefit most from part training (Welford, 1968). At present, no theory of skill acquisition purports to account for this relationship between task type and the most efficient means of training.

2.2.3 Massed versus distributed practice

Another research issue in the history of skill acquisition that focussed on the best means of practicing a task concerned the relative benefits of massed and distributed practice. That is, which type of practice is the most efficient training method: continuous practice in one long session (massed) or spaced practice in a number of sessions separated by time intervals of a certain duration (distributed)? All of the research in this area is beset with the problem of defining training efficiency when the cost of training is dependent on both the time spent training on the task and the length of time from the beginning of training to the final testing. Despite this problem, the most popular generalization is that distributed training is the most efficient method (McGeoch, 1931; Welford, 1968). Adams (1987), however, rejected this conclusion. After reviewing 100 years of research on this issue, Adams concluded that distributed practice does not improve learning relative to massed practice, but instead improves the momentary level of performance only. For example, subjects trained with massed practice and then examined under distributed conditions perform equally as well as subjects performing under distributed conditions throughout (Adams and Reynolds, 1954).

The issue has been further complicated by a meta-analysis study reported by Lee and Genovese (1988). After reviewing 116 studies that were directly relevant to a comparison of distributed and massed training, Lee and Genovese found that 47 studies were suitable for a meta-analysis of effect size. On the basis of this analysis, it was concluded that distributed practice led to better acquisition and retention than massed practice. Lee and Genovese suggested also, however, that this generalization may only apply to continuous tasks (e.g. tracking an object on a computer screen with a mouse). This suggestion was supported by the results of a subsequent study (Lee and Genovese, 1989) that indicated that acquisition and retention of skill on a discrete task (e.g. press a button in response to a stimulus) was better under massed practice conditions.

2.2.4 Knowledge of results

An important concern to some researching skill acquisition was whether performance improves without knowledge of results. Bartlett (1948) stated practice without knowledge of results does not improve performance. This generalization has been widely accepted, although explanations of this effect, ranging from motivational to associative, are subject to debate (Adams, 1987).

The effects of withdrawing and delaying feedback have been examined extensively and some clear results have emerged. Welford (1968) reports a number of these: (1) When knowledge of results in motor tasks is delayed, learning is slowed. However, movement accuracy on most trials is affected to a small extent only. The slowing of learning is due to a greater proportion of trials that involve relatively larger movement errors. (2) When subjects perform some other activity between a trial and knowledge of the results of that trial, learning is slowed. (3) Learning is slowed as the gap between feedback and the following trial is lengthened. (4) Increasing the precision of feedback increases the accuracy of motor performance. (5) If knowledge of results is provided during training and then subsequently removed, performance deteriorates.

2.2.5 Learning curves

One of the methods researchers have used to track improvement on a skill has been to plot performance as a function of amount of practice. Generally, when performance improves with practice, the graph of improvement is a smooth curve. Such curves are known generically as learning curves. Learning curves first appeared in psychology over a hundred years ago with the work of Ebbinghaus (1885). He was interested in the factors that determined how easily things could be stored in and forgotten from memory. Ebbinghaus was particularly dedicated; rehearsing lists of nonsense syllables (e.g. FOJ) to himself thousands of times to try to commit them to memory. One of the major influences of Ebbinghaus's work on Psychology was the presentation of his results in graphical form to show the number of syllables remembered as a function of the number of repetitions. Typically, memory increased as repetitions increased. The results portrayed on such a graph also had a characteristic shape, with memory improving substantially in the early stages of rehearsal, and improvements getting smaller and smaller as rehearsal continued.

Following Ebbinghaus, learning curves became commonplace in any study of learning. Psychologists of the behaviourist school (e.g. Ferster and Skinner, 1957) were particularly enamoured with learning curves as a means of representing the conditioning of rats and pigeons. Hungry animals would be placed in small boxes fitted with levers (for rats) or buttons (for pigeons). Pressing on these objects would typically result in a reward in the form of a food pellet. Psychologists were interested in the pressing rate exhibited by the animals in response to differing schedules of reward. Typically, the responses would be automatically recorded by a pen on continually moving paper. This resulted in curves that indicated the extent of learning exhibited by the animals.

Although the behaviourist influence on psychology has waned somewhat, learning curves are still used extensively in psychology. They are typically used for representing how the accuracy or speed of performance improves with practice. These curves, particularly those measuring speed, have characteristic shapes. Early in practice, speed improvements are dramatic, but taper off with continued practice—a case of diminishing returns. Snoddy (1926) was the first to note that when the logarithm of performance time is plotted against the logarithm of amount of practice, a straight line typically results. This indicates that performance time can be described as a power function of practice, as indicated by the following equation:

$$T = X + NP^c \tag{2.1}$$

In Equation 2.1, T is the performance time on a task, P is the amount of practice on the task, $X+N$ is performance time on the first trial of the task, and X is the performance time after an infinite amount of practice. Power functions where $X = 0$ often provide very good fits to data, especially where large amounts of practice are involved. The parameter c in Equation 1 is the learning rate. The value of c is less than zero, to match the negative accelerated feature of the learning curve, and is also usually a value between 0 and -1. The closer the value of c is to -1, the faster the learning rate.

Crossman (1959) re-analysed the data of many experiments in varying domains, such as card sorting, addition of digits, and cigar rolling, and noted that learning in all of these tasks conformed to what he referred to as 'de Jong's law'. De Jong (1957) had also noted the power function regularity in learning curves. Newell and Rosenbloom (1981) also examined learning curves in a wide range of domains. They examined the ability of power functions to fit learning curves in comparison with other functions that are also negatively accelerated, such as the exponential function and the hyperbolic function, and concluded that the power function regularly provided a closer fit to the data. Newell and Rosenbloom, like Crossman, were impressed with the apparent lawfulness of the regularity in the learning data, so much so that they referred to the regularity as the power law of practice, and noted that it was one of the few laws in Psychology.

Indeed the presence of power functions in human learning data is so ubiquitous that the power law of practice has almost become an accepted fact in Psychology. As a small taste of this ubiquity, consider the following examples. First, Figure 2.1 demonstrates the typical shape of a power function learning curve. Part (a) contains the reaction time data for a group of people performing a computer task involving simple arithmetic (see Speelman and Kirsner, 2001, for details of the task). Part (b) of the figure presents the same data on log–log axes. In both parts, the line represents the best-fit power function. Similar curves are apparent in the data presented in Figures 2.2, 2.3, and 2.4. This data

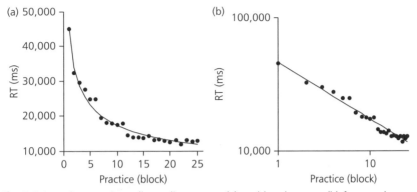

Fig. 2.1 Learning curves on linear–linear axes (a) and log–log axes (b) for people solving simple arithmetic problems (from Speelman and Kirsner, 2001). Lines represent best-fit power functions.

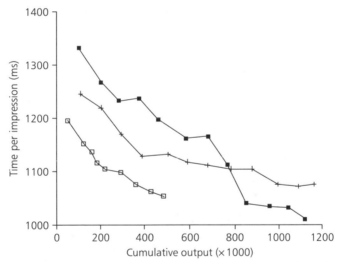

Fig. 2.2 Learning curves of three pressmen, representing time to make an impression in printing as a function of the number of impressions made (from Levy, 1965).

represents performance on a wide range of tasks: making print impressions (Figure 2.2); writing books (Figure 2.3); and even the production of ships (Figure 2.4).

Most discussion of the power law centres on data regarding the speed with which people perform tasks. It is also the case, however, that other measures of performance give rise to power function learning curves. For example,

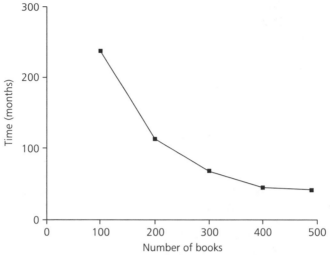

Fig. 2.3 Learning curve for Isaac Asimov, representing time to write a book as a function of number of books written (from Ohlsson, 1992).

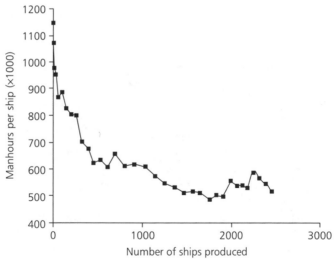

Fig. 2.4 Learning curve for the production of Liberty Vessels, representing time to produce each ship as a function of the number of ships produced (from Searle and Gody, 1945).

the number of errors committed on a task is typically reduced with practice (e.g. see Figure 2.5). Whenever the power law is considered, it usually refers to changes in performance time on tasks where error rates are very low, and change little with practice.

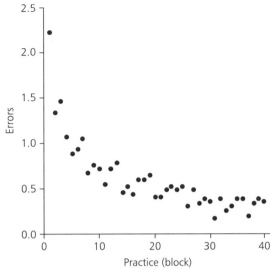

Fig. 2.5 Error rate as a function of practice on a simple arithmetic task (data from an unpublished experiment by Speelman, 1999).

The acceptance of the power law of practice within Psychology has grown to the extent that some researchers (e.g. Anderson, 1983a; Logan, 1988) have suggested that for any theory of skill acquisition to be considered seriously, it must be able to provide an account of the law. Certainly, anyone who has proposed a theory of skill acquisition in the last 25 years has promoted the ability of the theory to account for the power law as an important indicator of the theory's validity. A number of such theories are considered later in this chapter. It is also important to note that there have been suggestions recently that the power law may not be as lawful as has generally been believed. In addition, there is evidence that the shape of learning curves is affected by transfer. These issues are discussed in Chapter 3.

2.2.6 Transfer of training

As with the part versus whole training issue, transfer of training research has typically had an applied focus. The implicit motive in this research is usually to demonstrate that training in one situation will improve performance in another situation, with experimental manipulation aimed at either increasing or decreasing the extent of this transfer. An obvious example is research that looks at the relationship between training in a flight-simulator and subsequent performance in a real aircraft. Historically, the challenge in such research has been to investigate what features in the training and transfer situations determine the amount of transfer that occurs. In other words, what is transferred from one situation to another that can either benefit or impede performance in the second situation? The general aim, then, has been to determine when skills learned in one task can be transferred to performance of another task, with the hope of devising more efficient training methods. Efficiency in this context refers to some notion of the cost benefits of training, where training on a less expensive and time-consuming task may reduce the training time required on the target task. However, an influential theory of the principles underlying transfer—the identical elements theory of Thorndike (Thorndike, 1906; Thorndike and Woodworth, 1901)—suggested that there are no free rides in skill acquisition.

Thorndike's identical elements theory states that transfer between two tasks is determined by the extent to which the tasks share the same content. Thus, the more that is common between tasks in terms of stimuli, responses, or stimulus–response pairs, the greater will be the transfer. The theory has enjoyed widespread support from research in both verbal learning (e.g. McGeoch and Irion, 1952; Osgood, 1949) and motor learning (e.g. Adams, 1987; Duncan, 1958).

The identical elements theory was developed in the early days of behaviourism and so was couched in stimulus–response terms rather than cognitive terms. As a result, criticism was levelled at the theory's inability to account for transfer that apparently was not related to commonalities between tasks but was associated with more cognitive features of the tasks (e.g. Orata, 1928). A second, more telling, criticism of the identical elements theory concerned the assumption that stimulus–response pairs are the basis of transfer. This assumption was criticized as being so restrictive as to rule out transfer altogether (Meiklejohn, 1908). Unless a new task involved the same responses to the same stimuli as an original training task, there would be no transfer between the tasks. Thus learning to write with a pencil would be of no benefit for writing with a pen. Therefore, stimulus–response pairs were not sufficiently abstract to be identified as the identical elements of Thorndike's theory.

Little was achieved in the years that followed Thorndike's work to provide a suitable representation for skill. Research into transfer was more concerned with the effect of various training conditions on transfer performance. However, Briggs (1969) suggested that analysing the relationship between common features of tasks and the extent of transfer between them could only provide a preliminary understanding of transfer and that it was 'important to determine *what* is learned . . . during training . . . for a more complete understanding (p. 217)'. Hence, the progress of skills research was restricted by the lack of suitable concepts for describing the 'what' of learning.

The cognitive representation of knowledge became a popular topic of research and theory in the 1960s resulting in many suggested modes of representation, such as semantic networks (Collins and Quillian, 1969, 1972), productions (Newell and Simon, 1972), schemas (Minsky, 1975), and mental models (Johnson-Laird, 1983). As a result, theoretical tools not available to Thorndike were developed, enabling more abstract discussions of the processes underlying skills and transfer.

2.2.7 Fitts and the phases of skill acquisition

The above summary of results and theories was mainly concerned with motor skills. In fact, until the 1960s, skills research was almost exclusively concerned with motor tasks. The most influential definition of what constitutes skilled performance was restricted to muscular performance (Pear, 1948). It was not until the cognitive revolution during the 1960s that cognitive performance began to be considered under the skill heading. The most important early discussion of skill acquisition as involving cognitive processes was by Fitts (1964). This work is important in the sense that it specified the phenomena that a theory of skill acquisition should explain.

Although Fitts did not propose a theory of skill acquisition, his descriptions of the sequence of events involved in developing a skill were the first steps towards such a theory. One of his descriptions is worth quoting because it identifies the processes that need elucidation by theory:

> An adult, or even a child of a few years of age, never begins the acquisition of a new form of skilled behaviour except from the background of many already existing, highly developed, both general and specific skills. Thus, the initial state of our model is not that of a random model, but an already highly organised system processing language skills, concepts, and many efficient subroutines . . . . The number of such identifiable highly developed skills in an adult is certainly in the hundreds, each having its own executive program and library of subroutines, many of the subroutines being shared with other skills.
>
> The actual sequence of behaviour processes employed early in learning varies with the type of activity, of course, but might be somewhat as follows: The S observes or samples certain aspects of the environment, puts this information into short-term storage after some recoding, makes a decision such as selecting an appropriate subroutine which sets up a response pattern, executes a short behaviour sequence . . ., samples the internal and external feedback from this response plus additional stimulus information from the environment, recodes and stores this new information (in the process losing some of the information already in short-term storage), makes another decision which might be to use a different subroutine, and so on. As learning progresses, the subroutine becomes longer, the executive routine or overall strategy is perfected, the stimulus sampling becomes less frequent and the coding more efficient, and different aspects of the activity become integrated or coordinated . . . . As learning continues, overall performance may come to resemble more and more closely a

continuous process. The overall program having now been perfected, frequent changes no longer need to be made in it. However, subroutines may continue slowly to become more efficient, and the S to become increasingly able to carry on the entire behaviour process while engaged simultaneously in other activities, with little or no interference between the two.

(Fitts, 1964, p. 260)

Fitts (1964) suggested that skill acquisition involved three phases. The early phase was termed the 'cognitive stage' by Fitts. This stage lasts for only a few trials while the subject comes to terms with instructions and develops performance strategies. According to Fitts, these strategies develop from general 'sets' and strategies developed with previously learned tasks. Refinement of the performance strategy comes in the intermediate phase—'the associative stage'. Features of the previously learned strategies that are appropriate to the new situation are strengthened on the basis of feedback, whereas inappropriate features are weakened. This process forms new associations between specific stimulus cues and appropriate responses. In the end phase—'the autonomous stage'—the components of the performance strategy slowly become more autonomous so that they are less subject to cognitive control or external interference. As a result skilled performance of the task requires increasingly less processing, which means that more processing resources can be used for other activities. During this phase, skills continue to become faster and more efficient although the rate of improvement slows with practice.

Fitts provided no theoretical accounts of the processes he identified in the three phases, although he did point out where he thought existing theories were useful in this scheme. For instance, the selection of previously learned general sets and strategies for incorporation into new strategies draws on Crossman's (1959; see below) general probability learning model. In this model, subjects are presumed to possess a repertoire of methods for performing a task. Each method is selected at random and the probability of its subsequent selection is dependent on its performance speed—the faster ones being more likely to be selected. This process predicts the typical power function speed-up found in skill acquisition (e.g. Newell and Rosenbloom, 1981). However, other features of Fitts's description of skill development are not specified to the same extent. The development from the initial stages of task performance of the 'executive program', the 'subroutines', and the relationship between these is not given a clear process description. However, the suggestion that these skills have a hierarchical structure that is goal-driven is a large step towards such a description.

Fitts's work did not lead to a large increase of research into cognitive skills. Although there was certainly a growing interest in cognitive processes during this time, research was dominated by the advent of the information processing approach. Most researchers were interested in performance questions, where performance was examined in a limited context. As a result the field was soon well supplied with very specific theories concerned with isolated and disparate processes (e.g. Chase, 1973). There did not appear to be much interest in higher cognitive processes, that is, processes responsible for changes in performance.

Eventually, though, cognitive scientists began to be interested in more unified theories of cognition, attempting to describe cognitive architectures that could account for a wide variety of phenomena (e.g. Minsky, 1975; Newell and Simon, 1972). A number of these theories also consider the nature of skill acquisition, and these are discussed below.

2.3 Theories

In this section, we present the major theories of skill acquisition and evaluate the extent to which the theories meet the Skill Acquisition Phenomena Criterion. There are two issues that are of concern in this section. First, we focus on the various explanations for why practice leads to performance improvements, particularly improvements that have the negatively accelerated feature of power functions. Second, we look at how each theory handles the issue of transfer. A third issue—the effect of transfer on the shape of learning curves—is another feature of skill acquisition that the theories need to explain in order to meet the Skill Acquisition Phenomena Criterion. This issue is considered in Chapter 3.

A broad distinction can be made between theories of skill acquisition. On one hand, there are the theories that propose that practice leads to performance improvements because practice has the effect of refining procedures for performing a task (e.g. Anderson's ACT, Newell and Rosenbloom's SOAR). On the other hand, there are theories that view performance improvements as a by-product of some of the consequences of practice. For example, some theories claim that practice leads to greater knowledge (i.e. more memories to call upon) which in turn leads to faster performance (e.g. Logan's Instance theory). This distinction, is not exhaustive, as recent models of skill acquisition have begun to blur the boundaries between strategy refinement and memory-based performance as explanations of performance improvement (e.g. Rickard, 1997, 1999; Wenger, 1999). In this section, our presentation of the theories maintains the distinction; however, throughout the book there will be cause to consider abandoning such a clear separation of views.

The aim of this section is to begin to evaluate the theories in terms of whether they satisfy the Skill Acquisition Phenomena Criterion for suitability as theories of skill acquisition. The main issues in focus in this section are explanations provided by each theory with respect to why learning curves are typically negatively accelerated, and what features determine transfer.

2.3.1 Skill acquisition as strategy refinement

Crossman

Crossman (1959) provided an early view on how practice leads to performance improvements. He suggested that, when faced with a new task, we have many strategies that can potentially be used. With practice at the task, we monitor the outcomes we produce as a result of the various strategies used. With time we come to favour the more efficient strategies. These are used more often and this produces performance speed-up. Thus, Crossman's model qualifies as an example of a theory that proposes that practice leads to more efficient procedures for performing a task. The theory does not suggest that practice modifies strategies to make them more efficient. Instead, practice leads to the selection of the most efficient strategy among several.

Crossman's theory provides an account of the power law of learning. According to the theory, it is easier to find faster, more efficient methods early in practice, and so large gains in performance time are more likely at this stage. As practice continues, more efficient methods become harder to find, and so performance time improves by ever-smaller amounts.

Crossman's theory is not comprehensive on the topic of transfer. Obviously transfer is important to the theory as it relies on a range of strategies being available for performance of new tasks, however, Crossman did not deal with the issue in any great detail beyond a re-statement of Thorndike's identical elements hypothesis: '... transfer of skill from one task to another will take place where methods appropriate to one are also appropriate to the other' (Crossman, 1959, p. 163).

Crossman's model did not specify the origin of the various strategies. Furthermore, he did not provide evidence to support the claim that people will tend to follow the more efficient strategy—certainly there is evidence that this does not occur (e.g. Luchins, 1942). Thus, Crossman's theory cannot be considered as a serious contender for a comprehensive theory of skill acquisition. Nonetheless, taken with the other theories presented below, it illustrates that there are many ways in which particular behaviour changes (i.e. performance improvements with practice) can be modelled.

ACT-R

One of the most influential theories of skill acquisition, and to date, the most comprehensive, is the ACT theory, in its various incarnations. Early versions of this theory include ACTE (Anderson, 1976)—a successor to the HAM model of memory (Anderson and Bower, 1973), ACTF (Anderson *et al.*, 1979, 1980), and ACT* (Anderson, 1982, 1983a). ACT-R (Anderson, 1993; Anderson and Lebiere, 1998) is the latest version of the theory and inherits most of the features of the earlier versions. ACT-R is first and foremost a general theory of cognition that describes an architecture that underlies all cognitive processes. The ACT-R theory, therefore, qualifies as a candidate for a unified theory of cognition, as advocated by Newell (e.g. 1989, pp. 404–405). It is from this general theory of cognition that the ACT-R theory of skill acquisition emerges. Features of the cognitive architecture proposed by ACT-R that are relevant to skill acquisition are described below. This is followed by a description of the processes involved in skill acquisition and transfer.

The cognitive architecture proposed by ACT-R ACT-R proposes that the architecture underlying cognition is a production system. Such a system involves the application of production rules that are activated by the contents of a working memory. In this sense production systems can be considered 'cognitive S–R (stimulus–response) theories' (Anderson, 1983a, p. 6). Production systems are not peculiar to the ACT-R theory and have the property of being computationally universal. That is, they can be used to model all cognitive processes. However, the use of a production system in ACT-R is not simply to re-describe behaviour but is sensitive to psychological and empirical constraints. As a result, testable predictions can be made on the basis of this production system.

Basic to ACT-R is the distinction between declarative and procedural knowledge. Declarative knowledge can be considered to be the representation of facts (e.g. 'A red traffic light is a signal to stop'.). Procedural knowledge is basically the representation of what to do in particular situations. Thus, actions are contingent on certain conditions being present. In ACT-R, procedural knowledge is embodied as production rules—condition–action pairs that associate the presence of a particular data pattern in working memory (condition) with the performance of a certain action. Therefore, when the condition of a production rule is satisfied, the production can apply and the action will follow (e.g. 'IF traffic light is red, THEN stop').

Particular features of the ACT-R production system constrain the activation of productions. These are as follows: (1) Productions can only be activated by knowledge that is currently active in working memory. (2) The speed at which the condition of a production is matched to data in working memory is a function of the strength of the production. In ACT-R, productions gain strength with successful application.

In addition to the above constraints on production activation, ACT-R includes several rules of conflict resolution. Originally, in ACT*, there were three rules that determined which production will apply when the conditions of more than one production are matched by the data in working memory. (1) Refractoriness prevents the same production from applying to the same data in the same way more than once. As a result, the production cannot repeat itself over again. (2) When two or more productions can apply, the production with the more specific condition will apply. (3) Specificity and strength interact in the application of productions. If a production with a general condition is selected and applies before a more specific production can apply, then the general production will be the one that actually applies. Therefore, more specific productions can only take precedence if they have sufficient strength to ensure faster selection and application times than more general productions. This strength comes only with successful application (i.e. practice). ACT-R now includes one overriding conflict resolution mechanism. When several productions share the same goal, the most useful production is chosen for execution. Usefulness, or the expected gain of a production, is defined as:

$$\text{Expected Gain (E)} = PG - C$$

where P represents the probability that a production will satisfy the goal if it is executed, and G is the worth of the goal. Thus PG represents the potential gain of firing the production. C represents the cost of executing the production, and this generally reflects the time to achieve the goal. Hence E reflects the expected net utility of executing a particular production. When several productions compete for the same goal, the one with the highest expected gain will fire.

Individual productions do not usually function in a vacuum. Instead, sets of productions are organized with hierarchical goal-structures. This organization accounts for the hierarchical nature of human behaviour identified by Fitts (1964). Productions that underlie the performance of a particular behaviour are organized around the satisfaction of goals and sub-goals. This results in serial processing where only one goal can be attended to at a time (Anderson, 1983a, p. 33). This goal-driven structure also has the function of biasing pattern-matching processes towards matching structures involving the current goal. Considering the specificity constraint described above, this means that productions that refer to the current goal are more likely to apply and apply more rapidly than productions that do not refer to this goal.

The above description of the production system underlying the ACT-R theory of cognition is only a brief one, touching upon those features that are important for understanding the ACT-R theory of skill acquisition. A more complete account is available in Anderson and Lebiere (1998).

The ACT-R theory of skill acquisition The ACT-R theory of skill acquisition was developed by Anderson and his colleagues after studying the learning of geometry proofs (Anderson, 1982, 1983a, 1989a; Anderson *et al.*, 1981, 1993a; Neves and Anderson, 1981), computer programming in the LISP language (Anderson, 1986, 1987, 1989a; Anderson and Reiser, 1985; Anderson *et al.*, 1985, 1989, 1993b; McKendree and Anderson, 1987; Pirolli and Anderson, 1985a; Singley and Anderson, 1989) and other computer languages (Anderson, *et al.*, 1993c), text-editing (Anderson, 1987; Singley and Anderson, 1985, 1989), calculus (Singley and Anderson, 1989), algebra (Anderson, 1989a; Blessing and Anderson, 1996), language processing (Anderson, 1982, 1983a), schemata (Anderson *et al.*, 1979), problem-solving (Anderson and Fincham, 1994; Anderson *et al.*, 1997, 1999), and creating computer simulations of the processes underlying skill development in each of these areas. The computer simulations relied on similar architectures to that specified by ACT-R (and previously ACT*) and so provided a useful method of assessing the adequacy of the ACT-R account of skill acquisition.

In all of the work cited above involving Anderson, the basic theory of skill acquisition has remained consistent, varying little from the first appearance of the ACT* theory. However, some details have been modified recently and these are described below. The general sequence of events in skill acquisition is suggested to be as follows: Knowledge relevant to the performance of a skill begins in declarative form. This knowledge is interpreted by general productions called weak problem-solving methods. These methods are termed 'weak' because they are domain-general, that is, their operation is not specific to any particular type of task (e.g. analogy). Domain-specific productions are created by a process called compilation. This process involves two sub-processes. The first is procedularization, which describes the creation of domain-specific productions as a by-product of the interpretation of declarative knowledge via weak problem-solving methods. These new productions perform the goal behaviour without the need to consult declarative knowledge. Composition is the second compilation process, and describes the formation of efficient productions by collapsing sequences of productions into single productions that have the effect of the series. The likelihood of a production being applied in a particular situation, and the speed at which the production will be executed, are both functions of the production's strength. Productions accumulate strength depending on their history of success. Stronger productions are matched and applied faster. Therefore, highly practised productions are executed faster than newly formed productions. All of the above processes will now be described in more detail.

The processes underlying skill acquisition will be illustrated with respect to a student learning to solve algebra problems. The strategy described is not necessarily how people solve such problems but is useful in illustrating the changes that can occur with practice.

Imagine that a teacher is describing an algebra solution method to a student. The teacher may start with a problem like $79 = 3x + 4$ and tells the student that the goal is to solve for 'x'. To achieve this goal requires achieving a number of sub-goals. For example, the teacher may tell the student that the first step in realizing the overall goal is to isolate the 'x' term on the right-hand side of the equation. This will mean eliminating the '4' from this side of the equation. The teacher will then demonstrate how this is done, by adding '-4' to both sides of the equation:

$$79 + (-4) = 3x + 4 + (-4)$$
$$\Rightarrow 75 = 3x$$

Having achieved this sub-goal of isolating the 'x' term on the right-hand side of the equation, the teacher may then describe the second sub-goal, which is to eliminate the coefficient of the 'x' term, which is 3. This is achieved by dividing both sides of the equation by 3:

$$\frac{75}{3} = \frac{3x}{3}$$
$$\Rightarrow 75 = 3x$$

This is then the solution to the problem.

The student's memory of these instructions for how to solve the problem can be considered declarative knowledge. It represents knowledge about how to solve that particular problem, but cannot be used alone to solve other problems. For this knowledge to be useful in solving other problems requires processes that can interpret this knowledge and translate it into action. In ACT*, these processes were described as weak problem solving methods that can be useful in a wide range of domains. According to Anderson (e.g. Singley and Anderson, 1989), humans develop these at an early age and by adulthood these methods are well developed. These problem-solving methods include analogy, means–end analysis, hill climbing, and pure forward search.

In the algebra example, if the student were presented with another problem to solve, such as $85 = 4x + 5$ analogy would be the most likely method to apply. Analogy would function to enable the student to mimic the previous solution. This process will only apply, of course, if the student notices the usefulness of the previous solution (e.g. Gick and Holyoak, 1983; Holyoak, 1985). The process can be illustrated with the following plausible imitation of a talk-aloud protocol (for real examples of such protocols, see Anderson, 1983a).

'This problem ($85 = 4x + 5$) looks similar to the teacher's example, so maybe if I try the method that the teacher described I'll solve the problem. The teacher started by isolating the 'x' term on the right-hand side of the equation by adding the negative of the leftover term (4) to both sides of the equation. In this new problem the leftover term is 5, so I should add -5 to both sides of the equation:

$$85 + (-5) = 4x + 5 + (-5)$$
$$\Rightarrow 80 = 4x$$

'After doing this, the teacher eliminated the number in front of the 'x' term by dividing both sides of the equation by that number (3). In this new problem the number in front of the 'x' term is 4 so I should divide both sides of the equation by 4:

$$\frac{80}{4} = \frac{4x}{4}$$
$$\Rightarrow 20 = x$$

So, the solution must be 20'.

Although this is a purely fictitious protocol, it captures the essence of protocols reported by Anderson (1983a). This example was designed to illustrate how general interpretive methods can be used to translate declarative knowledge into action, given the limitations of declarative memory (i.e. that the student can remember all that the teacher did and why) and that a previous solution will be noticed as useful (see Singley and Anderson, 1989, p. 34).

A by-product of the application of weak problem-solving methods to interpret declarative knowledge and achieve a solution is the formation of new productions. In contrast to the domain-general weak methods, these new productions are domain-specific. That is, their application is peculiar to the domain of the problem, operating only on particular features of that domain. This development of productions from the application of general methods is called compilation and, as indicated earlier, involves two processes: proceduralization and composition.

Proceduralization eliminates the reference to declarative knowledge by building into productions the effect of that reference. In the algebra example, proceduralization of the problem solution would mean that the student no longer needs to refer to the memory of the teacher's instructions to solve further problems. Instead, the student will have developed a set of productions that will solve such problems directly. These productions are domain-specific—they operate only in the domain of solving such algebra problems. This contrasts with the weak methods that will apply in a large variety of domains. An example of a set of domain-specific productions for solving the algebra problems is presented in Table 2.1.

The development of productions, such as those in Table 2.1, precludes the need to hold declarative information (i.e. the teacher's instructions) in working memory and use analogy at each step of the problem. Thus, to solve new algebra problems, the student does not need to continually refer back to previous solutions for directions. This prediction is supported by the dropout of verbal rehearsal of problem-solving steps that characterizes early performance on this type of task (e.g. Anderson, 1983a). As the need to refer to declarative knowledge is reduced with proceduralization, so should the load on working memory be similarly reduced. This prediction is also consistent with observation (e.g. Woltz, 1988).

An important feature to note of the set of productions in Table 2.1, is that they have a hierarchical structure that matches the goal structure implicit in the solution of such problems. This is fundamental to the ACT-R description of skills and skill acquisition and underlies the form of the production sets that develop. The second process involved in compilation—composition—is determined by the goal structure of problems. Composition collapses several productions into a single production. These productions must occur in a sequence and share the same overall goal. The new single production does the

Table 2.1 Example of a set of domain-specific productions for solving algebra problems

P1	IF	goal is to solve for x in equation of form $a = bx + c$
	THEN	set as sub-goal to isolate x on RHS of equation
P2	IF	goal is to isolate x on RHS of equation
	THEN	set as sub-goals
		to eliminate c from RHS of equation
		and then to eliminate b from RHS of equation
P3	IF	goal is to eliminate c from RHS of equation
	THEN	add $-c$ to both sides of equation
P4	IF	goal is to eliminate b from RHS of equation
	THEN	divide both sides of equation by b
P5	IF	goal is to solve for x in equation
		and x has been isolated on RHS of equation
	THEN	LHS of equation is solution for x

work of the sequence but in fewer steps. For example, productions P2, P3, and P4 in Table 2.1 could be composed to:

P6   IF   goal is to isolate x on RHS of equation
          THEN   add $-c$ to both sides of equation
                     and then divide both sides of equation by b

With further practice, productions P1, P6, and P5 could be composed to:

P7   IF   goal is to solve for x in equation of form
                     $a = bx + c$
          THEN   add $-c$ to both sides of equation
                     then divide both sides of equation by b
                     and result is solution

An algebra 'expert' (i.e. someone with many years of experience solving such problems) should be able to recognize this solution immediately upon observation of the problem. The expert would be unlikely to consider the intermediate steps that the novice needs to perform.

Compilation predicts a speed-up in performance for a number of reasons. First, Anderson (1982) suggests that the time to perform a task is a function of the number of steps involved. Therefore, since composition reduces the number of steps (productions) required to perform a task, with practice performance will rely on fewer productions and so will take less time. A more significant reduction in performance time comes with proceduralizsation. Performing a task on the basis of a set of productions that execute the task directly should take less time than having to interpret declarative knowledge for procedural directions. This accounts for the dramatic improvements in performance time observed by Singley and Anderson (1989) after only one trial of learning. Singley and Anderson reported that subjects showed a 50% improvement in the time to produce a LISP function from the first trial to the second trial.

The combined speed-up in performance predicted by composition and proceduralization is not sufficient to account for all the speed-up that is observed in skill acquisition (Anderson, 1982). ACT-R includes a tuning mechanism—strengthening—that results in further improvements in performance time with practice. Productions are strengthened with successful practice. That is, each time a production is applied successfully it gains strength. Conversely, if a production is applied inappropriately it loses strength. The stronger a production is, the faster it is to apply. So, the combination of compilation and strengthening predicts a speed-up in performance that continues with practice.

Anderson (1982) demonstrates how the compilation and strengthening mechanisms account for the power law of learning (e.g. Newell and Rosenbloom, 1981). The basic ACT* version of such a power function is:

$$T = N P^c$$

where N is the time on trial 1, related to the original number of productions, P is the amount of practice, c is the rate of learning, $c < 0$; $c = f + g$ where f is the fraction by which the # of steps is reduced by composition, g is related to memory decay.

The ACT-R account of the power law of learning is examined in more detail in Chapter 3 when we consider the effects of transfer on the shape of learning curves.

Early versions of the ACT* theory of skill acquisition (e.g. Anderson, 1982, 1983a) included additional tuning mechanisms to strengthening—generalization and discrimination. These mechanisms were suggested to be automatic induction processes that refined the productions developed by compilation. Generalization is a process whereby general productions are generated from more specific ones. An example from Anderson (1987, p. 205) illustrates this process with respect to language acquisition. If a child has developed the following two productions:

| IF | the goal is to generate the present tense of KICK |
| THEN | say KICK + s |

| IF | the goal is to generate the present tense of HUG |
| THEN | say HUG + s |

the generalization mechanism would develop a more general rule that would be applicable in the above situations and others:

| IF | the goal is to generate the present tense of 'verb' |
| THEN | say 'verb' + s |

Discrimination has the effect of restricting the range of such general rules. Thus, in the above example, the general rule is overly general, and in certain circumstances is not appropriate. As a result, the discrimination mechanism would generate new rules appropriate for these circumstances. For example,

IF	the goal is to generate the present tense of 'verb'
	and the subject of the sentence is singular
THEN	say 'verb' + s

IF	the goal is to generate the present tense of 'verb'
	and the subject of the sentence is plural
THEN	say 'verb'

Despite the utility of generalization and discrimination in accounting for various phenomena in language acquisition (e.g. Anderson, 1983a), later versions of ACT* (Anderson, 1986, 1987, 1989a; Singley and Anderson, 1989) suggested that these two tuning mechanisms are unnecessary in a theory of skill acquisition. In fact, the effects of these mechanisms can be implemented by the same general problem-solving methods that initiate proceduralization (e.g. analogy) (Anderson, 1987). In addition, by having generalization and discrimination implemented by these general methods, the induction of more refined rules is more sensitive to semantic and strategic factors than the automatic processes of the generalization and discrimination mechanisms (Anderson, 1987).

A further refinement of the ACT theories has seen the composition process of ACT* dropped. This is not to say that composition-like phenomena do not occur. Indeed, there is behavioural evidence to suggest that people can acquire multistep productions, such as P7 above (e.g. McKendree and Anderson, 1987). Anderson (1993) claims, that there is no evidence that this form of production refinement occurs automatically with practice. Instead, in ACT-R, analogy to examples that illustrate a more direct solution strategy can lead to new, similarly direct, productions. These new productions, will compete with old productions that may perform the task in more steps, but are faster because of prior practice. Hence, the relative expected gain of the old productions and the new, more refined productions will determine which productions are executed. Thus, practice will not automatically lead to composed productions.

The removal of an automatic composition mechanism in the ACT theories means that performance improvements that result from practice are mainly due to strengthening of productions. In ACT* practice also led, automatically, to greater refinement of productions (e.g. composition). In ACT-R this refinement may occur, but will be determined by considerations of the gain and cost of performance. The only automatic consequence of practice in ACT-R is that productions are strengthened. Because the strength of productions increases as a power function of the number of executions, and productions are executed faster as their strength increases, practice leads to faster performance in a manner described by the power law of learning. In other words, skill acquisition is a process whereby practice leads to the development of procedural knowledge (productions) that is altered by repeated execution (i.e. it is strengthened), and this alteration in turn leads to faster performance. Thus, it is a change in the characteristics of knowledge that results in better performance.

In addition to the observations of cognitive skill acquisition that were mentioned above, the ACT-R theory of skill acquisition provides a useful account of the three phases of skill development described by Fitts (1964).

ACT-R and Fitts's phases of skill acquisition The early phase of skill acquisition identified by Fitts (1964) corresponds in ACT-R to the application of general problem-solving methods to declarative knowledge and to the initial development of productions. Fitts suggested that this phase only lasts for a short time, which is consistent with Anderson's reports of one-trial learning (e.g. Singley and Anderson, 1989). Fitts describes this phase as the cognitive stage, where most of the thinking about a task is performed. Anderson (1983a) claims that it is natural to equate this stage with the interpretive application of knowledge. Certainly there is considerable evidence that higher order cognitive activities, such as comprehension of task requirements and planning, are more prevalent early in skill development than later (e.g. Ackerman, 1988; Woltz, 1988). In addition, processing during this stage is more error-prone and deliberate than in subsequent stages (Ackerman, 1988; Woltz, 1988) as working memory resources are stretched by the interpretation of declarative knowledge.

The intermediate phase identified by Fitts describes the formation of specific associations between stimulus cues and appropriate responses. The similarities between such associations and production rules are obvious. In ACT-R, this stage corresponds to the dropout of verbal rehearsal of instructions and the associated reduction of working memory load.

The end phase was described by Fitts and Posner (1967) as the stage where 'component processes become increasingly autonomous' (p. 14). During this stage, skills are less reliant on working memory resources and become faster with practice. The ACT-R theory suggests that productions gain strength with practice and this results in faster application of the productions. In accordance with the power law of learning, the effect of strengthening on improvement becomes increasingly small with practice. Eventually, after many thousands of trials (Anderson, 1989b), no further improvement will be observed. During this phase, performance may appear to be automatic (e.g. Shiffrin and Schneider, 1977): when the conditions of a production are satisfied, the action will follow automatically.

Transfer The ACT-R theory of skill acquisition also describes how transfer can occur between tasks. Anderson (1987; Anderson and Singley, 1993; Singley and Anderson, 1989) resurrected the identical elements theory by identifying production rules as the elements of knowledge underlying transfer. According to this proposal, transfer between two tasks is determined by the extent to which productions underlying performance in one task are useful in performing the second. The greater the production overlap, the greater the transfer.

Productions have an immediate advantage over stimulus–response pairs with respect to representing the processing operations underlying skilled performance: productions are abstract cognitive representations. As described above, productions are formed as the by-product of an interpretive process that compares two declarative representations. For example, analogy compares the representation of a previous solution to the representation of the current situation and extracts common features. The productions that result from this process are generalizations and, therefore, are necessarily abstract (Singley and Anderson, 1989).

Three forms of transfer are traditionally considered in any discussion of transfer results: positive, negative, and zero transfer. The identification of identical productions as the basis for transfer leads to strong predictions concerning each of these situations. These are described below, along with studies that examine these predictions.

Positive transfer As a task is practised, a set of productions is developed that underlies the performance of this task. If the performance of a second task can utilize these same productions then positive transfer will result between the two tasks. Positive transfer in this situation refers to the fact that knowledge developed in one situation is transferred to another situation. This has a positive effect in the sense that there is no need to develop productions from scratch to perform operations that existing productions already perform. Therefore, the extent of this positive transfer is determined by the number of productions developed in the context of the first task that can be used in performance of the second task.

Singley and Anderson (1985, 1989; Anderson and Singley, 1993) provided support for the ACT-R account of transfer in a detailed study of text-editing skill. Two basic types of editors were examined: line editors that allowed examination of only one line of text at a time, and screen editors that enabled viewing of whole screens of text. Singley and Anderson predicted that there would be almost complete positive transfer between two line editors and only partial transfer from line editors to screen editors. The transfer predictions were based on models of the productions underlying performance with each of the editors. Despite the fact that the two line editors shared few commands, Singley and Anderson identified considerable production overlap in these editors, mainly concerned with the more abstract planning operations. This was shown to result in almost complete transfer between the two line editors: two days of practice with one of these editors was almost equivalent to two days of practice with the other in terms of preparation for further performance with this second editor. Much less production overlap was identified between the line editors and the screen editor and this was shown to result in only partial transfer from training with the line editors to performance with the screen editor.

Kieras and Bovair (1986) have also reported success at predicting the extent of transfer between tasks on the basis of the number of shared productions. Detailed predictions of the training time to reach a performance criterion were shown to be accurate when the task was analysed in terms of old and new productions. Old productions had been learned in the context of another task and so did not require learning. New productions were those that needed to be developed. Kieras and Bovair predicted and observed that the greater the number of old productions involved in the performance of a new task, the smaller the training time required on this task.

Negative transfer Negative transfer refers to a situation where performance of a task is worse than if a preceding task had never been performed. One interpretation of such a result is that the procedure for performing the second task is performed less effectively as a result of another procedure having been learned in the context of the first task (Anderson, 1987). However, the ACT-R account of transfer predicts that negative transfer in this sense does not exist (Singley and Anderson, 1989). The worst case that can be expected in a transfer situation is that two tasks share no productions, resulting in zero transfer (this situation is described below). ACT-R proposes that results that might indicate negative transfer in fact indicate positive transfer. However, what have been transferred are non-optimal methods for performing the task. Therefore, productions developed in the context of one task are transferred to the performance of another task. These productions do not interfere with the execution of productions relating to the second task (i.e. negative transfer). Instead, when these productions are used to perform the second task, performance is less efficient than if it relied on productions that were developed in the context of the second task only. This situation will occur when the stimulus conditions of the second task match the conditions of productions developed in the context of the first task. These productions will execute in response to these stimulus conditions, although the processing strategy they embody will not be optimal for the second task.

Some evidence consistent with the ACT-R account of negative transfer exists, the most famous being the demonstration of the *Einstellung* phenomenon by Luchins (1942). Subjects were required to solve a number of problems that involved determining the best method of combining three water jugs (A, B, and C) to make up designated volumes of water. The problem sequence was such that subjects were presented with five problems that each had the same solution (i.e. combine the jugs according to B - A - 2C). Following these problems, the subjects were presented with another two problems that could either be solved with this same method or with a more direct method (A + C).

Luchins found that almost all of the subjects solved the two transfer problems with the method discovered during training. In contrast, control subjects who were first presented with the transfer problems almost always solved them with the easier method. Therefore, the training problems encouraged the use of a non-optimal solution procedure with the transfer problems. The stimulus conditions of the transfer problems were obviously sufficiently similar to those of the training problems to trigger the execution of this non-optimal method. This meant that subjects could utilize a previous solution rather than develop a new strategy specific to the transfer problems. Further evidence that negative transfer is in fact the positive transfer of non-optimal methods has been reported with text-editing (Singley and Anderson, 1989) and computer programming (Kessler and Anderson, 1986).

Zero transfer The ACT-R account of transfer predicts that training with one task will provide no benefit for performance with a second task if the two tasks do not share common productions. More specifically, transfer between tasks is restricted to common productions and is not related to the abstract knowledge underlying the productions. Therefore, there will be no transfer between skills that use the same knowledge in different ways. This proposal leads to some counter-intuitive predictions. For example, there should be no transfer between the comprehension and generation of language. Singley and Anderson (1989) reviewed the small amount of research relevant to this issue and concluded that there was some evidence that comprehension and generation involved separate systems. In addition, Singley and Anderson reported an experiment that examined the training of subjects to solve calculus problems. Results of this experiment suggested that translating written problems into equations was completely independent of the solution of these equations. These processes shared common abstract knowledge about the function of calculus operators but used it in different ways. Similar evidence was provided by McKendree and Anderson (1987), who found that there was little transfer between evaluating and generating LISP code. There also appeared to be little transfer between evaluating certain combinations of LISP commands when the same components were presented in one combination during training and another during transfer. Thus although the same primitive knowledge was used in both cases, apparently the productions developed in one situation were not appropriate for the other situation. These studies demonstrate that the acquisition of skills is specific to their use.

In conclusion, by specifying productions as the elements underlying transfer, the ACT-R account of transfer provides an advance over Thorndike's identical elements theory. Productions appear to be more appropriate representations of procedural knowledge than stimulus–response pairs. In addition, there is some evidence that transfer between tasks can be predicted on the basis of identical productions underlying performance of the tasks.

SOAR

In several respects the SOAR theory (Laird *et al.* 1987; Newell, 1990; Rosenbloom *et al.*, 1991) is similar to the ACT theory. It is designed to provide accounts of a wide range of cognitive phenomena, and indeed has been successful in a number of domains (e.g. simple reaction tasks, the Sternberg item recognition paradigm, typing, verbal learning, cryptarithmetic, syllogisms, and sentence verification; Newell, 1992). In fact, SOAR has been proposed as a candidate for a unified theory of cognition (Newell, 1990). SOAR has been implemented as a computer program, enabling researchers to simulate phenomena and so compare observed and predicted data. Finally, SOAR is instantiated as a production system. That is, SOAR holds that behaviour results from the execution of a series of production rules.

In SOAR, all tasks are problems. Problems are solved by the execution of productions. Productions are executed if their conditions match task conditions or the actions of satisfied productions. There is no explicit conflict resolution mechanism in SOAR, although a pseudo-conflict resolution procedure does operate. This procedure occurs as part of the decision cycle. In each decision cycle, all productions that can be executed do so. However, if several productions fire in response to the same conditions, they do not all control behaviour. The execution of a production involves adding new knowledge to long-term memory. This knowledge will include preferences about which decisions or behaviours are better than others. The end of each decision cycle involves sorting through the preferences to determine the most appropriate behaviour. Performing this behaviour then triggers the next decision cycle.

Often the productions in long-term memory will not be sufficient for determining which step to take next. In this case an impasse occurs. SOAR treats such impasses as just another problem and sets subgoals to resolve the impasse. SOAR possesses several strategies for dealing with impasses, but each is designed to acquire knowledge about the appropriate next step. Impasses can occur while the system is already working on a sub-goal. As a result, procedures for performing complex tasks will typically possess a hierarchy of goals and sub-goals.

Encountering and resolving impasses provides the opportunity for learning. According to SOAR, when an impasse is resolved, a new production is created. The condition of this production represents the relevant working memory elements at the time of the impasse, and the action represents the solution taken. Thus, if the same situation is encountered again, it is not necessary to go through the problem-solving process again to resolve the impasse. Instead, SOAR suggests we simply retrieve and execute the previously successful solution.

Remembering past solutions to problems is known as chunking in SOAR. Being able to recognize a problem situation and execute a direct solution has obvious performance benefits compared to having to solve the same problem again each time it is encountered. Furthermore, in complex tasks, chunking can occur many times, effectively chunking together the behaviour of several chunks into new chunks. Thus, each time the same task is performed, there is less problem solving and more direct retrieval of solutions. In this way, SOAR can provide an account of the power law of learning. In essence, the negatively accelerated feature of the power law comes about because, in the initial stages of practice, there are many opportunities for chunking to occur, and so large gains in performance speed can result. As practice continues with a task, there is less opportunity for chunking to occur, and so less potential for further improvement in performance time. It is important to note that SOAR accounts for the negatively accelerated feature of learning curves with its chunking mechanism only and, unlike ACT, does not invoke a strengthening mechanism.

The SOAR account of transfer is similar to the ACT account. The productions that result from chunking are abstractions of the problem-solving process, and so may apply beyond the conditions under which they were originally acquired. However, productions can only be executed when their conditions are satisfied. Thus, SOAR resembles ACT in following an identical elements view of transfer: Transfer between two tasks will occur to the extent that productions developed to perform one task can be utilized in performance of the other task.

MacKay

Originally designed to provide an account of possibly the most complex human skill, speech production, MacKay's (1982) theory is also applicable to the full range of skilled behaviour. MacKay explained how a cognitive event (e.g. an idea to be expressed) could be translated into a muscular response (e.g. an utterance reflecting the idea) by proposing that such skilled behaviour is represented as a network of interconnected nodes. The network is hierarchical in nature, such that if an idea is to be expressed in speech, it is originally conceived in a conceptual system as a series of propositions. These propositions are then connected to a phonological system where they are translated into phonological information. In turn, the phonological information is translated into information about which muscles to move to make the sounds in a muscle movement system.

Greater fluency in behaviour comes about with practice, which results in connections between nodes being strengthened. Thus repeating a sentence aloud several times results in stronger connections between the propositional nodes, the phonological nodes, and the muscular nodes that represent the various features of the sentence. In essence, stronger connections between nodes means that activated nodes can prime those nodes to which they are connected lower in the hierarchy. This priming results in faster activation of the lower nodes, and so leads to greater fluency.

MacKay's (1982) theory accounts for the power law of learning in the following manner: The rate at which a node can be activated is related to the rate at which it can be primed. Priming rate is an exponential function of the frequency with which the node has been activated by a connected node in the past. Thus, an unpracticed node will show rapid improvement with practice, nodes with intermediate practice will show moderate improvement with further practice, and those nodes with extensive priming histories will be unlikely to have room for further improvements. The speed with which a task can be performed is a function of the performance of all of the nodes involved in performing that task. Thus, early in practice with a task, performance is dominated by nodes with little prior practice, and hence performance improvements will be large. As practice proceeds, learning rate becomes slower because all nodes are further along their learning curves and so are only improving slowly.

MacKay's (1982) theory also provides an account of transfer of training. To some degree the theory subscribes to the identical-elements view. In this theory, the elements are the nodes that represent particular aspects of a skill. Thus, the extent to which practice on one task will transfer to performance of a second task is determined by the extent to which both tasks engage the same nodes. For example, consider a bilingual person who repeats a sentence in one of their fluent languages several times. Then they are asked to read aloud a translation of that sentence in their other language. MacKay reports that there is considerable transfer in this situation, such that the translation sentence is read faster than control sentences. MacKay attributes this result to the fact that the original and translation sentences share nodes at the conceptual level (i.e. they both express the same idea). Although they may not share many nodes at the phonological and muscular level, nodes at these levels are so over-practiced that further practice is unlikely to result in performance improvements that would affect transfer.

Connectionist models

The final set of models to be considered in this section arguably does not belong in this section for several reasons. However, the models do possess some features in common with the other models in this section, and virtually no features in common with models in the next section. For this reason, connectionist models are discussed here and the appropriateness of including them in the category of 'strategy refinement' models is considered.

Connectionist models are models of memory processes that are based on some features of neural tissue (e.g. McClelland and Rumelhart, 1986; Rumelhart and McClelland, 1986). That is, these models involve networks of interconnected units, with each unit being activated by the firing patterns in units to which it is connected. Once a unit is activated, it can pass on this activation to other units. Typically, connectionist models have several layers of units. The input layer will be designed to represent features of the environment. The output layer will be designed to pass on features of the memory system to the environment. Some models also include one or more hidden layers between the input and output layers. Knowledge in the system is contained in the connection strengths between the units. There are three types of connection strength. A connection strength of zero means that activation of the connection has no effect on the units at the end of the connection. A connection strength with a positive weighting means that input has an excitatory effect, whereas a negative weighting means that input has an inhibitory effect. When input is received by the system, the various connection strengths result in firing patterns among the layers within the network. These firing patterns represent the system's response to particular environmental stimuli. Depending on the situation this response could be the perception of a word, the detection of an instance of a category, or a motor response to be executed.

Research involving connectionist models is often concerned with training a system to respond in particular ways to particular stimuli. In other words, the connectionist models can be configured to learn about an environment. Many different learning algorithms have been developed for use in connectionist models, but the majority appear to include some mechanism whereby connection strengths are modified to reduce error between the system's output and the desired output. Thus, the fact that connectionist models can simulate learning makes them relevant to the current discussion of skill acquisition. Furthermore, because learning in these models involves changes to existing representations (i.e. connection strengths), this learning can be considered to involve a form of strategy refinement in that one form of response is modified by experience to closer approximate the optimal form of response.

Having made the case for inclusion of connectionist models at this point in the discussion, it turns out that very few models have been proposed as accounts of the development of skilled behaviour. If we follow the criteria used so far, there are, to our knowledge, no connectionist models designed to account for both negatively accelerated improvements in performance time with practice, and transfer. There are some models, however, that deal with the first issue.

One connectionist model of skill learning has been proposed by Cohen *et al.* (1990). This model was specifically designed to provide an account of the classic Stroop effect (Stroop, 1935). In the Stroop task, words are presented in various ink colours. People are asked to state the colour of the ink as quickly as they can. The Stroop effect is observed in conditions where colour names are presented in other ink colours (e.g. RED presented in blue ink). Naming times in such conditions are typically slower than in conditions where words other than colour names are presented. The usual explanation for this effect is that reading words is an automatic behaviour, a skill resulting from many years of practice. When faced with a colour name, people have difficulty suppressing the typical response (i.e. 'red' for RED) in order to provide the correct response (i.e. 'blue' when RED is presented in blue ink). The Cohen *et al.* model was designed to simulate the development of an automatic skill (i.e. reading) that would interfere with the execution of another response (i.e. colour naming). Using the activation of units corresponding to particular responses to represent reaction time (i.e. the greater the activation, the shorter the reaction time), the model was successful in simulating the Stroop effect.

In addition to simulating the Stroop effect, the Cohen *et al.* (1990) model exhibited power function learning. The model was able to produce this result by virtue of the way in which connection strengths were modified during learning. Early in practice, there is likely to be a large difference between the actual output of the system and the desired output. As a result, large changes are made to the connection strengths. As practice increases and the system learns, the size of the discrepancy between the system output and the desired output will diminish. Connection strengths are then altered accordingly by ever decreasing amounts. This pattern of change in connection strength, together with the model directly relating reaction time to connection strengths (i.e. the stronger the connection, the shorter the reaction time), produces the negatively accelerated reduction in reaction times characteristic of the power law.

No connectionist model of skill learning currently provides an explicit account of transfer. Cohen *et al.* (1990), for example, did not consider the issue of transfer, either between different stimuli or different tasks, so the ability of their model to handle such situations is unknown. Connectionist models in general, appear well suited to dealing with such situations. Certainly, models do exist that provide an account of the ways in which behaviour is affected by changes in stimuli between training and transfer (e.g. Ratcliff, 1989; Willshaw, 1989). It may simply be a matter of time before a connectionist model is proposed that provides an account of both skill acquisition and transfer.

2.3.2 Skill acquisition as memory retrieval

The Instance theory

The approach in Logan's (1988, 1990) Instance theory to accounting for the phenomena of skill acquisition is very different to that of theories like ACT-R and SOAR. The latter theories generally describe improvement with practice as resulting from the refinement and tuning of procedural knowledge. In contrast, the Instance theory sees improvement in performance, particularly faster performance, as resulting from an increased range of episodic representations of past experience to call upon.

Three assumptions underlie the Instance theory. The first assumption—obligatory encoding—is that the act of paying attention to something results in a memory representation. Thus, each processing episode results in a separate representation in memory. This representation, or instance, consists of the stimulus conditions, the goal state, the interpretation given to the stimulus conditions, the response(s) executed, and the result of the response(s). The second assumption is that of obligatory retrieval. According to this assumption attention to an item or event causes whatever was associated with it in the past to be retrieved from memory. In other words, encountering a set of stimulus conditions that have been encountered again will result in the retrieval of all instances that were stored from those previous encounters. The third assumption, instance representation, says that each episode results in a separate instance, even if the episode is identical to previous ones. Together these assumptions effectively mean that attention to a stimulus will result in the retrieval of all previous associations to that stimulus. There could be many instances being retrieved if experience is extensive, and they all will be the same.

Logan (1988) claims that performance can be described as skilled (automatic) when it relies on the retrieval of instances only. This only occurs after a person has had some experience with a task, and therefore some instances to retrieve. With sufficient practice, exposure to the task will result in the retrieval of a past solution. When performance follows a remembered solution, behaviour is said to be automatic. Clearly, though, when we first encounter a task we do not have any instances to retrieve. So the Instance theory describes a process whereby initial performance with a task can commence, and, with practice, improve.

Development of skill According to Logan (1988), initial performance on a task is under the control of an algorithm. Logan makes no claims as to where these algorithms come from. As far as the other predictions of the theory go, the origin of the algorithm is not crucial. Still, the theory does overlook a substantial number of phenomena associated with developing a skill. Logan (1990) acknowledges the theory's shortcomings on this point and notes that a full understanding of the nature of instances requires some understanding of the algorithms that enable initial performance and result in instance representation.

To say that we perform a task initially by applying an algorithm means that somehow we acquire or develop a method for generating a solution to the task. For example, when children first learn to add single digit numbers, they typically generate an answer by counting (e.g. they might count out each addend on their fingers and then count the total) (Siegler and Jenkins, 1989).

Although initial performance proceeds by the execution of an algorithm, each time the task is executed, something is remembered about that processing episode (obligatory encoding assumption). What is stored in memory is an instance. Each episode results in a separate instance, even if the episode is identical to previous ones (instance representation assumption). In the single digit addition example, each time 2 + 3 is evaluated with the counting algorithm, a representation of the problem ('what's 2 + 3?') and the solution ('5') would be stored in memory. As the task is practiced, more instances are represented in memory.

For any particular processing episode, the algorithm can be executed, and the episode can access instances (obligatory retrieval assumption). In the single-digit addition, for example, 2 + 3 can be evaluated using the tried-and-true counting method, but at the same time, the present episode will retrieve past attempts at solving this expression (i.e. past solutions). As a result, performance in the present episode can take advantage of this retrieval of a past solution. Certainly, children appear to eventually remember the sums of all pairs of single digits, and perform addition by memory retrieval (Siegler, 1987). Thus, with practice, there are two options for controlling performance: algorithmic processing or instance retrieval (i.e. retrieval of a past solution).

According to the Instance theory, only one mechanism can control processing in any one episode. Initially performance is controlled exclusively by execution of an algorithm. As the number of instances increase with practice, a race develops between algorithmic processing and instance retrieval. In any particular processing episode, the two processes will proceed in parallel. Initially the algorithm wins all the time, because there are very few instances to draw from. Those that exist will be retrieved too late to control performance because the algorithm will have been executed already. With practice, more instances are stored. Logan (1988) says that instances have a distribution of retrieval times associated with them. Logan shows that as the number of instances increases, the time it takes to retrieve an instance decreases. Coupled with the claim that algorithm execution time does not change with practice, this means that, as the number of instances increases, the chance of retrieving an instance before the algorithm is executed also increases. Thus, practice leads to a reduction in performance time.

Logan demonstrates how the reduction in performance time conforms to the power law of learning. As practice leads to an increase in the number of instances, the size of the distribution increases. Logan suggests that the distribution of retrieval times is a Weibull distribution. Weibull distributions, and others that are roughly bell-shaped (e.g. the Normal distribution) have a characteristic relationship between an increase in their size and the values of their extremes. Logan has demonstrated how an increase in size is associated with an increase in value of the extremes. This relationship is a power function. That is, the value of the extremes increases as a power function of the size of the distribution. In terms of practice and retrieval times, the shortest retrieval time (i.e. the instance that will control performance) is a power function of the number of instances (i.e. practice). Logan (1990, pp. 5–6) provides a more intuitive description of how performance time on a task improves with practice according to the power law of learning:

> the power function speed-up follows from two opposing tendencies that govern the race: On the one hand, there are more opportunities to observe an extreme value as sample size increases, so the expected value of the minimum will decrease as the number of traces in memory increases. On the other hand, the more extreme the value, the lower the likelihood of sampling a value that is even more extreme, so adding traces to the race will produce diminishing returns. The first factor produces the speed-up; the second produces the negative acceleration that is characteristic of power functions.

Logan has also demonstrated that this relationship between distribution size and instance retrieval time predicts that the standard deviation of performance time will decrease as a power function of practice. Moreover, this power function will have the same learning rate as the power function describing improvement in performance time. Both of these predictions have been supported by experimental data (e.g. Logan 1988).

One of the tasks Logan has used in his demonstrations of features of the Instance theory has been the alphabet arithmetic task. This involves subjects evaluating expressions, such as

$$A + 3 = D \qquad C + 2 = G$$

Subjects are simply required to say whether the statements are true or false (i.e. the first example is true and the second is false).

Logan (1988) claims that subjects initially perform this task by counting through the alphabet. Eventually though, after much practice, subjects invariably perform by remembering solutions to expressions experienced before. Logan (1988) showed that RT on this task and standard deviations of RT were reduced as a function of practice, and that these functions had the same learning rate.

In many respects, Logan's Instance theory is a more elegant theory than most of the theories that describe skill acquisition as a process of strategy refinement. What this means is that Logan proposes a fairly simple learning mechanism (the accumulation of experience) and this accounts for several learning phenomena almost as a by-product. On the other hand, theories, such as Anderson's ACT-R theory, involve several mechanisms designed to account for several phenomena. This gives the theories a bit of an *ad hoc* flavour. Still, elegance is not the only criterion by which theories are evaluated. Accounting for all the data is the most important. And from this respect, the Instance theory does suffer from a few problems, particularly, with respect to the issue of transfer.

Transfer One curious feature of the Instance theory concerns its predictions regarding transfer. Basically, the theory predicts that there is no transfer between different tasks. The theory holds that skilled performance is based on the retrieval of instances. Thus, when we perform a new task, there should be no instances to call upon, and so performance should be at beginner level. Furthermore, since algorithms do not improve with practice in the Instance theory, performing the same task with different items will not be associated with any benefit. This can be illustrated with respect to the alphabet arithmetic task.

Logan and Klapp (1991) had participants practice the alphabet arithmetic task with letters from only half of the alphabet (i.e. half of the subjects practiced with A–M, the other half with N–Z). After 12 sessions of practice, with each problem repeated 6 times per session, participants were then presented with problems involving letters from the other (unpractised) half of the alphabet.

According to the Instance theory, when subjects acquire skill at alphabet arithmetic, they are relying more and more on the retrieval of solutions to particular problems. For example, with the problem A + 3 = D, rather than counting through the alphabet each time to determine 'true' or 'false', participants remember 'true'. In other words, when they see the problem A + 3 = D, they retrieve all the instances associated with that item. This is also the case for all the problems experienced. Each problem has its own distribution of instances to call on. Thus, participants are *not* getting better at counting through the alphabet. As a result, when the items are changed, to ones with letters from the other half of the alphabet, participants no longer have any instances to call upon. So their performance should return to beginner levels. This is indeed what Logan and Klapp found. When participants were exposed to the transfer items, the gains achieved during training were lost. This result supports Logan's (1988) claim that skills are item-specific, that is, the skills acquired are specific to the items experienced during training and cannot be used to perform the task with other items.

Although Logan's experiments have supported his claims about transfer being item-specific, on the whole his transfer prescription is too limited. That is, transfer has been observed by others to be far more general than Logan claims. Many researchers (see Chapter 3) have reported evidence that is consistent with general algorithms being developed that can be applied to many different items. Even the alphabet arithmetic experiments (Logan and Klapp, 1991) reveal some evidence that, although disrupted considerably by the change in items, participants did develop some item-general skill (i.e. they did not return to beginner levels—so they were getting better at counting through the alphabet). Other results that Logan has reported as evidence for item-specific skills have also indicated the presence of item-general skills (e.g. lexical decision (Logan, 1988, 1990); dot counting (Lassaline and Logan, 1993); detection of words in particular categories (Logan and Etherton, 1994)).

Although item-specific information seems to be represented, and restricts transfer, item-general information is also represented, sometimes. It is possible that Logan has found item-specific transfer because of the highly constrained tasks he had his research participants practice. When task conditions are different (e.g. Speelman and Kirsner, 1997), item-general transfer occurs. Speelman and Kirsner suggested that it is task conditions that determine the nature of skill and transfer, not the inherent nature of skill. That is, skills do not have a fixed nature, but rather develop as an adaptation to the environment. This issue is considered further in Chapter 3.

Mounting evidence that the Instance theory is too restrictive in its transfer prescriptions has prompted some suggestions for modifying the theory. Logan (Logan *et al.*, 1996, 1999), for example, has suggested that instances may be retrieved in a piecemeal fashion, that they may possess several parts that can be retrieved separately. Furthermore, there may be differences in the rate at which particular parts of an instance can be retrieved. In this way, the Instance theory could account for situations in which people appear able to perform tasks that are not identical to practiced tasks, and yet their performance exhibits some benefit of the prior practice. Importantly, the extent of transfer in such situations appears to be a function of the similarity between the two tasks. Thus, any modification to the Instance theory would need to include a mechanism whereby task similarity can determine the extent of transfer.

One modification to the Instance theory that provides a means of accounting for similarity-based transfer has been proposed by Palmeri (1997). His exemplar-based random walk (EBRW) model retains the race between an algorithm and memory retrieval. The major change to the theory in the EBRW model, however, involves a retrieval mechanism that is sensitive to similarity differences between instances. That is, experiencing an event can result in the retrieval of instances that are only similar to the event, rather than identical (as in the original theory). In addition, the speed with which an instance is retrieved is inversely proportional to the degree of similarity that exists between the event and the instance. Thus, the greater the similarity, the faster the retrieval time, with identical instances being retrieved the fastest (in such a case the EBRW model's predictions match those of the instance theory). By incorporating similarity-based retrieval of instances, the EBRW model allows for transfer between non-identical experiences (i.e. learning is not always as item-specific as implied by the Instance theory). This loosening of the boundaries on transfer, though, comes at a cost. Unless experiences are identical, transfer will be less than complete and be a function of similarity.

2.4 Conclusions

The history of research in skill acquisition is long and full of a vast amount of tinkering with variables to gauge their effects on learning and performance. In spite of the huge amount of information that has been collected on these issues, two generalizations are possible: (1) practice leads to performance improvements that are dramatic early in practice and diminish with further practice; and (2) transfer between tasks is a function of the degree of similarity between the two tasks. Both of these generalizations are, of course, subject to qualifications, and yet, they both form the basic assumptions of most theories of skill acquisition. As indicated in this chapter, however, the theories account for these basic 'facts' of skill acquisition to varying degrees. Although all of the theories presented provide an account of the power law, with respect to the issue of transfer there is greater unevenness. Crossman's theory relied on Thorndike's identical elements model and so could be considered to be limited in the same manner as that model (i.e. transfer between tasks is a function of similarities in observable stimulus–response elements only). The ACT-R and SOAR theories, as well as MacKay's theory, all account well for the transfer effects presented so far. The Connectionist theories of skill acquisition have not explicitly tackled transfer as yet. Finally, the Instance theory enjoys equivocal success on the transfer issue because it predicts transfer to be highly restricted and this is only observed in certain circumstances. More recent modifications of Logan's theory by others, however, suggest that this shortcoming can be overcome. As is indicated in the following chapter, however, the transfer issue is more complicated than has been presented up to now. For instance, whether transfer is general or specific to the items experienced during training appears to be related to several features of the environment in which performance takes place, not the inherent nature of skills. In addition, transfer has a dramatic effect on the shape of learning curves. We argue then, that it is on this issue that all current theories flounder and hence ultimately fail the Skill Acquisition Phenomena Criterion for suitability as a theory of skill acquisition.

At this point, it is possible to begin to evaluate the accounts provided by the various theories of the power law against the Explanation Criterion mentioned in Chapter 1. Although all of the theories provide an account of the law, some theories rely on building this feature into the theory as an explicit constraint on the way that practice affects performance. So, the ACT-R account of the power law rests in large part on the strengthening mechanism (i.e. compilation may be responsible for speed-up early in practice, whereas strengthening is responsible thereon). That is, the performance speed of a task is determined by the strength of the productions underlying performance of the task. A production's strength is determined by the history of successful application of the production (i.e. practice). ACT-R defines strength as being a power function of practice. And since performance speed is a direct function of strength, performance speed is thus a power function of strength. There is no explanation, however, of why strength is a power function of practice—it just is. Similarly, MacKay's theory builds in a negatively accelerated feature: the priming rate of nodes is an exponential function of the frequency of node activation. All of the other theories considered, however, account for the power law as a by-product of the way that practice leads to changes in the nature of mental representations (Crossman's theory, SOAR, Connectionist theories) or to changes in the number of mental representations (Instance theory). It can be argued then, that the accounts of the power law provided by ACT-R and MacKay are really just re-descriptions of the law. The other theories, however, explain the law as an emergent property of practice effects.

Chapter 3

Challenges

Every learning situation is a transfer situation

Singley and Anderson (1989, p. 267)

The theories of skill acquisition presented in the previous chapter give the impression that skills transfer is a straightforward matter: practice a task under one set of conditions and transfer will occur in another situation to the extent that the skills acquired in the first situation can be applied to the new situation. This generalisation is quite uninformative, however, as it basically translates to 'transfer will occur to the extent to which transfer will occur.' What is required for a useful account of transfer is an explanation of what it is about a skill that determines whether it can apply in a particular situation. Although all the theories are explicit in their claims on this point, we show in this chapter that all theories have overlooked a number of features of skill acquisition and transfer that complicate attempts to explain them with these theories. Nevertheless, we also show that there are actually some simple principles underlying these complications. In Chapter 4 we propose a new theory to account for these principles.

3.1 Generality and specificity

The major theories of skill acquisition and transfer that were reviewed in Chapter 2 differed in terms of their view of the nature of skill representations. The nature of these proposed skill representations determined the type of transfer that each theory suggested could be expected in particular situations. For instance, the ACT-R theory proposes that skills are represented by productions. Their abstract nature suggests that experience with one task can result in facilitated performance on a different task with the same underlying structure (e.g. Singley and Anderson, 1989). In contrast, the Instance theory sees skills as being represented by collections of mental snapshots of specific experiences. So specific are these instances that transfer of experience with one task is unlikely to occur to a different task, or even from one form of a task to another form of the same task (e.g. Logan and Klapp, 1991). Clearly the two theories, and their supporting data, represent a conflict. Is it possible for transfer to be so restricted on one hand, and relatively unrestricted on the other? Or is one of these theories wrong? A different view, which is presented below, is that transferability is determined, not by the inherent nature of skill representations, but by a number of different features of the environment: the type of task being performed, the type of training received, and also the context within which performance occurs. Before this view is presented, however, some of the evidence that is available on whether skills are general, specific, or both, is reviewed.

As has already been suggested, some research has indicated that skills can be general. That is, skills acquired to perform one task can be applied in the performance of a similar but different task. For example, Schneider *et al.* (1984) demonstrated a degree of transfer of perceptual skills, Carlson *et al.* (1990b) demonstrated transfer in electronic circuit trouble shooting, and Dumais (1979) demonstrated transfer of visual search skill. Transfer has also been observed in social judgement (Smith and Lerner, 1986), letter and category search (Schneider and Fisk, 1984), lexical decision (Kirsner and Speelman, 1993, 1996), syllogistic reasoning (Speelman and Kirsner, 1997), computer programming (Adelson, 1981, 1984; Anderson, 1987; Corbett and Anderson, 1992; McKeithen *et al.* 1981; Pennington *et al.*, 1995; Thomas, 1998), learning procedures from text (Kieras and Bovair, 1986), solving algebra (Kramer *et al.*, 1990) and arithmetic (Blessing and Anderson, 1996) problems, performing complex multistep computation tasks (Delaney *et al.*, 1998; Rickard, 1997), typing (Thomas, 1998), reading while taking dictation (Hirst *et al.*, 1980), and solving input–output mapping problems (Anderson and Fincham, 1994). In all of these examples, subjects practiced one task and then were required to perform another similar but different task. In each case, experience with the first task was shown to facilitate performance in the second task. Thus, the skills acquired by the subjects in these experiments can be described as general because they could apply beyond their domain of acquisition.

Evidence of the development of specific skills has also been reported. For example, Logan and Klapp's (1991) experiments with the alphabet arithmetic task revealed that practicing the task with one half of the alphabet did not transfer to the remaining letters of the alphabet (see Chapter 2). This result suggests that subjects developed specific skills during training. That is, the skills were specific to the items experienced during training and so could not apply to the new set of items presented during transfer. Other reports that skills are specific have been made with respect to reading normal text (Byrne, 1984; Byrne and Carroll, 1989; Proctor and Healy, 1995; Whittlesea and Brooks, 1988), reading typographically transformed text (Kolers, 1976, 1979a; Masson, 1986), solving multiplication problems (Campbell, 1987), performing search tasks with visual stimuli (Eberts and Schneider, 1986) and with items committed to memory (Treisman *et al.*, 1992), counting dots (Lassaline and Logan, 1993), making lexical decisions (Logan, 1988), learning serial responses (Brown and Carr, 1989), proofreading (Levy, 1983), in the Stroop task (Clawson *et al.*, 1995), and in manual skills when skin temperature is varied (Clark and Jones, 1962).

Skills have also been observed to be both general and specific in the one situation. For example, Greig and Speelman (1999) conducted an experiment that was divided into training and transfer phases. During training subjects were required to evaluate a simple algebraic equation ($x^2 + 2y$) by substituting values for x and y (e.g. $x = 1$ and $y = 3$). Training consisted of several blocks of trials where values for each of the variables were sampled from a small, fixed set of values. Each pairing of x and y values was presented several times during training. During transfer, subjects were required to evaluate the same equation on each trial. However, during this phase the values of the x and y pairs were sampled from a different set of values to those used during training. Again, each of the x and y pairs was presented several times. Thus the design of this experiment was such that the same equation was to be evaluated in both phases, however, this equation was applied to different pairs of variable values in each phase.

The results of the Greig and Speelman (1999) experiment were such that subjects responded significantly more slowly in the first block of the transfer phase than in the final block of the training phase although reaction time in the first transfer block was still significantly faster than in the first training block. This indicates that some transfer occurred. That is, when subjects came to perform the transfer task, their initial reaction times were faster than their initial reaction times on the training task. This indicates that the training provided some benefit when they came to perform the transfer task. However, transfer was not complete. That is, initial transfer performance was slower than performance in the final blocks of training. If transfer had been complete, performance would have continued at the same level as that observed at the end of training. Thus, there was partial transfer from the training task to the transfer task.

The Greig and Speelman (1999) experiment demonstrates that skills can be both general and specific in the one situation. First, the fact that subjects were able to perform the transfer task faster than they initially performed the training task indicates that the skills acquired during training were of some benefit in performing the transfer task. Furthermore, this benefit occurred despite the change in items from the first phase to the second phase. Thus the subjects' skills were, to some extent, item-general. However, the skills were also, to some extent, item-specific. The fact that initial performance on the transfer task was slower than final performance on the training task indicates that the change in items affected the application of the skills acquired during training.

Many other studies have shown similar results to those reported by Greig and Speelman (1999). That is, something about experience with a task is generalized to items not previously experienced, leading to better performance than if the task had not been practiced. However, the benefits of training are greater when items are repeated. This type of transfer has been observed with multiplication (Fendrich *et al.*, 1993; Healy *et al.*, 1993; Rickard and Bourne, 1996; Rickard *et al.*, 1994), visual search (Hillstrom and Logan, 1998), category search (Schneider and Fisk, 1984), rule evaluation (Kramer *et al.*, 1990), evaluation and generation of LISP statements (Muller, 1999), pound arithmetic (Rickard, 1997), complex sequential processing (Woltz *et al.*, 1996), and entering number strings on a keypad (Fendrich *et al.*, 1991).

It is also the case that a number of the studies mentioned above as demonstrating only general or only specific transfer, when examined more closely, actually reveal both forms of transfer. For instance, Kirsner and Speelman (1996) reported that time to perform lexical decisions was reduced with practice with words that were not repeated throughout practice, suggesting the operation of a skill that could be generalized across words. However, they also found that the rate of improvement in performance time was greater when words were repeated, indicating a degree of item-specificity in lexical decision. Lassaline and Logan (1993) reported that, if people are presented with patterns of dots and asked to state the number of dots present, they typically begin by counting the dots. This is revealed by the fact that time to provide an answer is a function of the number of dots in each pattern. After some practice with the same patterns, however, people usually recognize the patterns and retrieve an answer rather than generate an answer by counting. Performance on the basis of memory retrieval is indicated by the fact that time to provide an answer is unrelated to the number of dots in a pattern. Lassaline and Logan claimed that the skills that are developed in this task are item-specific. They cite as evidence for this claim the fact that when people who have practiced with one set of patterns are then presented with a new set of patterns, their performance time reverts to being a function of the number of dots in the new patterns. However, the slope of the function relating performance time to number of dots during transfer is never as steep as during the initial stages of training. Thus, although performance is disrupted by the change of items, indicating some degree of item-specificity, there is some benefit of previous experience with the task such that performance with the new items is not as poor as initial performance with the old items. That dot counting skill can be general and specific was also supported by Palmeri

(1997) who found that response times to new patterns were a function of the degree of similarity between the new and old patterns. A similar situation exists with the alphabet arithmetic task. In the initial stages of practice, when people count through the alphabet to determine a solution, response time is a function of the size of the addend (i.e. $A + 2 = C$ takes less time to verify than $A + 4 = E$). After some practice, people begin to memorize solutions and so their response times are no longer a function of addend size. Logan and Klapp (1991) claimed that the skill that develops in this situation is item-specific because when people are presented with a new set of items, the response times revert to being a function of addend size, indicating that people have to count again to verify the new items. The slope of the function with the new items, however, is not as steep as the function observed originally with the old items, suggesting some degree of generality of skill. Wenger (1999) also has reported that general and specific skills develop with practice on the alphabet arithmetic task. Finally, Kolers's (1976) work with reading inverted text is often cited as evidence of specific skills. That is, greater benefits of practice result for repeated pages than for new pages. This is not to say, however, that benefits do not accrue for new pages. They are simply not as substantial. So, the skills that are acquired for reading inverted text can be transferred to text that has not been read previously, however, transfer is best when the text has been read (in the inverted form) before.

It is clear from the foregoing that there is a major discrepancy in the research literature on transfer of training. Some research demonstrates that skills are general and can be applied beyond the circumstances of their acquisition. Other research shows that skills are restricted to the specific conditions within which they were acquired. A third body of results suggests instead that sometimes skills can be applied beyond their acquisition context but performance is better when circumstances remain the same. This discrepancy raises an important question: How can skills exhibit general, specific, or both forms of transfer? Certainly if one subscribes to a particular form of skill representation then this situation does not seem possible. That is, if instances are assumed to represent skills, and in particular, responses to certain events, then how can a skill be applied to events that have not been experienced previously? Or, if skills are mentally represented by productions, which are abstract in nature, how can a skill be developed that is specific to a certain set of stimuli? In our view, this situation is perfectly reasonable if one assumes that the mental representation of skill does not have some fixed form, and instead is a reflection of the manner in which a skill is acquired. That is, people adapt to a task situation, and their skill reflects the nature of this situation. Similar claims have been made by Anderson (1993, Anderson and Lebiere, 1998) and

Rasmussen (1983, 1986). In the following sections, we demonstrate the merit of this principle by analysing some of the characteristics of task situations and their relationship to the types of skills that are developed.

3.2 **Task effects**

The number of tasks that have been used to examine transfer over the last hundred years or so is enormous. No doubt, this has contributed to the confusion over the specificity of skill transfer. In our view, the degree of transfer that is observed in any particular situation is to a large extent determined by the nature of the tasks being performed. Some tasks are such that there is greater potential than in other tasks for knowledge acquired in one performance episode to be generalized to another performance episode. Unfortunately, researchers typically develop pet tasks that serve their purposes well and develop their theories about the nature of skill on the basis of results collected with these tasks. A theory then could be designed to account for the results of one set of tasks, but if tasks do indeed vary in terms of their potential for transfer, then the theory may well have nothing to say about transfer in another set of tasks. (Indeed the theories themselves can be restricted in their transferability because of the manner in which they were developed.)

We are not the first to suggest that the nature of transfer may be determined by the nature of a task. Rabinowitz and Goldberg (1995) suggested that specific transfer is typically found with tasks where people are given a lot of practice at providing a correct response to a particular stimulus (e.g. simple arithmetic, lexical decisions, alphabet arithmetic). In contrast, tasks that are associated with general transfer usually involve learning to process a range of stimuli in a particular manner (e.g. computer programming, geometry, text-editing). Rabinowitz and Goldberg, however, did not explain why the two different task situations lead to the different forms of transfer.

One clue as to why the nature of a task determines the nature of transfer comes from the fact that in many of the studies where general transfer is observed, stimulus repetition rarely occurs (e.g. Anderson and Fincham, 1994; Blessing and Anderson, 1996; Kirsner and Speelman, 1996; Speelman and Kirsner, 1997). The fact that performance improves with practice in these situations indicates that subjects are able to use knowledge acquired with some stimuli to benefit performance with other stimuli. Thus, in some tasks it is possible to develop a general mode of processing that can be applied to the range of stimuli that are presented in the context of a particular task.

One example of how a general mode of processing can be developed to deal with a range of stimuli is provided by a study by Speelman and Kirsner (1997).

In this study, subjects were presented with many syllogisms to solve. These syllogisms were presented in a two-part manner (see Figure 1.1). First, two premises were presented and subjects were required to press a computer key when they were ready for the next part of the trial. They were then presented with a conclusion and were required to decide whether the conclusion was a true or false implication of the premises. The premises were presented in one of two forms:

Form 1	*Form 2*
All of the beekeepers are singers.	All of the singers are politicians.
All of the singers are politicians.	All of the beekeepers are singers.

Both of these forms have the same true conclusion (i.e. All of the beekeepers are politicians). The false conclusions that were presented half the time were the converse of the true conclusions (i.e. All of the politicians are beekeepers). The two forms of premise pair were presented to subjects in a random order. No syllogism was ever repeated throughout the experiment, although each of the nouns was presented with other nouns in other syllogisms. The important feature of the results of this experiment to note is that response times on these syllogisms decreased with practice. Clearly subjects were learning about the abstract structure of the syllogisms and how it related to the form of the true conclusion (i.e. if premises are of Form 1, then the true conclusion involves noun 1 and noun 3, in that order. If premises are of the Form 2, then the true conclusion involves noun 3 and noun 2, in that order). Thus, they developed a skill that was independent of the particular items to which they had been exposed.

The results of the Speelman and Kirsner (1997) study suggest a principle that may underlie the relationship between task type and transfer type. That is, in any particular task, is there anything about experience with one item that can be of benefit with performance on another item? If so, then general transfer will result. Otherwise, specific transfer may be all that can occur. In the Speelman and Kirsner study, subjects had many trials of practice and so had the opportunity to learn about how the syllogisms related to each other. And given that there was a simple abstract structure that underlay the solution to all of the syllogisms presented, subjects could quickly take advantage of this general feature to solve all subsequent problems.

The type of situation that leads to specific transfer, according to the above principle, can be illustrated with respect to Masson's (1986) experiments with reading inverted text. This research is often cited as an example of the specificity of transfer. When the tasks and stimuli used in these experiments are examined, it is not surprising that such specific transfer was observed. Masson reported that skill at reading inverted text only transferred from studied words to non-studied words when the two sets of words shared the same letters. In other words, this skill was letter-specific. The reason for this is clear. There is very little that is common about reading inverted versions of each of the letters of the alphabet. For instance, what can be learned about reading the letter 'a' upside down that will benefit reading the letter 'm' upside down? Although some letters are similar in shape, and one might expect some degree of transfer between them, most letters will require the development of specific skills to decode the inverted form and relate it to existing mental representations of those letters.

The principle that describes the relationship between task type and transfer type is simply a reflection of the larger principle that relates transfer type to the way in which a person adapts to a task situation. In this particular case, people will adapt to those regularities of a task they perceive, whether there is one regularity that applies to all items, several regularities that applies to one set of items but not others, or no regularities across items at all. Furthermore, when it comes to developing strategies for performing tasks, people appear driven to reduce effort (Anderson *et al.*, 1998, see Chapter 2). That is, developing one skill that can apply to many stimuli is far less effortful than developing a separate skill for each stimulus. As a result, when the task is such that a general skill can be developed, it will be developed. Otherwise, specific skills will be required.

There is at least one complicating factor with the task-transfer principle. The way in which a task is presented and practiced may also influence the degree to which people can perceive regularities between items. As a result, transferability of resultant skills may also be affected. This issue is taken up in the following section.

3.3 Training effects

For as long as skill acquisition has been studied it has been known that the way people are trained has an effect on the type of skills they develop. At least two important factors that modulate this effect have been identified. One is the number of different types of situations people are exposed to during training, and the other is the schedule of presentation of different situations during training.

The greater the variation in stimuli people are exposed to during training on a particular task, the more likely it is that they will develop general skills. This has been demonstrated in a variety of contexts. For example, Schneider and Fisk (1984) reported data from a category search task. Subjects were given practice at detecting words from a particular category in a list of three words. In one experiment subjects were trained with either four or eight exemplars of a category. After training, subjects were required to perform the same task but with new words from the same category. Schneider and Fisk found that there was much greater transfer to the new words for the group who trained with eight exemplars. A similar effect was reported by Rabinowitz and Goldberg (1995) with the alphabet arithmetic task. They found that subjects who practiced the task with a small number of items developed skills that were more item-specific than subjects who practiced with a larger set of items.

The reason that increased variety during training leads to more general skills can be understood in terms of the principle introduced earlier concerning efficient adaptation to a task environment. When faced with only a small variation in item type, people will develop skills to cope with this limited environment. Given that they have experienced an environment that varies little, and the skills they have developed can deal with this small variation, there is no incentive to develop skills that will cope with a broader variation. As a result, it is unlikely that those skills that are developed will enable satisfactory performance with a different set of items. In contrast, when the training environment involves a large variation in item type, people will learn to cope with this variation. To do so efficiently will probably rely on the abstraction of features that are common to many items. Thus, skills will be developed that can deal with a variety of task situations. As a result, when faced with transfer to a different task situation (e.g. a new set of items), it is likely that these skills are sufficiently general that they can cope with stimuli that have not been previously experienced. Certainly, the likelihood is greater that this is the case than when training involves only a small number of items.

Another factor in the effect of training type on transfer type is the schedule of exposure to different task variations. Jelsma *et al.* (1990) suggest that item-specific skills result from 'procedural tactics that invite learners to mechanically and consistently repeat performance on a particular task' (p.108), whereas item-general skills result from 'the application of variability of practice' (p.109). An example of this distinction is the contextual interference effect. Originally noted with respect to motor learning (e.g. Lee and Magill, 1983; Shea and Morgan, 1979), this effect has also been found with cognitive tasks (e.g. Carlson and Yaure, 1990) and now appears to be a general feature of skill acquisition (Proctor and Dutta, 1995a, pp. 229–230). The contextual interference effect describes the situation where a task involves several forms, and these are performed in either a random order, or a blocked order. In the blocked order, one form of the task is performed several times, followed by several repetitions of another form, and practice alternates between blocks of each form of the task. There are at least two performance differences that result from the different forms of training. First, performance during training is usually faster in the blocked condition. This performance advantage, however, is reversed when retention of skills is tested. That is, random training appears to lead to better retention of skills, and also skills that are more generalizable to different situations.

Why random and blocked practice should have different effects on transfer can be illustrated with respect to the Speelman and Kirsner (1997) syllogism experiment. The random training was as described earlier—the two different forms of premise pairs were presented in a random order. In the Blocked condition, however, subjects were presented with a block of 24 syllogisms where the premises were of one form, followed by a block of 24 syllogisms with premises of the other form. Blocks alternated throughout the training phase. Subjects in both conditions were exposed to the same syllogisms; the only difference was the order in which they appeared. In this task, an important skill to develop is the ability to identify the form of a pair of premises, because the form of the premises determines the form of the true conclusion. Clearly the blocked condition simplifies this part of the task: except for the first trial of each block, subjects know in advance the form of a premise pair before it is presented. In the Random condition, subjects do not know from one trial to the next what form of premise pair will appear, and so need to learn how to distinguish between the two forms. This difference between the two conditions is revealed by a clear speed advantage for the Blocked condition throughout training. This advantage comes at a cost, for the Blocked subjects. The greater speed shown by the Blocked subjects during training means that they are able to solve the syllogisms with fewer processing steps. Given the predictability of premise form in this condition, it is likely that subjects in this condition did not go to the trouble of trying to identify form in the way that was required of the Random subjects. As a result, the Blocked subjects would not have developed the ability to identify premise pair form. That this is the case is demonstrated by what happened when the two groups of subjects were then presented with new syllogisms in a random order. Subjects in the Random condition continued to perform at a rate predicted by the learning curve that described their improvement during the training phase. Subjects in the Blocked condition, however, were slowed dramatically: They were slower than would be predicted from their training learning curve, and also slower than the Random subjects. Thus, the nature of the training conditions experienced by the Blocked subjects was such that they did not need to develop a skill that was crucial for effective performance under random conditions. Since there was no incentive to develop such a skill, it was not acquired.

The contextual interference effect illustrates how training type can influence skill type and hence transfer. This effect is another example of the principle that people are sensitive to regularities in a task environment, and the skills they develop to perform the task are a reflection of their adaptation to these regularities. An important implication of this principle is that training conditions should be designed carefully with transfer goals in mind. If a certain set of skills are desired in a trainee, then training conditions have to be designed that not only allow these skills to develop, but that encourage these skills and not some other set to be developed. This prescription is appreciated in the research literature concerned with the fidelity of task environments in simulators, such as those for learning to fly. The fidelity of a simulator refers to the degree to which the simulated task matches the target task in all respects. Research in this area has found that it is not necessary for simulators to possess perfect fidelity (Proctor and Dutta, 1995a, p. 289). In fact, in some situations, perfect fidelity may actually impede skill acquisition because extraneous conditions affect the ability to learn about the important regularities in the task (Lintern *et al.*, 1990). What is required, however, for simulators to provide effective training and maximize transfer to some target task is functional equivalence (Spears, 1983). Essentially two tasks have functional equivalence when responses that have been learned to stimuli in one task can be generalized to stimuli in the other task. In other words, when functional equivalence exists, subjects are able to adapt to the regularities in the simulator environment that also apply in the target task environment.

In conclusion, the nature of a task and the nature of training on the task can determine the type of skill that is acquired, and this in turn determines the type of transfer that is possible. No theory of skill acquisition currently addresses this relationship between performance environment and resultant skills and their transfer. Thus, the theories under consideration all fail the Skill Acquisition Phenomena Criterion with respect to these features of transfer. As we have described them, however, the effects that task type and training type can have on the nature of skill acquisition and transfer both reflect the same general principle. That is, people will acquire skills that represent their adaptation to the environment in which they are currently performing. They are sensitive to regularities in a task environment that exist both within a trial context, and also across several trials. As a result, they may develop skills that reflect more than the immediate demands of the task. Restrictions on transfer to different versions of the task will occur if the transfer task does not possess these same regularities. This principle forms the basis of the theory we present in Chapter 4.

3.4 Transfer of training and its effect on learning curves

A further reason why factors that affect transfer are important in evaluating theories of skill acquisition is that transfer can affect the shape of learning curves. Given that the nature of learning curves is one of the important facts about skill acquisition that all theories strive to account for, it is imperative that a valid theory can account for factors that impact on transfer as well as their influence on learning curves.

3.4.1 The power law of learning and its alternatives

As would be expected with any law, once the power law of learning was suggested, many objections and challenges to its status as a law of human behaviour were mounted. In the remainder of this chapter, we present a number of these challenges that demonstrate that describing the relationship between practice and improved performance with a power function is not a straightforward matter.

As described in Chapter 2, the reduction in performance time that is associated with learning can be described by a power function of the amount of practice. This is the power law of learning. The most general form of such functions is given by the following equation:

$$T = X + NP^c \tag{3.1}$$

where T represents the time to perform the task, P represents the amount of practice on the task, X represents performance time at asymptote, N represents a constant relating to the task (N is proportional to the number of processing steps involved in the task), $X + N$ represents the performance time on Trial 1, and c represents the rate of learning. The value of c is a constant for any particular situation and is negative, most commonly in the range $-1 < c < 0$ (c can be positive when the dependent variable increases in value with learning, as for example, in the case of accuracy).

According to Anderson (1982) the value of X is usually very small relative to $X + N$. In addition, power functions approach asymptote slowly. Anderson suggests that it is for these reasons that power functions with zero asymptote (i.e. $X = 0$) can provide very good fits to practice data. However, Anderson makes the point that when practice involves a sufficient number of trials, careful analysis of data will reveal evidence of non-zero asymptotes.

The apparent lawfulness of power function learning has been called into question recently, with strong arguments being presented for exponential function learning (e.g. Heathcote *et al.*, 2000). When Newell and Rosenbloom (1981) first presented the case for the power law of learning, they explicitly compared the ability of the power function and the exponential function to account for a number of sets of learning data. The general form of the exponential function used to describe performance improvements with practice is:

$$T = X + Ne^{cP} \tag{3.2}$$

where the meaning of each parameter is the same as in the general form of the power function presented above (Equation 3.1). Although Newell and Rosenbloom's comparisons found that learning data were consistently described better by power functions, doubt has been cast upon the validity of that conclusion.

At least three objections have been raised to the proposal that performance time is a power function of practice. The first objection concerns the quality of the evidence that supports the power law. Several researchers (e.g. Heathcote *et al.*, 2000; Myung *et al.*, 2000) have pointed out that when power functions are most evident, the data being analysed represents average data from several individuals. This result is considered misleading because an artifact of the process of calculating a linear average of individual learning functions is that it will result in a learning curve that is described better by a power function than an exponential function, even if the individual functions were exponential (Myung *et al.*, 2000). The second objection to the power law concerns evidence that favours exponential learning functions. Following the first objection, when individual learning curves are analysed, exponential functions regularly provide a better fit to the data than power functions (Heathcote *et al.*, 2000; Josephs *et al.*, 1996; Rosenbloom and Newell, 1987). Finally, the third objection to the power law concerns the suggestion that there may not be one pure function that describes all learning curves. For instance, there is evidence that exponential functions are best for describing performance in some conditions, whereas other conditions result in learning curves that are best described by power functions (Carlson, 1997, pp. 59–60). Other researchers have suggested that learning curves on complex tasks may represent the operation of several underlying learning functions (Delaney *et al.*, 1998; Rickard, 1997, 1999). The combination of component learning functions could even involve a mixture of power and exponential functions (Heathcote *et al.*, 2000).

Several years ago, we also proposed that learning curves should be considered as summaries of many learning functions. This argument is detailed in the next section. It should be immediately obvious that, despite the foregoing, we have maintained the use of power functions as descriptions of learning. The main reason is that the model takes as its starting point Anderson's (1982) ACT* theory of skill acquisition, and in particular the ACT* account of the power law. Ultimately this feature of our argument for a componential view of the learning curve is of no consequence, as the final message applies no matter what form learning functions take, as long as they are negatively accelerated.

3.4.2 Learning rate

As indicated in Chapter 2, Snoddy (1926) was the first to report that learning data, when plotted on log–log axes, approximated a straight line. Snoddy also reported that the learning rate of his subjects, as indicated by the slopes of their learning curves on log–log axes, were identical:

> We have already indicated that the facilitation lines (learning curves) for all types of practice are parallel on log paper, which means that the slopes of the log equations are

equal. From this it would be a good guess that all individuals, whether high or low in efficiency, might have the same slope for their facilitation lines. This turns out to be the case and *n*, which is equal to 0.25, is the universal slope. We have studied about 300 children, 500 insane, and over 1000 low, normal and superior adults among college students, and have invariably found the same average slope of the log equation in facilitation practice. It is of interest that many of our insane subjects are well below the normal distribution curve for adults, and yet these have the same slope *n*. In our study of children of all age levels, the slope of the facilitation lines is seen to be the same as for normal adults. This constancy of the slope of the log equations for all subjects is not only a thing of much interest mathematically and physiologically, but it simplifies enormously the mathematics involved in the treatment of clinical data.

                                                    (pp. 22–23, parentheses inserted)

This finding of identical learning rates among such a disparate sample of people is indeed remarkable, for at least two reasons. First, it is unlikely that measurement of any other feature of human performance would yield an identical value across a group of people. Second, no mention is ever made of this remarkable observation in modern discussions of learning curves. The reason for this omission is clearly because no one observes any degree of consistency in learning rates among people. This may be due to the greater precision in curve fitting afforded by today's computers compared to the analytical techniques available to Snoddy. Certainly, our experience is that learning rates are just as variable as any other measurable characteristic of human performance.

Although the learning rate parameter of power functions is usually found to be between −1 and 0 there appears to be substantial variation within this range between tasks and subjects (e.g. Newell and Rosenbloom, 1981). However, a systematic relationship between type of task and subjects' learning rate has yet to be established. This section presents an account of this relationship, an account that shows how transfer and learning rate are intimately connected. This model was originally developed as part of Speelman's (1991) doctoral research, and was evaluated in Kirsner and Speelman (1996), Speelman (1995), and Speelman and Kirsner (1993).

Anderson's (1982) ACT* theory of skill acquisition included an account of the power law of learning that is probably the only account to be explicit about the determinants of learning rate. This account basically suggests that, all things being equal, learning rate is a constant for each person. Given the fact that subjects exhibit varying learning rates dependent on task situation, this account is obviously not sufficient. However, Anderson's account can be used as a starting point for the development of a more precise model. This model assumes that learning rate is affected by the relative amounts of practice of particular task components and also the relative number of processing steps involved in these components. Thus, this model, which we refer to hereon as the component model, is in fact designed to account for the shape of learning curves following transfer, but will account for changes in learning rate as a matter of course. In the remainder of this section, Anderson's account of learning rate is described, followed by a description of the component model. Predictions that follow from the component model are compared with previously published data. It should be noted that development of the component model pre-dated Anderson's (1993; Anderson and Lebiere, 1998) revision of the ACT* theory, and so may not accurately reflect some of the details of the ACT-R account of the power law of learning. The ultimate message of the component model, however, is unaffected by the choice of theoretical starting point.

3.4.3 **ACT*and learning rate**

As described in Chapter 2, ACT* predicts that performance will become faster with practice as a result of both algorithmic improvement and strengthening. ACT* states that the process of compilation improves the procedure for performing a task by reducing the number of steps involved in the procedure. It is assumed that the number of steps is reduced by a constant fraction with each improvement. Anderson (1982) suggests that this algorithmic improvement follows a standard power function for improvement to an asymptote:

$$N = N^* + N_0 P^{-f} \tag{3.3}$$

In this equation, N represents the number of processing steps performed on Trial P (where P represents the amount of practice), $N^* + N_0$ represents the number of steps performed on Trial 1, and N^*, the asymptote of this function, represents the minimum number of steps that constitute the optimal procedure for performing the task. The exponent f represents the constant fraction by which the number of steps is reduced with each improvement.

The other contributing factor to performance time reduction in the ACT* theory is that of strengthening. In ACT* it is assumed that the representation of task-specific information is strengthened in memory with practice. The strength of a memory element then determines the speed at which it can be accessed and applied. Anderson (1982) shows that this reduction in application time with increased strength can also be described by a power function:

$$T = C + AP^{-g} \tag{3.4}$$

In this equation, T represents the time to execute a series of productions, P represents the amount of practice, A is a constant that represents the time it takes to execute a certain number of productions and is therefore proportional to the number of productions involved in performing a task, the asymptote C represents the minimum time for execution of a certain number of productions, $C + A$ represents the maximum time for execution, and the exponent g is a constant that represents the rate at which the strength of a memory element decays, and is a value greater than zero.

In order to derive a function that describes total time to perform a task Anderson (1982) combined Equation 3.3, which represents the number of productions involved in performing a task, and Equation 3.4, which represents the time per production. This combination resulted in Equation 3.5:

$$TT = (N^* + N_oP^{-f})(C + AP^{-g}) \qquad (3.5)$$

This equation simplifies to Equation 3.6:

$$TT = N_oAP^{-(f+g)} \qquad (3.6)$$

if N^* and C are assumed to be zero. Anderson makes this assumption because Equation 3.5 is not a perfect power function, although it is a good approximation to one. Eliminating N^* and C results in a pure power function that can be further simplified to the equation introduced above as the general form of a power function that describes learning:

$$T = NP^c \qquad (3.7)$$

As described above, N is a constant related to the initial number of productions involved in performing the task and P is the amount of practice. This equation has a zero asymptote.

The step from Equation 3.5 to Equation 3.7 suggests that the learning rate for any task (c) is a negative constant that is determined by two other constants: the fraction by which the number of productions is reduced with compilation (f), and the decay rate of production strength (g). The latter two constants, according to Anderson (1982), are parameters of the cognitive system. Therefore, learning rate is itself a parameter of this system. This implies that learning rate is determined by particular characteristics of a subject's mental functioning, that it is a constant which is 'built in' to each subject. Thus, in Anderson's account, there is no apparent facility for type of task to affect learning rate.

If learning rate is some form of constant for each subject, then presumably the range of learning rates that are observed between experiments is a result of different combinations of results from subjects with different learning rates. However, this suggestion is not supported by experiments where learning rate was observed to vary from task to task within individuals and groups (e.g. Fitts, 1964; Grose and Damos, 1988; MacKay, 1982; Newell and Rosenbloom, 1981; Smith and Sussman, 1969; Snyder and Pronko, 1952). Therefore, it does not appear that variation in observed learning rates results only from a sampling distribution of combinations of various constant learning rates. Variation in learning rate is also likely to result from an interaction between subject characteristics (i.e. their intrinsic learning rate) and task features. The form of this interaction is considered below.

Old and new task components

The form of the interaction between a constant learning rate and task features could involve the fact that, except for infants, most tasks have components that involve previously learned skills as well as components that are peculiar to the new task (Fitts and Posner, 1967, p. 19). The latter components will include both components for performing the new part of the task and components that integrate the functioning of the old and new components. This conception suggests that for any task there will be some components that have had more practice than others. The obvious consequences of such a suggestion are that (1) the older components will be faster than the new components (if the number of steps involved in the two sets of components is equivalent), and (2) the older components will have less room for improvement than the new components. These predictions in turn suggest further consequences. However, they also rely on a number of assumptions.

The first assumption underlying the above predictions is that for any one person the rate at which new skills are learned is a constant. This is as suggested by Anderson's (1982) conception of the power law of learning. A 'new' skill here is conceived of as a skill that involves no components that have had previous practice. This includes those skills that are necessary for integrating the functioning of old and new skills into the same goal structure. The second assumption is that all components underlying the performance of a task will improve according to the power law of learning and, with practice, will continue to do so at the same learning rate.

In summary then, the above conception suggests that, in most cases, learning a new task involves continued practice on old skills. These are skills that have been practised in the context of some other task. Learning a new task will also involve the development of new skills. These are skills that are required to fill the gap between the repertoire of old skills possessed by the trainee and the skills necessary to perform the new task. These new skills will involve both task-related skills and skills for integrating the functioning of old and new task-related skills. In order to evaluate the predictions based on this concept of task learning it will be informative to contrast this concept with an idealized situation where all components of a task are learned from scratch.

The idealized situation is a simple one—improvement is a function of practice and follows the power law of learning. The initial time to perform the task is a function of the number of components or steps involved in the task. Thus, the whole situation can be described by one power function. In contrast, the more realistic situation is unlikely to be accurately described by one power function. The simple reason is that in this situation each component will not have had equal amounts of practice. As a result, a power function with one term that describes amount of practice is not sufficient. This then raises the question of how varying amounts of practice can be incorporated into a function that describes improvement on a task with old and new components.

One possibility is suggested by Anderson *et al.* (1989) who propose that 'acquisition of…skill can be predicted by composing simple learning functions for (the) units (p. 503)' underlying tasks. One interpretation of this proposal is that it is suggesting that components of a task have their own learning functions and that the learning function for the task as a whole is a combination of these separate functions. With respect to the current discussion, this would suggest that old and new components of a task improve with practice according to their own learning functions. These separate functions would then include the fact that the components have had unequal amounts of practice. The learning function for the task would then be a combination of these 'old' and 'new' learning functions.

The form of this combination needs to be considered before the implications of this suggestion can be examined. Underlying a great deal of the research into skill acquisition is the assumption that the more steps involved in a task the longer it takes to perform (e.g. Anderson, 1982; Carlson *et al.*, 1989; Staszewski, 1988). The assumption implies a serial process where each step contributes a particular amount of time to the total task time. Following this logic with the combination of old and new skills requires the combination to be a serial one. That is, the processing of one set of components should not impinge upon the processing of the other set except to provide input information. If this is the case then the learning function for the whole task should be a simple linear combination of power functions describing improvement in each of the underlying components. If the components can be separated into old and new then this function will have the following form (Speelman, 1991):

$$T_{task} = T_{old} + T_{new}$$
$$= N_o P_o^c + N_n P_n^c \tag{3.8}$$

This equation represents the linear combination of two power functions of the form described in Equation 3.7. Terms with the subscript 'o' represent parameters of the old components of the task, and terms with the subscript 'n' represent parameters of the new components.

There are a number of implications of Equation 3.8 that should be made explicit. The first is that the contribution of each set of components to the total task time is weighted by the number of steps involved in each set. That is, the greater the number of steps in a set of components, the greater will be the contribution of this set. The second implication is that this weighted combination will be qualified by the amount of practice that the sets of components have had prior to the combination. This qualification has two related forms: (1) the more practice a set of components have had, the faster they will be, and so practice serves to reduce the contribution of a set of components to the overall performance time of a task; (2) as the amount of practice of a set of components increases the room for improvement decreases.

The most important implication of Equation 3.8 concerns the rate at which improvement will occur in the total task. In this equation, the learning rate (c) of the two separate power functions is the same in each function. This represents the assumption described above that the learning of all components of a task for any one person is a constant. Incorporating this assumption into the equation results in a power function describing improvement in the overall task that has a different learning rate to that of each of the components. This difference is always in the direction of a reduction: the learning rate of the total task will be slower than the learning rate of its underlying components. The amount by which the learning rate will be reduced is a function of the relative number of steps in the old and new components, and of the relative amount of practice each set of components had prior to combination.

For example, consider the case of a subject who has practiced a task for six sessions. Let the task have 100 steps ($N = 100$) and the learning rate be -0.8 ($c = -0.8$). The improvement in the time to perform the task can now be described by the equation $T = 100\, P^{-0.8}$ (this is only a loose description as N in Equation 3.7 is only proportional to the number of processing steps/productions involved in a task, not equal to this number). Now suppose the subject is given a new task to practice, that includes all of the steps in the old task plus a new set of steps that number 20. The subject will be able to perform the old steps quickly but will be starting from scratch with the new steps. The time to perform such a task that includes old and new components can be described by the combination of the power functions that would describe improvement on the separate components. Thus,

$$T = T_{old} + T_{new}$$
$$= 100\, P_{old}^{-0.8} + 20\, P_{new}^{-0.8}$$

where

$$P_{old} = P_{new} + 6$$

This function now has an overall learning rate of $c = -0.44$ (i.e. plot values for T against P_{new} on log–log axes and the gradient of the resulting straight line is −0.44). Therefore, learning rate has been attenuated as a result of combining two skills that differ in the amount of practice they have had and the number of steps involved with their execution. The rate of improvement in the overall task is slower than in the components underlying performance in the task. However, the attenuation will not always be as dramatic as in this example. As mentioned above, the amount of attenuation is moderated by two factors.

The first moderating factor on the amount of attenuation in learning rate is the relative number of steps in the old and new components of a task. The effect of this factor on the overall learning rate is depicted in Figure 3.1. The data points were generated from the above example, where $P_{old} = P_{new} + 6$ and $c = -0.8$. The number of steps in the new component was varied from 0 to 500 and the number of steps involved in the old component was kept constant at 100. It is clear from this figure that an increase in the ratio of old to new steps increases the attenuation of the learning rate. The function depicted in Figure 3.1 has minimum and maximum boundaries. The minimum boundary corresponds to the situation where there are no old steps involved in the task. The learning rate in this situation corresponds to the intrinsic learning rate of the system, which is −0.80. The maximum boundary represents the maximum attenuation effect. This corresponds to the situation where the old steps outnumber the new steps to the extent that the new steps have no effect on the overall learning rate.

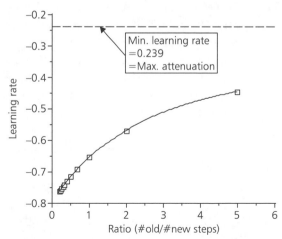

Fig. 3.1 Learning rate as a function of the ratio of the number of steps in old skills versus the number of steps in new skills. The data points were generated from a learning example described in the text. The line represents an interpolation of the data points.

The point of maximum attenuation is equivalent to measuring the learning rate of a task as if it were a new task and ignoring the fact that it has been practiced for six sessions. The subsequent sessions of practice would elicit performance times that improved at what appeared to be a slower rate than the earlier sessions. However, this attenuation is simply a result of using an inappropriate point to represent 'session one'. Figure 3.2 illustrates that in this situation a practice function with a 'slow' learning rate is in fact the tail end of a practice function with a faster learning rate. This phenomenon can result in inaccurate measures of learning rate when prior experience with a task is not taken into account. Newell and Rosenbloom (1981) suggest that using a more general form of the power function that incorporates the amount of prior practice can improve the accuracy of power function descriptions of practice data. Such a function would have the following form:

$$T = N (P + E)^c \qquad (3.9)$$

This equation is the same as Equation 3.7 except that the term which represents the amount of practice on a task is now divided between practice that is observed (P) and practice prior to observation (E). This form of the power function has been shown to provide a better fit to some practice data but is also no better than simpler functions (Equation 3.7) with other data (Singley and Anderson, 1985). The reason why Equation 3.9 is no better than Equation 3.7 for some practice data is that the assumption of prior experience with a task is too general an

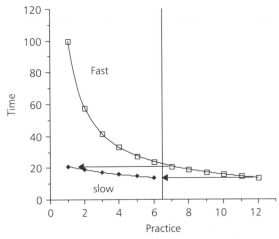

Fig. 3.2 Demonstration that a practice function with a 'slow' learning rate may be the tail end of a function with a faster rate. The last six data points of the fast curve (learning rate = −0.80) have been displaced six practice units. The new curve now has the slower learning rate of −0.239.

assumption. As demonstrated above, prior experience may only apply to some components of a task. Other components will not have had any practice. Hence, Equation 3.8 may be a more accurate depiction of some situations.

The second moderating factor on the attenuation of learning rate is the relative amount of practice that the old and new skills underlying a task had prior to their combination. Figure 3.3 illustrates the effect on learning rate of increasing the amount of prior practice of old skills in the example introduced above. All of the data points in this figure were derived from the example situation with the number of old steps constant at 100 and the number of new steps constant at 20. The learning rates were calculated for the learning functions that resulted from varying the amount of practice of old skills in Equation 3.8. Figure 3.3 shows the result of varying P_{old} from 0 to 100 sessions. When the old skills have had no practice prior to combination, the learning rate is simply the intrinsic learning rate of the system (-0.80). This corresponds to the situation where all components of the task are new. As the amount of practice of old skills increases the attenuating effect on learning rate increases until the combination of old and new skills has its maximum effect. In this situation, when old skills have been practised for eight sessions prior to the combination of old and new skills, the resulting learning rate is at its slowest at -0.439. Beyond this point, increasing the amount of practice old

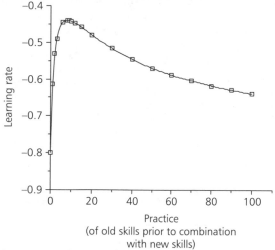

Fig. 3.3 Learning rate as a function of the amount of extra practice of old skills in comparison to new skills. The maximum attenuation of learning rate occurs when $P_{old} = 8$ and results in a learning rate $= -0.439$. The data points were generated from a learning example described in the text. The line represents an interpolation of the data points.

skills have prior to combination has a diminishing effect on learning rate. This diminishing effect continues until the old skills have had so much practice that any further practice results in only negligible improvement. At this point, the combination of old and new skills has no effect on the overall learning rate. The learning rate for the overall task will now be completely determined by the rate at which performance on the new skills improves, and this will be at the intrinsic learning rate of the system (-0.80 in this situation).

In summary, Equation 3.8 leads to the prediction that when a task involves old and new components, this task will be learned at a slower rate than that at which each of the two sets of components improves (i.e. the constant intrinsic rate of each person). The amount by which this learning rate will be attenuated will be moderated by the relative number of steps between old and new components of the task, and by the amount of practice that the old skills had prior to learning the new task. Some evidence exists in the research literature to support these predictions. This evidence is presented below.

Evidence in support of Equation 3.8 In order to evaluate Equation 3.8, data is required from a very specific type of situation. First, there needs to be performance data from both a training phase and a transfer phase in order to compare learning rates in both phases. Second, sufficient information about the tasks performed in the two phases is required in order to make judgements about the relative number of old and new skill components utilized in the training and transfer tasks. We were able to find three studies in the research literature that provided sufficient information to enable a comparison between the data from these studies and predictions derived from Equation 3.8.

Singley and Anderson (1985) Singley and Anderson (1985) examined the extent of transfer between different computer text-editing programs. Two basic types of editors were used: (1) line editors, where only one line of text in a file can be viewed at a time and editing is on a line-by-line basis; and (2) screen editors, where the screen is filled with the contents of a file and users are able to designate the location to be edited by moving around the screen with a cursor. Subjects in this study were trained to operate two line editors (ED and EDT) and one screen editor (EMACS). Singley and Anderson were interested in the extent to which training on one versus two line editors would transfer to performance on a screen editor. They found that there was positive transfer both between the line editors and from the line editors to the screen editor. These results were interpreted as suggesting that all of the editors shared a certain number of productions necessary for their performance. Thus, training with one editor provided the subjects with a set of productions, of which some were useful for operating another editor. In more detail, there was almost complete transfer between the line editors, which suggests that these editors share a large number of productions. In contrast, there was only partial transfer between the line editors and the screen editor, suggesting that the productions developed with the line editors were not totally sufficient for operating the screen editor. The development of more productions would have been necessary for efficient performance with this editor.

The most interesting result of this experiment for the current discussion concerns the differences in the shape of the learning curves during training and transfer. Singley and Anderson fitted simple power functions to the data and the equations of these functions are presented in Table 3.1. The design of the experiment was such that the subjects who performed in the Transfer phase with ED were trained with EDT and vice-versa. The subjects who performed in the Transfer phase with EMACS were subjects who had either been trained with one of the line editors or both, the total amount of training being equal for both groups of subjects. The equations in the Training column of Table 3.1 were derived from data from control subjects who practiced with only one editor.

It is clear from the equations in Table 3.1 that in all cases the learning rate during Transfer was slower than the rate during Training. Furthermore, the amount of attenuation was greater when transfer was between line editors (-0.53 to -0.20 and -0.79 to -0.34) than when transfer was from line editors to the screen editor (-0.55 to -0.41). These results are as would be predicted on the basis of Equation 3.8. First consider the line editors. The fact that there was almost total transfer between these editors suggests that they share a large number of productions. Therefore, when subjects switch to one line editor after operating with the other line editor, very few new productions need to be developed. In other words, when these subjects operate the new line editor, underlying their performance will be a large number of old skills and a small number of new skills. As was shown in Figure 3.1, this is the type of situation where attenuation of learning rate is very large. In contrast, transfer from line

Table 3.1 Power functions describing performance with three text-editors during training and transfer phases of an experiment reported in Singley and Anderson (1985)

Editor		Performance	
Training	Transfer	Training	Transfer
EDT	ED	T = 4.3 P–0.53	T = 3.7 P–0.20
ED	EDT	T = 4.8 P–0.79	T = 3.9 P–0.34
ED/EDT	EMACS	T = 3.9 P–0.55	T = 3.4 P–0.41

editors to screen editors involves fewer shared productions. Thus, subjects who trained with line editors and then switched to the screen editor would be able to use some of their previously developed productions but would also need to develop a relatively large set of new productions. As a result the ratio of old to new skills in this situation would be smaller than in the situation where transfer was between line editors. As shown in Figure 3.1, this predicts a smaller attenuation of learning rate in the former than in the latter situation.

A similar interpretation of the Transfer results was suggested by Singley and Anderson. Initially they attempted to account for the different practice functions that were observed in Training and Transfer with Newell and Rosenbloom's (1981) general power function (i.e. Equation 3.9 above). However, they concluded that the simple notion of including prior experience into the power function was not sufficient to account for the Transfer data. Singley and Anderson then suggested that in such transfer situations it was necessary to identify components of tasks that were general and specific. General components are those that are shared between tasks. Specific components are those that are peculiar to the particular task. Singley and Anderson then proposed that a more appropriate account of their transfer data would involve a power function that included two separate power functions, one for the general components and one for the specific components:

$$T = X + N_g\, P_g^{\,c} + N_s\, P_s^{\,c} \tag{3.10}$$

This equation is equivalent in form to Equation 8 with an asymptote. Furthermore, equating general components with old components and specific components with new components results in the two equations being equivalent in function as well. Unfortunately, Singley and Anderson did not evaluate whether Equation 3.10 provided a better account of their transfer data than Equation 3.9. Furthermore, there was no explicit discussion of the implications of this conceptualization of transfer on learning rates.

MacKay(1982) MacKay (1982) reported data combined from two earlier studies (MacKay, 1981; MacKay and Bowman, 1969) in which the speed of reading sentences aloud was measured. Three types of sentences were examined: normal, scrambled, and nonsense. The scrambled sentences were derived from the normal sentences by rearranging the order of the words. The nonsense sentences were derived in turn from the scrambled sentences by substituting or rearranging letters in words to form pronounceable non-words.

MacKay reported two main results. The first was that normal sentences were read faster than scrambled sentences, which were read faster than nonsense strings. The second result was that the rate at which subjects improved their reading speed with practice was a function of the type of sentence being read. Subjects improved at the fastest rate with nonsense strings, at a slower rate with scrambled sentences, and at the slowest rate with normal sentences.

The difference in learning rates can be accounted for by considering, at a fairly superficial level, the skills that underlie reading aloud the three types of sentences. First consider the normal sentences. Competent readers rely on skills that (1) convert familiar words into sounds, and (2) use syntactically based meaning to increase fluency (e.g. noun phrases such as 'the dog' are read faster than 'the' and 'dog' read separately, Just and Carpenter, 1980). With adult readers these skills are unlikely to improve much with practice. Hence any improvement observed with this type of sentence will be at a very slow rate.

Now consider the scrambled sentences. Subjects who read such sentences aloud now perform without the benefit of the second type of skill involved in normal reading. That is, because the scrambled sentences did not contain familiar noun or verb phrases, words can only be processed as individual meaning units rather than as part of higher level concepts. Therefore, with this type of sentence, subjects would be required to develop some other strategy to increase fluency beyond the level at which they can read a list of unrelated words. This suggests that reading these sentences results in the combination of old and new skills. The ratio of old to new skills with these sentences will be smaller than with the normal sentences and so the attenuation of learning rate will be less than with the normal sentences. Thus learning will be faster with the scrambled sentences than with the normal sentences.

With the nonsense sentences subjects are at even less of an advantage in terms of being able to use already established skills. Because these sentences were derived from the scrambled sentences there is no syntactically based meaning to increase fluency. In addition, the sentences contain no familiar words and so pronunciations are not as easily accessible as with real words. Instead subjects must rely on pronunciations derived from the pronunciations of real words that look similar. This derivation process is unlikely to be a well-practiced skill. Without many other old skills to influence performance with these sentences, it seems plausible that the ratio of old to new skills in this condition is lower than in both of the previous conditions. Therefore, the combination of old and new skills in reading nonsense sentences will have little attenuating effect on learning rate and so subjects will improve with these sentences faster than with the other types.

The MacKay results support our claim that a consideration of the relative number of old and new skills used to perform a task according to the relationship depicted in Equation 3.8 will enable predictions about the relative learning rates in tasks with different ratios of old to new skills.

Snyder and Pronko (1952) It appears that Equation 3.8 can also provide a good account of the acquisition of perceptual-motor skills. Snyder and Pronko (1952) investigated the effect of wearing inverting lenses (i.e. these make the world look upside down) on performance in a motor task. For 15 days, subjects were trained with normal vision on the Purdue pegboard task—a task that requires precise visual control of motor responses. Following this training phase, the subjects were then given 27 days practice on the same task while wearing inverting lenses. This latter condition had the obvious effect of slowing performance compared to the normal vision condition.

A more interesting result concerns the rate at which performance improved in the two conditions. The practice data from this experiment has been replotted in Figure 3.4. The lines represent the best-fit power functions of the form described by Equation 3.7. It is clear from this figure that, although performance with inverted vision never attains the speed of that with normal vision, the performance in the former condition improves at a faster rate (-0.20) than in the latter condition (-0.10).

The differences in learning rate can be accounted for by assuming that performance in the inverted vision condition involves the same skills as in the normal vision condition plus a new set of skills that cope with the inverted visual information. Performance in the normal vision condition can be

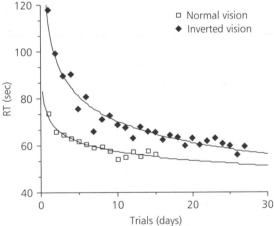

Fig. 3.4 Data reported in Snyder and Pronko (1952). Data points have been plotted on linear axes. The lines represent the best-fit power functions with the following equations:

Normal Vision: $T = 72.418\, P^{-0.10}$, $r^2 = 0.913$;
Inverted Vision: $T = 111.98\, P^{-0.20}$, $r^2 = 0.935$.

considered to involve both old and new skills. The old skills are concerned with co-ordinating visual information and motor responses. The new skills are more task-related and concern rules specifying peg placement. In the same vein, the inverted vision condition involves the same old and new skills plus another set of skills concerned with translating the inverted visual information into normal orientation information. This means that subjects can adapt existing skills to operate in the new environment rather than having to develop a whole set of new skills. It also implies that more new skills underlie performance in the inverted vision condition than in the normal vision condition. The fact that the performance on the first day of inverted vision was almost 60% slower than on the first day of normal vision suggests that the skills to be learned in order to cope with the inverted vision substantially outnumber the skills needed to place the pegs. Thus the ratio of old to new skills in the inverted vision condition is smaller than in the normal vision condition. The prediction can now be made on the basis of Equation 3.8 that the combination of old and new skills in this task will result in a greater attenuation of learning rate in the normal vision condition (see Figure 3.1). This then accounts for Snyder and Pronko's finding that performance with inverted vision improved at a faster rate than with normal vision.

Summary and conclusions

The studies discussed in this section, when considered as a whole, provide consistent support for the notion that the combination of old and new skills can affect the rate at which a task is learned. The way in which learning rate is affected depends on the extent to which old components have been practiced prior to combination with the new components, and the relative number of steps involved in the old and new components. One of the studies discussed above (Singley and Anderson, 1985) showed a slowing of learning rate from Training to Transfer. Another study (Snyder and Pronko, 1952) showed an increase in the learning rate from Training to Transfer. The MacKay (1982) data did not come from a transfer design but did show differences in learning rates between conditions which were accounted for by considering the relative amounts of practice and number of steps involved in the underlying components.

3.5 Task learning curves as summary functions

One of the major implications of Equation 3.8, or as it will be referred to henceforth, the Old/New Function, is that learning rate, as exhibited on a particular task, is by no means a constant of the cognitive systems of research participants. It is clear that overt learning rate can be affected by the combination of old and new skills. In addition, as will be demonstrated below, it is also reasonable to suggest that learning rate is also affected by other factors, such as motivation and anxiety. Thus, as suggested above, there is evidence that is counter to what is implied by Anderson's (1982) account of the power law of learning, that the rate at which performance on a task improves is a constant of the learning system. It may well be the case, and was an assumption of the argument developed above, that new component skills that contribute to overall performance on a task are acquired at a rate that is a constant for any individual.

The fact that the rate at which performance on a task improves can be a function of previous experience with components of the task is not surprising. Certainly it would be expected that learning a task would be facilitated if a trainee is familiar with parts of the task. However, what is important to realize is the apparent distinction between the learning of a task and the learning of components underlying performance of the task. The Old/New Function predicts that a combination of old and new skills will affect learning rate. This effect involves an attenuation of learning rate compared with the rate at which the old task components were originally learned. Thus, the learning rate of a 'new' task will be different to that of a previously observed new task, that is, the task in which the old task components were learned. The significance of this finding is that the rate of improvement on a task is determined by the history of the components that underlie performance of the task, rather than experience with the task itself. Thus, variability in task learning rates appears to result from the combination of underlying component skills with varying application histories that all improve at the same rate. Therefore, contrary to what is implied by Anderson's account of the power law of learning, the rate of improvement on a new task is not directly determined by parameters of the cognitive system. Instead it is the rate of improvement of component skills that underlie performance of the task that is determined by the parameters of the cognitive system. Only when performance on a task relies on the execution of completely new skills will the task-learning rate be the same as the cognitive system's learning rate. However, given that for adults most tasks involve the execution of component skills that vary in the extent to which they have been practiced, improvement on a new task is unlikely to ever be at the same rate at which the underlying components improve.

It should be noted that the argument about the attenuation of learning rates that results from the combination of old and new skills should not be construed as a claim that transfer leads to someone becoming a slower learner. Certainly part of the claim is that the rate of improvement on a task in which some of the requirements have been mastered before will be slower than if the task was entirely new. But this slower improvement rate is on the overall task. New task components will be learned at the rate that someone normally learns new things. That is, someone's capacity to learn new things is unaffected by the transfer situation. It is only when measurement of performance takes into account performance on both old and new task components is a slower overall learning rate observed. In other words, learning rate on the overall task is attenuated, but learning rate on the new task components is unaffected.

The picture of skill acquisition that emerges from this discussion of learning rates is one where skilled performance involves the execution of a number of component skills. These component skills may be represented cognitively as production rules (although there is nothing in the above account that implies this constraint). When a number of new productions are executed together to perform a task, performance will improve according to a power function that has a learning rate determined by the parameters of the cognitive system. If the task conditions applicable to the successful execution of these productions continue to be present, then performance on the task will continue to improve according to the same power function. This will be the case even if task conditions change, as long as the appropriate conditions for the execution of the productions remain in the stimulus environment or are produced by the execution of other productions. Thus, collections of productions can develop the appearance of skill modules, where changes in task conditions do not affect their execution, nor the pattern of their improvement. New productions may develop alongside these already well-practiced productions as task conditions dictate. These new productions will improve according to a different power function, although one with a learning rate again determined by the parameters of the cognitive system. In other words, new productions will improve at the same rate as the one that describes the improvement of old productions. Thus, old and new productions will improve together according to their own learning curves. Although these learning curves will have the same basic learning rate, the momentary learning rates of the two sets of productions will be different because these productions are at different points along their learning curves. Performance on the task as a whole will improve at a rate that is not the same as the learning rate of new productions. In fact, the learning rate on the total task will be a function of the combination of the separate learning curves that describe the improvement of the different sets of productions that underlie performance on this task. Thus the power function that describes improvement on the total task can be seen as an aggregate of the learning curves of the components that underlie performance of this task. In other words, just as performance time on the total task is a function of the time to execute all of the productions that contribute to the overall performance, so is the learning curve for performance on the total task a function of the learning curves describing improvement in all of these productions.

Although the simple addition of two power functions that describe improvement in old and new skills provides a reasonable account of changes in learning rate, more complicated tasks than those examined so far will no doubt involve more complicated combinations of functions. The large variation in learning rates for different tasks that is typically observed, both between and within subjects, may be a result of examining performance on tasks that involve various combinations of skills with varying practice histories. This apparently simple explanation for variations in learning rate belies the complexity that underlies the learning of a task. For example, it would be an immensely difficult exercise to determine the relative contributions to the overall pattern of improvement in a task that are made by, on one hand, the number of skills involved in various task components and, on the other hand, the practice histories of these skills.

The fact that new tasks rarely involve the execution of only new skills calls into question the ability of simple power functions to account for improvement with practice. Although such functions may be able to describe the improvement that is observed, the parameters of such functions will not be accurate reflections of features of the components underlying performance. For instance, in Anderson's (1982) account of the power law of learning, the intercept value of a power function (i.e. N in $T = NP^c$) was said to be proportional to the number of productions executed in the performance of a task. However, this will only be the case if all of the productions being executed are new. If some of the productions are old, and therefore are further along their learning curves than the new productions, then this coefficient will underestimate the number of productions being executed. Similarly, Newell and Rosenbloom's (1981) revised version of the simple power function (i.e. $T = N(P + E)^c$) may be able to account for improvement on a task that relies on the execution of old productions only, but all of these productions must have been practiced to the same extent for the parameters of this function to be informative (i.e. E must be the same for all of the productions). Therefore, when a task involves the execution of productions with varying practice histories, as most tasks will, the best way to describe improvement on the task is to combine separate power functions that describe the improvement of the various sets of productions. The difficulty, however, is in estimating a trainee's experience with particular task components and the number of productions that are executed to perform these components. The degree to which such an exercise is undertaken will depend on the accuracy that is desired from a function designed to describe improvement on the task.

The argument presented above, that learning curves reflect summaries of learning curves of component skills, was derived from a discussion of learning rates. Others have made similar claims about learning curves, but have reached these conclusions from different directions. As mentioned earlier, Heathcote *et al.* (2000) argued that power function learning curves were only found in averaged group data, and that individual learning curves were best described by functions that represented the combination of exponential and power functions. Also mentioned earlier was Singley and Anderson's (1985) suggestion that the type of transfer observed in some situations could only be understood by considering the skills that were specific to particular tasks and skills that were general to several tasks. As a result, they proposed that performance improvements on a transfer task should be described by a function that combined separate learning functions for the specific and the general skills. Some researchers (e.g. Delaney *et al.*, 1998; Rickard, 1997, 1999) have reported that, in some tasks, people utilize different strategies at different times. These researchers found that the resultant learning curves were best described by functions that included separate functions for each strategy. There is evidence, then, from various sources to support the claim that when people perform new tasks, they utilize old skills and develop new skills. The combined improvement on all of these skills that occurs with practice on the new task is the improvement that is observed on the new task.

It is important to note that the implications of the Old/New Function still apply regardless of the form of the learning functions that describe improvement of component skills. That is, if learning proceeds according to a power function, an exponential function, or some combination of these (Heathcote *et al.*, 2000), combining learning functions that differ in their intercept values (i.e. starting times) and/or amounts of practice will result in an overall function with a learning rate that differs from the learning rates of the component functions. This result is due to the combination of negatively accelerated functions. The momentary learning rate at any point along such curves is different to any other point along the curve. When a task learning curve is a summary of the learning curves of several component skills, and the components are at varying points along their learning curves (i.e. different practice histories), then the task learning curve will reflect the combination of several momentary learning rates. Furthermore, the difference between task learning rate and the learning rate of components will occur regardless of the form of the underlying learning curves, as long as they are negatively accelerated.

One important implication of the Old/New Function is that all human performance is the product of the operation of many component processes. The level of performance exhibited at any one moment is the result of the execution history of each component process, and the ability of the person to develop new processes when necessary. In this view every performance episode becomes a transfer situation (cf. Singley and Anderson, 1989)—in familiar situations old skills are utilized as is, whereas in new situations some degree of adaptation is necessary. Thus, transfer determines the form of the Old/New Function that applies in any particular situation. That is, the degree to which transfer occurs in a particular situation and the nature of this transfer determines the components that comprise the specific version of the Old/New Function that applies to this situation. Clearly then, any factor that affects the nature and scope of transfer also imposes constraints on the nature of the Old/New Function. The early part of this chapter presented some of the prominent determiners of transfer but there are several other factors not traditionally considered in discussions of transfer. Context and individual differences also have important effects on the extent of transfer observed and hence the shape of learning curves, and so to complete the picture on transfer effects we now turn our attention to these factors.

3.6 **Context effects**

A complicating factor in the operation of the Old/New Function is the effect that changes in task context have on the performance of old skills. As part of an attempt to evaluate the validity of the Old/New Function, we (Speelman, 1995; Speelman and Kirsner, 1993) obtained transfer results that gave us cause to question one of the assumptions underlying this equation. This was the assumption that, when old skills are performed in the context of a new task, they will continue to improve according to the learning curve that described their initial improvement prior to transfer. This assumption seemed reasonable on the basis of many of the existing theories of skill acquisition. For instance, both the ACT theory and the Instance theory would predict that, if a skill can be applied in a particular context, the best predictor of performance time would be the learning curve that had tracked the skill up to that point, extrapolated one unit. Certainly no theory had suggested why performance of a skill might be slower than previously was the case (except due to lack of use). In any case, further research to test this assumption explicitly (Speelman and Kirsner, 2001) found that the assumption was only partially correct.

Speelman and Kirsner (2001) described several experiments in which people performed a simulated analysis of the purity of a water sample. The task involved several arithmetic calculations, using parameter values presented on a computer screen, a set of constant equations, and boxes on the screen for entering intermediate and final values. In every experiment in this study, there was a training phase and a transfer phase in which the number of calculations performed would vary. The task was such that calculations could be added or subtracted without affecting the face validity of the task. Furthermore, performing one calculation could be achieved independently of all the other calculations in a trial. Subjects typically would be presented with one version during training, and a different version during transfer. The main aim of the experiments was to examine the learning curve on one set of calculations throughout both phases, and in particular, to determine whether there were any effects on this learning curve when a set of new calculations had been added to the task. In other words, would old skills be performed in the new task just as they had always been performed? If so, performance time would be predicted by extrapolating the learning curve observed during training. Alternatively, the presence of the new calculations could somehow disrupt the performance of the old skills, in which case the training learning curve may underestimate transfer response times. In general, the results of the Speelman and Kirsner (2001) experiments revealed that performing old skills in new tasks did disrupt the performance of the old skills. In each experiment, old skills were performed slower during transfer than was predicted by extrapolating the training learning curves.

Certainly the disruptive effect of integrating old and new skills has been reported before (Carlson *et al.*, 1990a; Elio, 1986; Frensch, 1991; Gottsdanker *et al.*, 1963; Herman and Kantowitz, 1970; Pashler and Baylis, 1991; Proctor and Dutta, 1995b; Rickard, 1997; Rickard *et al.*, 1994). Miller and Paredes (1990) found that students learning to multiply performed addition slower during this period than before this period. This result was interpreted by the authors as indicating that learning to multiply was interfering with the well-established skill of performing addition. Miller and Paredes went on to suggest that

> within a domain of knowledge, learning new skills may often require one to rethink or reorganise previous knowledge, leading in turn to a temporary disruption of performance. Finding that such disruptions occur as one acquires new knowledge suggests that new knowledge is being incorporated into a structure containing the previous skill
>
> (p. 239).

Just as in the Miller and Paredes (1990) study, the disruption observed by Speelman and Kirsner (2001) was short-lived. In most cases, with further practice on the transfer task, response times on old calculations returned to the levels predicted by the training learning curves. This result supports Miller and Paredes's suggestion that a disruption to the performance of old skills caused by a change in task conditions is an effect on performance, not on learning. Thus, in our study, the old skills were continuing to improve with practice during performance of the transfer task, but there was some sort of overhead on performance associated with the change in task. Once subjects had learned to cope with the altered conditions of the task, their performance could reveal the improvement on the old skills that had accumulated during this period.

The disruption to skilled performance created by a change in task conditions has recently been investigated further. In two unpublished research projects (Forbes, 2000; Giesen, 2000) the aim was to determine whether the disruption observed by Speelman and Kirsner (2001) was due to a change in the visual appearance of the task (i.e. adding more calculations on a trial), or to a change in the mental set possessed by subjects when performing the task (i.e. knowing that some new calculations were to be solved after the old ones). In both of these projects, subjects performed simple multiplication problems from the six times tables (e.g. 6×3). During the training phase, a small number of problems were repeated several times each, in a random order. Despite using adult subjects, clear learning curves were obtained during this phase. In the transfer phase, these same problems were presented several times each again. Interspersed between these problems were other similar problems. There were many different conditions. In each condition the new problems were of a particular sort. So, for instance, in one condition, the new problems were taken from the other times tables (e.g. 7×8). In another condition, the new problems involved a change in operation (e.g. $6 \times \_ = 18$). The important feature of the experiments to note is that, on those trials during the transfer phase in which the training problems were presented, the visual appearance of the trial, and the task required of the subjects, were identical to the way they were during training. Theoretically, then, performance on these trials should be predicted by extrapolating the training learning curves. What was found, however, was that in several conditions, performance on the training problems was disrupted in the same manner as in the Speelman and Kirsner (2001) study. The fact that these old problems were being performed in a context where, on other trials, new problems were being solved, was apparently sufficient to disrupt performance on the old problems. This is despite the fact that these old problems could be solved in exactly the same way as in training (i.e. everything about the task, on each of these trials at least, was as before). This result suggests that the disruption to learning curves does not require a change to the visual appearance of the task to occur, as in the Speelman and Kirsner experiments. Instead, a change in task context is sufficient.

A further feature of the Forbes and Giesen experiments is worth noting. In many of the conditions in which a disruption was observed, performance eventually returned to the levels predicted by the training learning curves.

There was one condition, however, where performance was disrupted to such an extent that, for the amount of practice experienced in the experiment at least, there did not appear to be any chance that performance would return to the levels predicted by the training learning curve. The new problems in this condition involved double-digit addition (e.g. 17 + 62). Therefore, during transfer, problems alternated randomly between simple six times table problems, and fairly difficult addition problems. This mixture caused performance on the six times tables problems to be disrupted substantially compared with performance in training. This condition, it would seem, caused such a dramatic reassessment of what was required in the task as a whole that subjects could not approach the old problems in anything like the old way.

In conclusion, it would seem there is qualified support for the assumption underlying the Old/New Function that old skills will continue to improve in new tasks according to their original learning curves. A change in context can affect performance of old skills, but this does not appear to affect learning. That is, given sufficient practice, performance of old skills will eventually return to the levels predicted by learning curves that describe initial improvement. However, some changes in context may be so dramatic that a major re-evaluation of a task's requirements is necessary, and this can retard further improvement, or possibly even prevent further learning. One implication of this conclusion is that transfer is not an automatic function of having appropriate skills to apply in a certain situation. Certainly having appropriate skills is better than not having them. Unfortunately, predicting the extent of transfer is far more complicated than simply determining task requirements and cobbling together the requisite skill modules.

A further implication of the effect of context changes on skilled performance is that it calls into question the concept of pure automatic processes. Ever since the work of Shiffrin and Schneider (1977; Schneider and Shiffrin, 1977) and Posner and Snyder (1975), a distinction is commonly made between automatic and controlled forms of processing. Briefly, this distinction rests on the extent to which attention or consciousness plays a role in performance. Controlled performance relies on attention, whereas automatic performance does not. In the latter case, exposure to particular stimulus conditions is sufficient to evoke an immediate response, possibly without the intervention of any conscious thought processes. Moreover, the response is obligatory in the sense that once initiated it cannot be stopped. This sort of performance only comes after extensive practice and could be seen to be the sort of performance that occurs at the end of a learning curve, or at least at that part of the curve where improvements are minimal. Thus, with sufficient practice under appropriate conditions (Schneider and Shiffrin, 1977; Shiffrin and Schneider, 1977;

Schneider *et al.*, 1984) one can develop the ability to respond in an automatic fashion to particular stimuli. That is, if certain stimuli are perceived, an appropriate response occurs automatically. Thus, after many years of reading experience, seeing CAT is registered as the sound 'cat', and possibly leads to consideration of feline associations. Furthermore, this process can occur without any intention to read the word, without any knowledge of the underlying steps that may take place, and without any ability to prevent the sound or associations from springing to mind. In one sense, then, an automatic response can be considered 'dumb' in that it takes no thought.

The notion that practice can lead to a situation where a stimulus can invoke an automatic response is called into question by the effects of context on transfer. For instance, the Forbes and Giesen experiments described above involved people solving multiplication problems that conceivably involved automatic retrieval of solutions (e.g. 6 × 2; Rickard and Bourne, 1996; Rickard *et al.*, 1994). The results of these experiments demonstrated how performance on these problems could be affected when changes occur in stimulus conditions other than those that are responsible for triggering the automatic responses. Similar effects of context have been demonstrated with the 'gold standard' (MacLeod, 1992) of automatic performance, the Stroop effect (see Chapter 2). Dishon-Berkovits and Algom (2000) have shown that the degree to which colour-naming performance is affected by intrusions of the automatic reading response is determined by the relative proportion of trials in which colour names and words match and do not match. Thus performance on any particular trial is not determined simply by an automatic response to the stimuli on that trial. Instead, performance is determined by conditions that exist across many trials. And yet the automatic processes that are supposed to operate in the Stroop effect (i.e. reading processes) are assumed to be automatic following years of pre-experimental practice. Thus so-called automatic processes may not be as dumb as they are commonly conceived. People appear to consider the context in which they perform to a much greater extent than is suggested by the traditional dichotomy of controlled and automatic processing.

3.7 Individual differences

Earlier in this chapter, we discussed the fact that there are individual differences in learning rates. We considered the possibility that learning rate is a constant of the cognitive system, as implied in Anderson's (1982) ACT* theory. That learning rate is a constant is also assumed in the Old/New Function, although this function reveals how, even within individuals, learning rate will vary depending on the particular task situation. In this section, we describe evidence that indicates a number of individual differences in peoples' abilities and characteristics have an impact on skill acquisition and so contribute to individual differences in learning rates and other learning curve parameters.

Ackerman (1988) has demonstrated that individual differences in particular abilities predict performance at different stages of skill acquisition. With reference to the three phases of skill acquisition described by Fitts (1964, see Chapter 2), Ackerman states that a general cognitive-intellectual ability accounts for a substantial portion of the variance in performance observed in the first phase. The reason for this is that during this stage, people are typically working out the demands of the task and the best strategy to adopt. This type of performance requires the use of memory, reasoning, and knowledge retrieval. Therefore, the more intelligent someone is, the better will be their initial performance. As the first stage gives way to the second stage, the influence of general intellectual abilities is diminished. In their place, perceptual speed ability becomes more predictive of performance. This ability involves 'speed of consistent encoding and comparing symbols' (Ackerman, 1988, p. 290). That is, once a strategy for performing a task has been developed, the ability to apply it consistently and quickly will determine the speed of performance in the second phase of skill acquisition. Finally, with further practice, the third phase of skill acquisition is reached, and the influence of perceptual speed ability wanes. The third phase is marked by performance that appears to require little cognitive input, and Ackerman says that individual differences here are related to differences in psychomotor ability. Essentially this ability 'represents processing speed . . . (that is) . . . mostly independent of information processing' (Ackerman, 1988, p. 291). Evidence in support of Ackerman's claims about the relationship between abilities and skilled performance has been reported by Fleishman (1972), Hertzog *et al.* (1996), and Woltz (1988).

Ackerman's (1988) model suggests that three basic parameters of the learning curve are affected by individual differences in three sets of abilities. For instance, if general intellectual abilities are associated with differences in performance early in practice, then they must determine the intercept value of learning curves (i.e. performance time at the beginning of practice). If perceptual speed abilities predict performance during the middle phase of skill acquisition, then individual differences in these abilities will be associated with individual differences in learning rate. Finally, if performance during the final phase of skill acquisition is associated with psychomotor abilities, then individual differences in these abilities will be predictive of asymptote values. Unfortunately, the relationship between individual differences in particular abilities and learning parameters is not as clear-cut as this description implies. It turns out that variations in one parameter of a learning curve can influence the value of other parameters. For example, the learning rate parameter of a power function reflects the speed with which performance approaches asymptote. Consider, then, two learning curves with similar intercept values, and similar rates of improvement. This refers, in a general sense, to a situation where performance begins at the same point, and gets faster by the same degree with each subsequent practice episode. Imagine, that the curves have different asymptotes. As a result, power functions fitted to both curves will actually have different values for the learning rate parameters, with the curve with the slowest asymptote having the fastest learning rate. Despite this wrinkle in the story, it seems clear that individual differences in abilities do contribute to individual differences in learning curves.

Other types of individual differences have also been found to affect learning curve parameters. For example, Eyring *et al.* (1993) reported that ability and familiarity with a task predicted learning rates. In addition, self-efficacy predicted both learning rates and asymptotic values. Eyring *et al.* interpreted the association between self-efficacy and performance as indicative of the role motivation plays in skill acquisition. Others (e.g. Thomas, 1998) have speculated on how important motivation is to the acquisition of skills. Ericsson *et al.* (1993) proposed that motivation is one of the most important individual differences in determining whether someone embarking on the learning of a musical instrument will survive the rigours of years of practice and ultimately develop world-class playing abilities. It would seem self-evident that motivation to succeed is important in whether or not practice leads to skilled performance (Anderson and Corbett, 1993, p. 254). At this stage, the role of motivation has not been articulated, nor even considered, in any modern theory of skill acquisition (Anderson and Lebiere, 1998, p. 40). And yet, the role of motivation in skill acquisition raises some tantalizing questions. For instance, is there anything more to motivation effects than differences in likelihood to engage in practice? That is, someone who is more motivated than another person about a particular task is more likely to undertake greater amounts of practice. Even if overt practice was equivalent for two people, the more motivated person may pay more attention to what they are doing and less attention to off-task thoughts, and so would improve the quality of their practice. They may also engage in more covert practice (e.g. mental rehearsal on and even away from the task). Thus motivation effects could be completely reducible to practice effects.

Individual differences in anxiety have also been reported to influence learning curve parameters. Greene *et al.* (1998) reported that higher state anxiety was associated with slower learning rate, higher intercept values, and greater variability in performance. Thomas (1998) also noted that some people experience anxiety when task conditions change, such as with the implementation of a new computer system, and this adversely affects their ability to transfer old skills to the new situation.

Age is another factor that has some potential to affect learning rate parameters. With age there is a general decline in cognitive abilities (Proctor and Dutta, 1995, p. 324), and so it might be expected that skill acquisition would also suffer. The evidence on this issue is not clear, however (Salthouse, 1989). The small amount of evidence that is available does suggest some differences in skill acquisition ability that are related to aging. For example, Salthouse and Somberg (1982) found that the learning curves of older people on a perceptual motor task had slower intercept values and slower near-asymptote values. Interestingly the curves of the older people were similar in shape to those of the younger group, suggesting that learning rates were similar in the two groups. There is also some evidence that older people are less likely than younger people to develop item-specific skills with practice, relying instead on refining item-general skills (Hertzog *et al.*, 1996; Proctor and Dutta, 1995, p. 326).

The picture that emerges from the individual differences literature is one where learning curve parameters are just another set of features upon which people differ. Moreover, differences in these parameters appear to be related to both enduring and temporary characteristics of people, and these may interact with situation-specific factors to affect the pattern of improvement that follows practice on a task. Thus, learning curve parameters, and in particular learning rate, may not be constants of the cognitive system, but instead are variables that come under the influence of many intra- and extra-individual factors. In any one situation, however, it may be safe to assume that a relatively constant intrinsic learning rate applies. Certainly, Snoddy's (1926) belief of one learning rate that applied to every person and task is a fantasy.

3.8 **Conclusions**

This chapter has demonstrated that the level of skill exhibited in any particular behaviour is fundamentally a matter of transfer. Just about all behaviour is composed of many component processes contributing to the overall performance. Skills developed in different contexts are recruited into service in the performance of new tasks. The absolute level of performance exhibited on a new task is determined by the extent to which old skills can be executed in the new context, and the extent of prior practice with these old skills. Furthermore, the rate at which performance of the new task improves is determined by several factors: (1) the performer's intrinsic learning rate; (2) the relative proportion of old and new skills used to perform the task; and (3) the extent of prior practice with old skills prior to the combination with new skills. The degree to which any of these transfer features can determine performance levels will be further complicated by: (1) the nature of old and new tasks; (2) the nature of past and present training; (3) performance context; and (4) individual differences. Currently no theory attempts to take all of these factors into account in explaining performance and so all of the theories considered fail the Skill Acquisition Phenomena Criterion for suitability as a theory of skill acquisition. In the next chapter, we show how all of these factors, and the principles that underlie their effects, can be integrated into one theory—the component theory of skill acquisition and transfer.

Chapter 4

A new framework

a complex task like text editing can be decomposed into parts, and each part seems to be learned separately.

Singley and Anderson (1989, p. 103)

In previous chapters we outlined a case against current theories of skill acquisition on the grounds that they do not account for all features of the effects of transfer on performance, particularly effects on the shape of learning curves. As a result we concluded that these theories fail the Skill Acquisition Phenomena Criterion for suitability as theories of skill acquisition. The aim of this chapter is to present a framework for a new theory of skill acquisition that does account for these transfer effects, a theory that takes as its starting point the view expressed in Chapter 3 that skilled performance results from the execution of many component processes.

To view skilled performance as being the product of underlying component processes is to see a learning curve as a macrocosm of many individual learning experiences. Performance at one point in time reflects what has been learned at some previous time that is able to impact on performance at the moment. Thus, although a learning curve may be viewed as reflecting an incremental improvement process that leads to a smooth transition from novice to expert performance, it is actually a summary of the operation of a vast number of component processes, each with their own improvement functions, and each with varying histories of application with or without success. According to this conceptualization, looking at performance over the course of a learning curve, or at particular points along the curve could lead to very different views of the processes underlying performance. Examination of performance on novel tasks typically reveals fragile behaviour that is erratic and not often successful, but shows clear improvement with practice. Mid-level performance is more consistently successful, but elements, such as speed, still reveal improvement with practice. In contrast, when expert-level performance is studied, very little changes as a result of further practice. Such expert performance includes adult-level reading and speaking. Arguably such skills have reached the asymptote of their learning curve, and are characterized by performance that does not change monotonically with repeated execution. One might be excused for concluding, on the basis of observing such behaviour only, that the processes responsible for this behaviour were not the end product of years of practice, but were instead innate brain structures activated by interaction with the world. It is our view, though, that focussing exclusively on adult-level performance of tasks leads to limited conceptualizations of the underlying mechanisms. Restricting one's scientific gaze to a small range of behaviours in restrictive and possibly artificial contexts, and without consideration of a possible developmental trajectory can only lead to theories about isolated systems and a proliferation of such systems that seemingly have no relationship to each other. We will argue in this chapter that more can be gained from considering the possibility that much of adult skilled behaviour is indeed the end product of years of skill acquisition. We will demonstrate how consideration of the learning principles identified in the previous chapters can lead to parsimonious explanations of many adult-level skilled behaviours. Furthermore, we will begin to sketch a theory of skill acquisition that is consistent with these principles and that, as we show in later chapters, can also illuminate many other aspects of human behaviour and functioning.

4.1 **Principles**

Several characteristics of learning were identified in the previous chapters. In this section, we propose a number of principles of learning that subsume these characteristics and so provide a summary of the basic facts used in previous chapters to evaluate theories against the Skill Acquisition Phenomena Criterion. Ultimately, then, accounting for these principles becomes the Skill Acquisition Phenomena Criterion. The theory we propose later in the chapter can account for these principles. Furthermore, given that in subsequent chapters we make the claim that the theory also meets the remaining Criteria, the theory is essentially a statement that many seemingly independent cognitive phenomena can be understood by reference to a small number of principles.

Principle 1: Practice leads to faster performance

Principle 1 is the most obvious feature of learning. When something has been learned from a previous experience and it can be utilized at some later moment in time, performance at that later moment is typically faster than previous performance. This principle applies to all aspects of behaviour, not just overt behaviour, such as performance of a task. For instance, recognition of experiences as familiar is faster as the number of recognition attempts increases (Pirolli and Anderson, 1985b). Perception of objects is faster with increased experience (e.g. Crovitz et al., 1981). It is probably not unreasonable to suspect that this principle reflects a basic characteristic of neural functioning (Altmann et al., 2004; Barnes, 1979; Bolger and Schneider, 2002).

A common explanation for the effect that practice has on the speed of performance is that practice leads to faster, more reliable activation of knowledge structures. This effect of practice is often referred to as strengthening in theories of skill acquisition and memory (e.g. Anderson, 1982). That is, as access to an item in memory increases, the representation is in some way strengthened, which means that it becomes easier to access (i.e. access is faster and more reliable) and more resistant to forgetting (Anderson, 1983b; Pirolli and Anderson, 1985b). So, another version of Principle 1 is that practice leads to strengthened knowledge structures. When performance relies on access to memory representations, the greater the strength of those representations, the faster will be the performance.

An important feature of the way in which performance speed improves with learning is that it is negatively accelerated. That is, performance improvements are typically dramatic early in practice, and taper off as practice increases until some asymptote is reached. There is a great deal of debate as to the particular mathematical function that best describes this pattern of improvement (see Chapter 3). For our current purposes it is not important which function provides the best description of a learning curve. Only the negatively accelerated feature of learning curves is crucial for our argument.

Principle 2: Practice leads to efficiencies in knowledge access

According to Principle 1, practice leads to faster performance. As mentioned above, one of the reasons for this is that repeated access to memory representations strengthens these representations, and this facilitates further access, which in turn facilitates performance that relies on this access. Another reason why practice leads to improved performance speed is what we identify as Principle 2. When people practice a task, the way in which they perform the task changes. Typically, practice leads to a more efficient form of processing. This gain in efficiency can be characterized as a move from beginner-level performance, which involves some deliberation about what responses are required, to mastery-level performance, which is marked by immediate recognition of a situation and knowing the appropriate responses.

There are a number of different theories as to how practice leads to this sort of improvement in the efficiency of processing. According to the ACT family of theories, improvement in processing is a result of practice leading to a reduction in the number of processing steps through either deleting unnecessary processing steps or collapsing a number of simple processing steps into fewer more complicated processing steps that have the same effect as the original steps. The proponents of the SOAR theory make similar claims. According to the Instance theory, the efficiency of processing is improved by moving from a situation where processing steps are executed in a serial manner to another situation where stimulus conditions trigger the appropriate response without any intervening deliberation. In other words, where people may originally engage in a process of generating a solution to a problem, eventually with practice, when the same problem is presented the appropriate solution is retrieved directly from memory.

Although the various theories propose different means by which practice leads to more efficient processing, all of the theories lead to the same prediction: With sufficient practice of a task where the stimulus–response relationship is consistent, performance will eventually reach the stage where perception of a known stimulus will trigger an automatic response (i.e. seeing '3 $\times$ 4 = ?' will automatically lead to a response of '12'). It is clear that moving from a situation where several processing steps are required before a response is generated to a situation where a stimulus invokes a response automatically will result in considerable savings in the amount of time to perform the task. But this process does not only save time. One view of the result of this process is that people are able to make use of consistencies in the world to set up short cuts in the ways in which they deal with the world. A problem and all of its associated stimuli, goals, and processing steps necessary to lead to a response, can be represented mentally in a compressed form, much like a shorthand version of a word. For instance, a child still in the early stages of learning to read, will struggle with the various components of the letter string 'independent', sounding out each syllable and trying to piece them together, probably producing a stilted version of the word. At this stage there may also be a struggle to connect the relatively odd sound of the utterance with the word and its associated meaning. That is, the child may recognize the word in the speech of others, and use it herself in conversation, but because the processes of converting the visual version of the word to speech are not mastered as yet, comprehension of the written word is not guaranteed. With practice, however, the child will no longer find it necessary to process the word in parts. She will, instead, instantly recognize the word and be able to read it aloud, along with emphasis placed at the appropriate places. Thus, the stimulus leads directly to the response. Furthermore, recognition of the word will also entail automatic retrieval of its meaning (if the child is engaged in reading for meaning). In this way, marks on a page can become a shorthand pointer to a great deal of knowledge (e.g. the sound of the word, its definition, associated words). Hence, practice can take a person from a situation that requires considerable time and mental effort to sort out, to a situation that can be addressed immediately and with apparently no mental effort.

Research on expertise is full of examples where the acquisition of expert knowledge is accompanied by a change in the way the domain of expertise is perceived. Experts perceive particular configurations of stimuli like most people recognize words. That is, the configurations are recognized automatically as meaningful, and depending on the goal of processing, may be relevant to decisions about appropriate responses. In contrast, novices behave like someone who is learning to read and is just able to recognize that certain visual patterns (e.g. letters and letter combinations) are relevant to this task. That is, novices are typically barely able to recognize as relevant components of those configurations that experts automatically appreciate as a whole. The clearest example of this feature of expertise comes from the domain of chess. A common memory task that is used to examine expertise differences in chess involves presenting people with a chess board and a configuration of pieces that corresponds to some point in the middle of a game. Exposure to this configuration is usually restricted to a few seconds. The board is then covered up, and the subject's task is to reproduce the configuration on another board. Accuracy in this task is a direct reflection of chess expertise. Novices can typically reproduce 33% of a configuration. Players of an intermediate standard can reproduce 49%, and players of the Grand Master level can reproduce 81% (Chase and Simon, 1973). Importantly, these differences in accuracy are not observed when players are presented with random configurations of pieces. The usual explanation for these results is that, as players gain expertise, they learn to associate certain configurations of pieces with the state of the game. For instance, there are attack configurations that pose danger for the opposition's queen, and there are defence configurations designed to protect the king. So, the acquisition of chess expertise is associated with the ability to automatically recognize particular meaningful configurations of chess pieces. Evidence for this view comes from the fact that when players are observed attempting to reproduce mid-game configurations in the memory task, novices tend to position pieces in groups that typically are related in superficial ways, such as they all appeared in the same region of the board, or they all had the same colour. In contrast, chess masters positioned pieces in groups that corresponded to meaningful configurations (e.g. attack, defence). These configurations were not restricted to pieces of the same colour or the same region of the board but would involve pieces of both colours that may have been positioned some distance from each other. Thus, chess experts appear to be 'reading' a chessboard in terms of groups of pieces that correspond to meaningful configurations— indeed they may even have names for these configurations (e.g. 'The Nimzo–Indian Defence', 'The King's Gambit', and 'The Giuco Piano'—see Kasparov, 1985). This ability to recognize meaningful groups of pieces is not just a party trick, however. It is most likely to be an essential component of the chess playing skill. That is, a configuration is meaningful in that it indicates the current state of play (i.e. who is winning, who is under attack) and may suggest an appropriate next move or even a series of moves. Thus, the acquisition of chess expertise appears to be a process whereby years of playing experience, as well as reading and talking about the game, leads to a knowledge base that is full of configurations that are associated with appropriate strategies and moves. Years of practice at viewing, producing, and thinking about these configurations lead to the ability to perceive these configurations automatically as individual objects, rather than as a grouping of several pieces.

Many other domains reveal the same sorts of perceptual differences between experts and novices. When expert radiologists and novices are presented with the same X-ray slides, they 'see' very different things. Novices find it difficult to recognize individual features of the body. For instance, it is quite difficult to see the lungs within the rib cage, and to distinguish the heart from the lung structure behind. In contrast, radiologists can not only identify individual anatomical structures, but they can see relationships between the structures, particularly, when something is abnormal (Lesgold *et al.*, 1988). In the domain of Physics, novices and experts view physics problems quite differently. When novices are presented with a collection of problems and asked to arrange the problems into groups of similar problems, they tend to put all the pulley problems together, all the inclined plain problems together, and all the spring problems together. In other words, novices perceive the problems in terms of superficial features. Physics experts, however, group problems according to the physics-based principle that underlies the problem and its solution (Larkin, 1983). Thus, all problems involving the conservation of momentum will be grouped together, whereas the problems involving Newton's first law of motion will be grouped together. Similar observations have been made with respect to the grouping of photographs of basketball concepts and skills by basketball players and fans (Allard and Burnett, 1985). Furthermore, sports people tend to have better memories for plays within the sport of their expertise compared with plays within other sports (Allard and Stakes, 1991). In the domain of wine tasting, experts and novices can sometimes have such different experiences with the same wine that it appears as if they are drinking different wines. Novice wine tasters might be able to distinguish (by taste!) between a red and a white wine, or even between a fruity and a dry white wine. Experts, by contrast, can distinguish all sorts of subtle flavours in a wine and have labels for them all (e.g. 'This wine has a strong melon character, with citrus overtones and a straw finish. It is fairly fruity on the front palate, with a crisp, dry finish'.). Some expert wine tasters can even identify the vineyard that bottled a wine in a particular year. Novices simply miss this information—their taste buds might work exactly like those of experts, but a great deal of information seems to be overlooked. Clearly, experienced wine tasters have had years of practice at sorting through the range of experiences associated with tasting a sip of wine. They have learned to identify particular combinations of sensations and have attached labels to these combinations. As a result, experts can recognize these perceptual objects automatically and produce a name for them with ease. Similarly, in the musical domain, musicians learn to recognize features of music, such as arpeggios, scales, modes, keys, chords, and tempi. Some musicians can even recognize the pitch of a musical note. Beginner musicians may realize what all these features of music indicate, but are quite incapable of detecting them or providing the appropriate label while listening to a piece of music.

All of this research on expertise has a number of features in common. Experts 'see' things differently to novices. This difference in perception appears to be related to the ability to identify configurations of stimuli as representing meaningful wholes rather than as groups of individual stimuli. These configurations are meaningful because they are related to the purpose of the processing they perform in their domain of expertise. That is, after years of experience in a domain, and years of practice performing particular tasks, certain configurations of stimuli automatically trigger responses, and these responses could be in the form of actions, decisions, thoughts, or production of a label. Thus, the automatic response to a stimulus configuration is a large component of expert performance. That this feature appears to be a characteristic of all areas of expertise illustrates the pervasiveness of Principle 2.

Principle 3: Learning leads to less demand on working memory

The combination of Principles 1 and 2 can be considered as comprising a third principle. The ability to recognize groups of stimuli as meaningful, and to do so automatically, results in a freeing up of mental resources. In particular, working memory is often described as being limited in capacity such that it can only hold a certain number of items at any time (e.g. 7 ± 2 items according to Miller, 1956). Principle 3 states that learning will lead to a situation whereby this capacity limit can be circumvented. For example, if someone is presented briefly with the following set of letters:

UREMFOLTA

and then asked to recall them, they might have difficulty remembering all of the letters, particularly in the correct order. If the letters were rearranged, however, into the following order:

FORMULATE

then memory for the set of letters is likely to be far more accurate. With the first set of letters, there are nine separate pieces of information, a number that may exceed most people's working memory capacity. In the second set, however, because we recognize the letters as together forming a word, the nine pieces of information can be processed as one piece of information. In this way, working memory will only contain one piece of information—a pointer to an item in our long-term memory for words—which means that working memory will have spare capacity for any other information that is to be held there. Presumably, then, another six or so sets of letters that are similarly arranged into words could be held in working memory without seriously affecting the ability to recall them. In this way, we could conceivably recall 63 letters or more (i.e. 7 words at 9 letters each) without too much trouble. Thus, we are able to make use of our knowledge of words to apparently circumvent the normal capacity limits on working memory. This phenomenon is often referred to as 'chunking' in the memory literature (Baddeley, 1990). It refers to the ability to interpret information in meaningful chunks, and it is the chunks that make up the limited number of items of information that can be held in working memory. It is important to note, though, that chunking is only help-ful to memory when the chunks are meaningful, and by this we mean they relate to something that is well entrenched in long-term memory and can be accessed reliably and quickly. If someone's knowledge of a particular configura-tion of items is sketchy, then the chunk will probably be stored as more than one item in working memory, and the effort to keep the components of the chunk together in working memory will take up capacity. Therefore, some-one's ability to make use of chunking to make more efficient use of their working memory will be determined by the degree to which they can automatically detect meaningful configurations of stimuli in information they are exposed to. This ability to detect meaningful configurations of stimuli will, in turn, be determined by the degree of practice at processing those stimulus configurations.

According to Principle 3, then, learning within a particular domain often leads to the ability to automatically process information in that domain in ways that result in fewer demands on working memory. An everyday example of this principle in operation is the use of acronyms, such as ASIO, CIA, STM, and RAM. Acronyms represent small sets of letters that correspond to the first letter of each word in a set of words (i.e. ASIO for *Australian Security Intelligence Organisation*). Thus, a smaller number of letters can be used in place of a larger set. After sufficient experience with an acronym, the acronym can take on the meaning of the set of words it represents. Thus, seeing 'ASIO' will invoke the same associations as 'Australian Security Intelligence

Organisation' but without the necessity to process four words. Thus, small numbers of letters can represent much larger sets of letters. In this way less information is processed, and more cognitive resources are available to process other information. Further motivation for adopting this linguistic convention is that it becomes a more efficient mode of communication (i.e. less time is spent on the same concept), and saves cognitive effort (Anderson *et al.*, 1998, see Chapter 2).

The study of expertise has highlighted many areas where chunking occurs and where the nature of the chunks (size, complexity) is related to the degree of expertise attained by an individual. For example, in the memory task used to examine the cognitive processing associated with playing chess, novices and masters place pieces on the board in distinct groups, suggesting they have processed particular pieces together and remember them as chunks. In addition, novices and masters recall the same number of such chunks, suggesting that the two groups of players are subject to the same capacity constraint on working memory. Importantly, though, the number of pieces in each chunk is greater for the masters than for the novices (3.8 pieces versus 2.4 pieces, Chase and Simon, 1973). Hence masters can remember a greater total number of pieces than novices. A similar observation has been made with expert waiters. Ericsson and Polson (1988) reported that a waiter who was required to memorize dinner orders had developed a strategy of recoding them into word-like acronyms that retained information about seating position (e.g. for salad dressings, Blue cheese, Oil-and-vinegar, Oil-and-vinegar, Thousand island = BOOT). In this way many bits of information could be recoded as a much smaller number of items, thus enabling memorization of a large number of dinner orders. Number mnemonists have been reported as following a similar strategy. For example, Professor Rueckle knew a great deal of number facts so well that he could recognize large numbers as being related to smaller numbers. For instance, he would see 451,697 as being two numbers that are themselves the products of two prime numbers (i.e. $451 = 11 \times 41$, and $697 = 17 \times 41$) (Ericsson and Staszewski, 1989). As a result, he would be able to relate many bits of information (i.e. 6 digits) to a smaller number of facts that he knows well, thus freeing up storage capacity in working memory for other digit strings.

Principle 3 has important implications beyond the fact that expertise in a domain can result in sometimes extraordinary memory skills for information in that domain. One of these implications is that, by developing a strategy whereby large amounts of information can be processed with only a small amount of working memory resources, the expert has considerably more working memory capacity available for other forms of processing than is the case with a novice. As a result, the expert is capable of a greater level of complexity in their behaviour than the novice. This phenomenon we label as Principle 4.

Principle 4: As expertise increases, fewer mental resources are required to perform a particular task, enabling the development of a hierarchy of skills

The first three principles, taken in combination, characterize learning as leading to a situation whereby more and more of the knowledge that underlies performance can be retrieved faster and more reliably as expertise increases. As a result, an expert has more knowledge at their mental fingertips that can be accessed quicker than the novice. Furthermore, this increased accessibility of expert knowledge frees up mental resources for other forms of processing. Certainly this characterization of the attainment of expertise matches the common experience that when embarking on a new task (e.g. driving a car) we can often feel so overwhelmed by the various elements of the task that require our attention that we feel as if we cannot do the task at all. Eventually, though, with increased experience, the task seems to get easier. The task is not changing, of course, we are. We slowly gain more of the knowledge that is required about how to perform the task, and our ability to use this knowledge increases. Ultimately we reach the stage where the knowledge is executed automatically and we can feel as if performing the task requires no effort whatsoever. Thus, someone who has been driving a car for 10 years or more probably engages so few mental resources for the actual operation of the car that they have plenty of resources available for increased vigilance on the road (and so are involved in fewer accidents than novice drivers, Adams, 2003), and are capable of performing other tasks while driving (e.g. singing along to the radio, conducting conversations, planning a new route to avoid a traffic jam) that have little impact on the driving task itself. Principle 4, then, identifies the fact that as expertise is acquired in a domain, more and more mental resources become available, and so further development of behaviours becomes possible.

Everyday life is full of examples where increased experience with a particular domain or task leads to a transition through a hierarchy of skills. Infants who can barely comprehend or produce language, or orient themselves in three-dimensional space eventually learn to communicate with speech and text, and may even learn to pilot a plane. The distance between novice and expert performance in these domains is clearly great, but so is the amount of time and opportunity for practice. The amount of improvement on a novel task that can be observed in 1 hour in the laboratory can be anywhere from 50 to 90% (e.g. dropping from 41 s per trial to 15 s, Speelman and Kirsner, 2001, exp.1). Given years of practice to master the many components of a complex task, vast leaps in performance levels are possible. Principle 4 suggests that the acquisition of adult-level skills is a matter of learning component skills to a level of performance that enables sufficient mental resources to be made available for the development of a new set of component skills. According to this principle, then, complex behaviours should develop in a stage-like manner. When component skills are new, resources will be used to cope with the demands of the task. As component skills improve with practice, a level of mastery of the task is reached such that fewer resources are required to perform the task. The freeing up of mental resources makes possible the performance of higher level behaviours, which may require the development of a new set of component skills. By proposing Principle 4 as a principle of learning, we are making the strong claim that the acquisition of skills, such as language comprehension and production, and performance of mathematical operations, from infancy to adulthood, should be characterized by clear stages in development, not necessarily related to biological maturation, where the trajectory is through a hierarchy of behaviours, from low-level to higher level behaviours, where mastery of some behaviours must always precede development of other behaviours, and performance within a stage will be marked by improvement of component skills without necessarily any improvement in the overall target behaviour. Thus, the degree of improvement apparent at any point in time will depend on the level of granularity of the analysis of behaviour. At a high level, improvement may appear discontinuous but at a lower level, improvement may be gradual but continuous.

Principle 5: Mastery in a domain involves the application of an array of component processes, with varying degrees of specificity to tasks and contexts, that are recruited in a manner that allows for consistent performance under stereotypical situations and flexible performance under unusual circumstances

Principle 5 expresses an assumption that underlies the previous four principles. That is, many behaviours represent the execution of a vast array of component processes. Component processes range from those that are developed specifically for the particular behaviour being performed, to those that are useful across a broad spectrum of behaviours (e.g. reading skills). As indicated in Chapter 3, the extent to which skills are specific to a particular context is determined by several factors, but in essence, people adapt to a task situation, and their skill reflects the nature of this situation. According to Principle 5, then, all behaviours involve a transfer situation, where the level of performance is determined by the extent to which existing component processes can be recruited, and new component processes need to be developed for the task at hand. Furthermore, the speed of performance of a task is as described by the Old/New Function (see Chapter 3). That is, the time to perform a task is a sum of the time to execute the component processes necessary for performance of the task. When performance of the task commences, old component processes will be some way along their own learning curve, and new component processes will be at the beginning of their particular learning curves. The learning curve exhibited for performance of the task, then, will reflect a combination of the component learning curves.

Some behaviours will involve component processes that are applicable across a wide range of domains. Reading skills, for instance, are recruited by a vast array of tasks facing adults. As a result of at least 20 years of reading in a large number of contexts, most adults' reading skills would be just as applicable to reading on a computer screen as part of learning document editing skills as reading recipes in acquiring cooking skills. Hence, performance improvements in these behaviours are unlikely to be a result of improvements in component reading processes. Instead, improvements in performance of these behaviours are more likely to be the result of refinement of component processes that are specific to the particular behaviour. This prediction reflects a general feature of the Old/New Function: The amount of performance improvement observed with a task will be a function of the amount of improvement that occurs on component processes and the relative contribution of well-practiced and new component processes to the overall performance (see Chapter 3).

Summary

The five principles of learning describe a number of features that are general to all forms of skill acquisition. Essentially these principles state that practice leads to faster and more efficient uses of knowledge. This enables faster performance and results in less demand on mental resources. In turn these outcomes enable higher level behaviours to be attempted. Ultimately skills are developed through refinement of many component processes. There should be nothing controversial about these principles. Indeed most of them have been enunciated before by others. It seems to us, however, that there has been little consideration of these principles together in terms of what they imply about the acquisition of skills. In particular, there appears to be little appreciation of how pervasive these principles are. Our claim is that they underlie every form of learning and hence every learned behaviour reflects the operation of these principles. Realization of this fact leads to new insights into the origin and nature of behaviours. Below we begin to sketch a theory of the acquisition of skills in which we demonstrate that a great deal more of the process of acquisition can be explained by just these five principles than may have been realized previously.

4.2 The Component Theory of Skill Acquisition

In this section we present an overview of a new theory—the Component Theory of Skill Acquisition which we continue to develop throughout the remainder of the book. In this chapter we describe a high-level framework that accounts for issues, such as constraints on the development of a hierarchy of skills. In subsequent chapters we present our views on the mechanisms that underlie and support this framework.

To some extent, our view of skills as assemblies of component processes recruited to perform a particular task is similar to Munro's (1992) approach to understanding complex systems. Munro claimed that complex systems can be understood at various levels of analysis:

> For example, I am working at this desk, which means that certain behavioural processes are going on which involve the desk and my body as physical objects or structures. Dropping to level n-1 and 'opening a window on to' my body, it is seen as a set of living or action processes involving parts or organs; each of these parts in turn can be regarded as biochemical processes, based on chemical structures, which in turn can be interpreted as processes based on atomic structures, and so on. The same kind of analysis might be applied to the desk—we can identify processes 'going on' within this desk, such as biochemical decay and its constituent processes down to the sub-atomic level. Furthermore, if we accept a wider frame of time, the desk, my body and everything else can be seen as the traces of change processes which have occurred in the past.
>
> (Munro, 1992, p. 177)

Munro drew a strong distinction between processes and structures, but noted their relationship across level of analysis:

> we might define structure . . . at any level of analysis as the trace of processes which have occurred at the level of analysis below. If the relationship of level n to level n-1 is that of process to structure, what is the relationship of n to $n + 1$? Applying the same logic, it follows that processes at level n have the potential to become structures supporting processes at level $n + 1$.

The way we have been referring to component processes corresponds to Munro's processes. That is, a skill can be considered to be comprised of a number of component processes that perform the various sub-tasks involved in the skill. For example, in the task of text comprehension, there are many sub-tasks. Consider two of these sub-tasks: (1) Recognizing groups of letters as words; and (2) combining words and their meanings to form the meaning of a phrase or sentence. Arguably, the second task cannot occur without the first task being completed to some extent (for the sake of this argument we will ignore the obvious examples whereby meaning can provide contextual constraints on hypotheses about the identity of ambiguous words). In Munro's terms, then, the outcome of the word recognition processes is the identification of words. These words are then the objects, or structures in Munro's terms, that are operated on by the processes responsible for extracting meaning from combinations of words. Thus, the processes that operate at one level of analysis provide the structures that are operated on by processes at the next highest level of analysis.

One view of Munro's thesis is that it provides a snapshot of the way various processes and structures interact at a specific moment in time for a particular person. We would like to extend this view to include an analysis of the manner in which such hierarchies of processes and structures develop throughout a person's lifetime. The hypothesis we present here is that cognitive development is a process whereby tasks are mastered through mastering lower level tasks. Skilled performance is built up over time through practice. Performance begins with low-level tasks, or at least tasks that appear to be rudimentary to an adult but are beyond the capabilities of a child (e.g. recognizing letters). These tasks are practiced until performance of them becomes automatic. That is, processes are developed that perform this task automatically. Initially these processes require most of the available cognitive resources to proceed. Little capacity is available for any other task (e.g. reading words). Once these processes have become automatic, however, sufficient cognitive resources are available for the person to attempt higher level tasks (e.g. reading words). Importantly, it is the outcome of the initial processes (i.e. letter identification) that provides the structures that are operated upon by the processes involved with the higher level task (i.e. reading words) (e.g. Karmiloff-Smith, 1979). With further practice, processes will be developed that are specific to this higher level task and these in turn may become automatic, enabling further developments in the level of skill.

It is important to emphasize that as people move up through skill hierarchies, they are not actually faced with the prospect of behaviours having to be continually more complex. On the contrary, the development of skilled behaviour can be considered to involve a relatively constant level of complexity increase from one level to another. As low-level skills are mastered, a person can only attempt a restricted range of higher level aspects of a task because they have a limited set of capabilities (i.e. the low-level skills they have acquired). As the higher level aspects of the task are mastered, however, even higher level aspects can then be tackled. For example, although the transition through arithmetic problems from addition to multiplication to division to fractions might appear to be an increase in complexity, movement through each stage will only be possible if lower level tasks have been mastered and so requirements of the next level are within the capabilities of the person. Hence, each attempt at higher level processes is always limited by the current capabilities of the person (i.e. the processes that have been mastered) and so behaviour is restricted to increasing in complexity by a maximum amount each time. This suggests something like a quantum in the amount by which behaviour can develop at any particular time. It may also explain why a smooth transition through a hierarchy of skills can feel like a development from the easy to the difficult, but where the difficult becomes easy before the next difficult task is tackled. Of course, if a difficult task is attempted before a lower level task has become easy, then the difficult task may seem too difficult, and a disruption to the transition through the hierarchy may result.

Elements of this developmental hypothesis are presented in Figure 4.1. Rather than being a formal graph of data, this figure is more a conceptual representation of the development of the various components of a skill. The circles represent groups of processes involved in performing particular tasks. Each circle, then, represents the operation of many component processes, each with their own learning history. The figure depicts some of the processes involved in performing the task of text comprehension. Note that this representation is not designed to be a complete theory of text comprehension, but is designed merely to illustrate some of the constraints on the development of all skills. In the figure, there are a number of tasks that are connected and positioned along the same horizontal line. These tasks represent a number

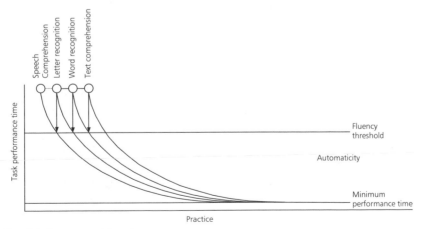

Fig. 4.1 Component learning curves.

of component skills that need to be mastered before a person can attempt the high-level task of text comprehension. These tasks have been arranged in the figure to depict the order in which they must be mastered, moving from left to right. That is, the task of speech comprehension must be mastered to a particular extent before the task of letter recognition can be attempted. Given that the vertical axis in this model represents time to perform a task, one reading of the figure might be that these tasks look to be positioned such that they have the same performance time at the beginning of practice. This is not a claim we would make. What we are trying to convey in this figure by having all tasks start at a particular point is that, indeed, all skills have a starting point in their development. Although this will not translate into being the same initial performance time for all tasks, there will be some maximum performance time for each task that can only get smaller with practice. Given that the horizontal axis represents amount of practice on a task, the distance between each task on the same horizontal line is designed to indicate that some amount of practice of the preceding task is required before the higher level task can be attempted and therefore get started on its own learning curve.

There are two distinct regions in Figure 4.1. The region in the middle of the figure depicts tasks that have had so much practice that they are performed automatically. For instance, for an adult, letter recognition occurs automatically and would seem to be one of the simplest tasks imaginable. In this context, automaticity is defined along the same lines as discussed by Logan (1992) and Anderson (1992). That is, a task is performed automatically when the stimulus conditions of the task result in direct retrieval from memory of appropriate responses, rather than relying on the generation of responses through several processing steps. One feature of automatic letter recognition, then, involves a label for a letter becoming available immediately upon exposure to the letter, rather than having to generate the label through some algorithm (e.g. singing the alphabet song until the part that corresponds to the particular letter). It is important to note that automaticity is not an all-or-none quality. As is clear from Logan's view of automaticity (e.g. Logan and Klapp, 1991), and evidence with the Stroop task (MacLeod and Dunbar, 1988), there are transition points in the development of a skill when performance can sometimes be a result of working through several mental steps and sometimes be automatic in the sense of relying on direct retrieval of a response. As practice increases, the relative mix of these two forms of processing will move towards being primarily automatic. Even then, completely automatic performance can still show improvements in performance time with further practice (Klapp et al., 1991). This feature of automaticity is incorporated in Figure 4.1.

In the figure, the upper edge of the Automaticity region is labelled as the fluency threshold. The fluency threshold corresponds to the point at which tasks can be considered to be performed automatically to a sufficient extent to allow enough mental resources to be freed up for other behaviours to be attempted. As depicted in the figure, performance of a task (e.g. letter recognition) moves along a learning curve with practice. When the learning curve crosses the fluency threshold performance of the task now requires so few mental resources that the person is now able to attempt a higher level task (e.g. word recognition).

Tasks that appear in the upper region of Figure 4.1 correspond to tasks that are at varying levels of performance quality. Tasks at the beginning of their learning curve cannot be attempted, or if they are attempted are unlikely to lead to consistently successful performance, with the current level of expertise. All of the tasks connected by a horizontal line in the figure require certain conditions to be met before they can be attempted. In particular, they require some level of mastery of the lower level tasks (i.e. those tasks to their left in Figure 4.1). That is, a number of component processes that can run automatically must be available for these higher level tasks to be attempted. Until there are sufficient component processes available, or sufficient cognitive resources available (e.g. working memory capacity), or both for the task to be completed, the learning curve for a task cannot commence. The process underlying this reliance on certain conditions to be met before tasks can be attempted is analogous to the changing of gears in a car with a manual transmission. In the car, the revolutions of the engine need to be at a certain minimum frequency for a smooth change of gears to occur. If the aim is to change from a low gear to the next higher gear, and the revolution frequency is too low, then the engine will run inefficiently at the higher gear, or possibly stall. In a similar vein, then, fluent text comprehension relies on automatic word recognition. For example, in reading, the beginner is often confronted with sentences in which there are many words that are unrecognizable. This situation usually requires some long-winded process for determining the identity of each word, such as sounding out the letters of each word. Engaging in this process can finally result in each word being read aloud satisfactorily, but with no comprehension of the meaning of the sentence. The reason is that by the time the final words have been deciphered, the earlier part of the sentence will have been forgotten. The process of deciphering words requires too much mental capacity for there to be sufficient resources left over to keep in mind the meaning of the earlier part of the sentence. The sentence will then require another reading for meaning.

The constraints on whether or not a task can be performed may be related to Newell's (1989) arguments for temporal constraints on basic cognitive processes. Newell suggested that on survival grounds, humans must be capable of overt behaviour within about one second of an initiating stimulus. To achieve this, the human cognitive architecture must be capable of performing basic cognitive operations within around 100 ms. Although the survival imperative for fast cognitive operations is possibly no longer as strong as it was hundreds of thousands of years ago in the wild, we have inherited the cognitive system that evolved in those times. We also live in a world where there exist obvious physical constraints on the minimum speed for successful performance of certain tasks. For instance, gravity imposes a constraint because it determines how quickly objects fall to earth. As a result, preventing falling objects from hitting the ground requires performance that is fast enough to beat the gravity-determined falling speed. Tasks involving objects that move through space in more than one dimension impose several speed-related constraints on successful performance. So, catching a ball requires that someone process the current velocity and trajectory of the ball, predict the likely future velocity and trajectory, and move their hands to an appropriate position before the ball either moves past or hits the ground. In addition, similar temporal constraints may also exist for psychological reasons, such as the patience levels of someone performing a task, and the patience of someone interacting with the performer (i.e. if a task takes too long to perform, the performer may give up, or the audience walks away and so the performer stops). Also the rate at which information decays from memory could determine the size of a spoken sentence that can be comprehended—if a sentence is too long, the beginning may be forgotten by the time the end arrives.

The limit in the theory on whether or not a task will be attempted is likely to be flexible in the sense that the absolute level will be dependent on a range of factors, including momentary motivation to perform the task—if someone is highly motivated to perform a task, they are more likely to complete it than if they were not motivated. They may even be able to overcome a lack of lower level skills to some extent. This motivation will also be determined by a range of factors, such as interest in the task (someone who is interested in the domain will be more likely to attempt a complex task than someone who is bored by the domain), and the possibility of some reinforcement or punishment for a successful or unsuccessful attempt.

According to the Component Theory of Skill Acquisition, development of skilled behaviour proceeds in the following manner. A task is attempted once there are sufficient cognitive abilities available. For instance, children of around 3 years of age, or even younger, are usually able to start recognizing letters. At this age, though, the skill is by no means automatic because mistakes are common, the speed of response is variable, and some letters may not be encountered nearly as often as others (e.g. the first letter of one's name is likely to be a high frequency letter compared to some others). With continued exposure to letters and practice at identifying them (e.g. through games with parents, or watching children's television shows, such as Sesame Street), children become adept at recognizing letters. Eventually, letter recognition becomes an automatic process. This has the effect of moving the task of word recognition closer to the child's capabilities. Prior to this point word recognition may have been possible, but it would be very difficult for the beginning reader because there will still have been some stumbling over letter identity. Thus, as depicted in Figure 4.1, the processes involved in letter identification are connected to the processes involved in word recognition in the sense that improvement in the lower level processes makes performance of the higher level task possible. That is, as the lower level processes move further down their learning curve with practice, and so further into automaticity, they enable higher level tasks to be attempted and so commence down their learning curves. That is, as letter identification becomes automatic, word recognition begins to fall within a child's capabilities, enabling the task to be performed, and performance to improve with practice. Once the performance of word recognition starts to improve, the processes involved in performing this task begin to require fewer mental resources. As this occurs, the likelihood that there are sufficient mental resources available to attempt text comprehension increases. This idea is depicted in Figure 4.1 by the arrow connecting the text comprehension circle to the word recognition learning curve. This arrow indicates the point at which the word-recognition task is performed automatically, the point in time at which the text comprehension task can be attempted. One way to think of this process is as if the improvement in the performance initiates the learning curve for the text comprehension task. That is, the relationship between the word-recognition processes and the text comprehension processes ensures that as the first reaches a mastery level of performance the second will begin to follow. The lower level processes, then, virtually drag the higher level processes towards them but down their own learning curve.

It must also be the case that the likelihood of attempting all of the tasks involved with text comprehension relies on someone having some facility with speech comprehension. That is, the ability to comprehend written discourse is related to the ability to comprehend spoken discourse. Thus, in Figure 4.1, this relationship is depicted as a connection between the letter recognition processes and the speech comprehension processes. This connection is represented with a dotted line to indicate that the line of succession from speech comprehension to letter recognition is not as direct as it is between letter recognition and word recognition. That is, although speech comprehension needs to be mastered to a particular extent for a child to realize the relevance of letter recognition, not all of the component processes involved in speech comprehension are involved in the task of letter recognition. In contrast, all of the component processes developed to master letter recognition are required in the early stages of word recognition. It is also the case, though, that there will be processes involved in the task of speech comprehension that, although may not be relevant to letter recognition, will be relevant to word recognition and text comprehension. In other words, the likelihood of attempting and successfully completing a text comprehension task will be influenced by the level of mastery of many other tasks, such as speech comprehension and recognition of written words. The degree of influence will be dependent on the degree to which component processes developed for completing one task are useful for completing another task.

Ultimately the situation depicted in Figure 4.1 is a representation of the influence that improvement on lower level processes has on improvement on higher level processes. Depending on the point of development of a higher level skill, this influence could be in terms of increasing the likelihood of performing the task (i.e. getting started), or it could be in terms of improved performance time (i.e. the task can be performed but still has a long way to go in terms of performance time improvements). The extent to which lower level processes can influence improvement in higher level processes is also a function of the amount by which the lower level processes has been practiced. That is, as lower level processes increase in practice, the room for improvement in these processes is reduced (i.e. the negative accelerated feature of learning curves), and so there is less scope for improvement on the low-level processes to contribute to overall improvement in the higher level processes.

In essence, Figure 4.1 represents the relationships between the factors that determine whether or not a task can be performed. The figure depicts the conditions that need to be satisfied before the task can be attempted, and how this is affected by the practice history of lower level component processes and the degree to which component processes can be recruited into performance of the task. Ultimately, this figure describes the factors that determine the probability of a task being performed successfully. This is the point at which learning curves traditionally begin. That is, the learning curve depicts time to perform the task, but only does so if the task is performed successfully. Only when this occurs can a performance time be recorded. From this point, performance time usually starts to improve with practice. Clearly, though, many things are taken for granted as having occurred for learning on the task of interest to commence. For instance, all of the learning of lower level component processes, as depicted in Figure 4.1, will have occurred to a certain extent for the task to be attempted.

In summary then, the Component Theory of Skill Acquisition acknowledges that much goes on before the performance described by the traditional learning curve can occur. Therefore, a more accurate depiction of the learning associated with performing a particular task might be something like the curve presented in Figure 4.2. The left hand side of this figure represents the probability of performing a particular complex task. This is determined by whether or not sufficient low-level component processes exist that can perform all the operations necessary for performing the task in the time available. The available time will be determined by the nature of the task and the context within which it is being performed. For example, if the task is driving across a road, then this time will be the time available to get across the road before an oncoming vehicle arrives. The time available to perform a task will also be determined by intrinsic limits, such as the time it takes for the performer to become bored with the task, or the time it takes for intermediate products of processing to be forgotten.

There are two curves in Figure 4.2 that represent different elements of performance in the development of a skill. One curve represents the probability of performing a task successfully (i.e. often measured as Accuracy in skill acquisition experiments). This task begins at 0% on the left of the figure and approaches 100% at the right of the figure. The other curve represents the

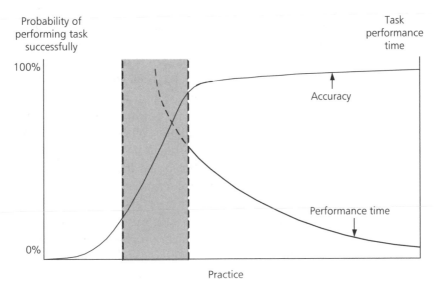

Fig. 4.2 Performance curves underlying skill development.

time to perform a task and starts at some indefinitely high value in the middle of the figure and ends at a much smaller value towards the right of the figure. The S-shape of the Accuracy curve reflects several realities about getting ready to attempt a new task. First, there may be a long lead time before the probability of the task being performed starts to rise. The reason for this is that there may be a need for lower level processes to be developed to a particular level of proficiency first, and these could require even lower level processes to be refined. Second, a person may be ready to perform the complex task but for some reason other than the availability of necessary component processes is not able to perform the task successfully (e.g. fatigue, lack of motivation). Obviously, the length of the tails of this curve will vary for each task, person, and circumstance. In addition, the rate at which this curve increases will vary as a function of the rate at which low-level processes are developed: the more practice these processes receive, the faster they become, and the more likely it is that a high-level task can be attempted. Thus, the Accuracy function is a product of all of the operations represented in Figure 4.1.

The region shaded grey in Figure 4.2 represents a situation where there are not sufficient mental resources available for the task to be performed successfully all the time. That is, the level of mastery on lower level component processes is insufficient to guarantee successful performance of the task. This is not to say that the task cannot be attempted at this point. Rather, if the task is attempted it is unlikely to be performed successfully, or if it is performed successfully it is likely to take a long time to complete. To the right of this grey region the likelihood of successful performance has reached a threshold point. This point corresponds to a time when the level of mastery of component processes is sufficient to ensure that performance of the task is likely to be successful in most attempts. Once this point has been reached, solutions or performance strategies can be repeated and so performance time will begin improving with practice. Thus, the learning curve for this particular task will commence. The performance time at the beginning of the learning curve will be a function of: (1) The number of component processes necessary to perform the task—the more processes, the longer the time; and, (2) the amount of practice received by each component process—the more practice, the shorter the time. The rate at which performance time improves with practice is a function of: (1) The performer's intrinsic learning rate; and, (2) the relative contribution of the various component processes in terms of how much of the task they are responsible for performing and how much practice these processes have received (see Chapter 3 and discussion of the Old/New Function for details).

Figures 4.1 and 4.2 should be viewed as companion figures. Figure 4.1 describes the state of affairs that determine the position of a performer on the Accuracy curve of Figure 4.2, and the constraints that determine whether or not that person will begin to perform the target task and then show subsequent performance improvements, as described by the Performance Time curve of Figure 4.2. Thus, the two figures provide a snapshot of the sorts of processes that underlie performance of tasks and the resultant acquisition of skills. The picture provided by these figures will be duplicated over and over again as new skills are acquired. Each new skill will build upon the acquisition of prior skills, and the acquisition of new skills will have the same general features as the acquisition of old skills. This picture is not complete, however, and before we end this chapter, we present a few additional features.

Recognition and production—waiting for all components to come on-line

At around the age of 3 years, Stella's drawings began to include circles with facial features. Fairly soon after this, though, she showed reluctance to draw people at all. If she could be convinced to draw a person, she would draw the bare minimum and then ask her older sister, Maggie (7 years), to complete the drawing, with hair and bodily features. This stage continued for at least 6 months until suddenly she started drawing people with bodies that were joined to but separate from the head, and limbs that were attached to appropriate parts of the body. What was curious about this episode was that she appeared to have completely skipped the stage typical of many children, including Maggie, of drawing people with one large head, no body, and limbs attached to the head. While Stella was reluctant to draw people, she had certainly been envious of the complete people Maggie was able to draw, and sometimes would sulk when she attempted a drawing that did not match Maggie's figures. It would appear, then, that Stella was able to recognize a complete drawing of a person, but was unable to produce one. Moreover, she seemed to be unwilling to commit to paper what seemed to her 'a stupid person', and would only persist with a drawing when her drawing skills matched her perception of a person. This change in Stella's drawing habits came about at around the time that she started to learn about letters, and, in particular, how to write them. The first task she wanted to master was to be able to write her name, and so match the feats of some of her pre-school buddies. There were many stumbles on the first attempts, accompanied by many tears and tantrums. The 'S' in particular

> **Recognition and production—waiting for all components to come on-line**
> *(continued)*
>
> caused some problems. Even though she had examples on the page in front
> of her, and her parents would physically guide her hand on occasion to
> illustrate the required movements, she would get the orientation wrong
> (i.e. horizontal instead of vertical), or the curves would face the wrong way
> (i.e. mirror-reflections would occur), or there were not enough curves. It
> was not that she did not have an idea of what the letter looked like—this
> episode occurred after the 'S-for-Stella' episode (see Chapter 1). Instead, it
> appears that it took some time for her to calibrate her writing actions to
> the intended shapes. In other words, just as in the drawing-a-person
> episode, there was some delay between recognizing when a goal had
> been achieved (i.e. drawing a complete person, writing a correct 'S'), and
> developing the skill necessary for producing the appropriate response.

When component processes become automatic, their operation may no longer
rely on execution of lower level processes. For instance, when word-recognition
processes become automatic such that words are read as quickly as individual
letters can be recognized (Doehring, 1976), it may be the case that word-
recognition processes no longer rely on letter recognition processes. With
sufficient reading practice, words are recognized as singular objects rather than
as collections of other objects (i.e. letters). This is not to suggest that letter
recognition does not occur during reading. On the contrary, this will occur if
this is the processing goal. However, the main aim of reading is to derive meaning from a collection of words rather than a collection of letters. As a result, a set
of word-recognition processes will be developed that operate by recognizing
words directly rather than through a process of recognizing letters first. Thus,
although originally relying on the initial recognition of letters, word-recognition
processes will develop to be independent of the letter recognition processes.
These 'direct-route' word-recognition processes will not replace the original
processes that involved letter recognition first, they will simply receive greater
practice because they are executed faster, and so will develop a privileged status
in terms of being the processes executed whenever word recognition is required.
The component processes responsible for letter recognition will maintain their
automatic status because they will still be used for tasks in which recognition of
individual letters is the main aim, such as deciphering partially legible print, and
reading serial or product numbers and vehicle registration plates, or when word
recognition is the main aim but the words are unfamiliar or foreign.

So, what happens when we encounter a word that we have not seen before? Clearly, we do not possess processes that can recognize the word in an automatic one-step fashion. Nonetheless, the goal of trying to understand the stimulus that comprises letters will mean that other relevant processes will also be trying to process the word. That is, whenever a word stimulus is encountered, all processes relevant to processing a word will try to process it, but the fastest one will complete the process. For familiar words, this will invariably be processes that recognize words in a one-step fashion. For unfamiliar words, for which such processes do not exist, word recognition will be attempted using processes that can identify letters, processes that can combine letters to form sounds, and processes that can match sounds to known word sounds. Thus, when there are no high-level processes available for performing a task, lower level processes are still available to complete the task. In this way, performance will result from a decomposition of the unfamiliar task into a number of more familiar tasks.

It is important to note that there is a limit on the extent to which high-level processes can completely supersede lower level processes, such as in the above example of word-recognition processes eventually acting independently of letter recognition processes. In text comprehension, this limit occurs at the level of comprehending sentences. It is unlikely that readers develop processes that can automatically recognize whole sentences such that reading no longer requires individual words to be recognized. The reason for this is that there is a greater level of variation at the level of sentences than there is at the level of words. The average reader might have a vocabulary of 50,000 words, although there is likely to be only a few thousand words that are experienced so frequently that recognition can be said to be automatic. Many of the rest may be recognized quickly, and some will require some degree of deliberate deciphering, probably involving recognition of individual letters. Indeed the time to identify letter strings as words (as opposed to non-words) is a function of the frequency with which they occur in language (Kirsner and Speelman, 1996). The number of sentences that involve combinations of just the few thousand high frequency words will potentially run into the millions. This number skyrockets when the low frequency words of a reader's vocabulary are included. The difference of several orders of magnitude in the frequency of exposure to sentences compared to words results in the acquisition of very different types of processes. As described in Chapter 3, the nature of training conditions can affect the nature of resulting skills. When training involves exposure to a relatively small set of stimuli, with consistent interpretations, skills develop that are specific to the item in the sense that they do not transfer to other items. Frequent exposure to a word such as 'cat' will result in the acquisition of processes that will allow direct recognition of 'cat' without necessarily involving recognition of the individual letters. In contrast, when training involves exposure to a large number of stimuli, with varying interpretations, skills develop that are general in the sense that they will apply to a large range of items that share some common features. Sentences vary considerably in terms of the words that they consist of, however, they usually consist of phrases with stereotypical linguistic structures. The experienced reader, then, will develop a set of processes for extracting the phrase structure of a sentence. These processes will operate quickly because certain phrases will occur regularly enough for a high level of expertise to develop. However, these processes will not be completely automatic because language producers (writers in this context, but speakers too!) are typically idiosyncratic, if not creative, in their use of phrase structure, and so the text comprehender has to remain flexible. This flexibility is revealed in the fact that the speed of text comprehension can be directly affected by factors other than those associated with phrase structure (e.g. context—Speelman, 1998a)—a result that would not be expected if processes responsible for deciphering phrase structure were automatic. Thus, the nature of printed discourse is such that some components (words) appear so frequently that readers are encouraged to develop automatic means for processing these components, whereas other components vary so much (sentences) that more flexible processes are required. Many other complex tasks will require similar types of skills to be developed. For example, in chess, there are particular configurations of pieces that suggest future courses of action. As a result, expert players learn to recognize configurations as individual objects rather than as collections of individual pieces. These configurations may also suggest sequences of moves, however, the best players will not follow stereotypical sequences and face the risk of being predictable, hence the need to develop strategies that are flexible in the face of defence and counter-attack from an opponent. Thus, as in text comprehension, a range of component processes will be required to become an expert chess player. Some of these processes will be automatic (i.e. those responsible for object recognition), and others will be flexible (i.e. those responsible for strategy).

4.3 Implications

There are a number of implications of the above conceptualization of skill acquisition. One implication of the component theory is that it provides an explanation of the occasional observation of plateaus in learning curves. As mentioned in Chapter 2, the first report of plateaus was by Bryan and Harter (1897) in their study of telegraphic operators. Bryan and Harter (1899) suggested that plateaus were related to the fact that learning to receive letters, words, and sentences occurred at different rates. Thus, being able to improve one part of the task (e.g. perceive sentences) required prior mastery of another component of the task (i.e. perceiving letters and words). Similar observations of plateaus in the acquisition of technological skills have been reported (e.g. learning to program computer software; Thomas, 1998). Many of these observations may also be indicative of a brief retardation of learning that occurs while performance of some component process reaches a level of maturity (through increased practice or representational change; Karmiloff-Smith, 1992) necessary for further improvement in the overall task. This certainly may explain the typical pattern of acquisition of reading skills, where letter recognition is mastered before word recognition, although words are ultimately processed just as quickly as letters (Doehring, 1976). Because some tasks require that certain components be mastered before other components can be performed or even attempted, there is likely to be a typical developmental sequence in acquiring certain skills. Furthermore, if substantial work is required for component processes to reach a level of mastery before higher level tasks can be attempted, then there is likely to be some period of consolidation in the acquisition of the higher level skill. That is, there will be periods in which there appears to be little progress being made in performance of the task. Closer scrutiny, however, may reveal that performance is improving, but only on lower level components of the task. According to this view of skill acquisition, then, the processes that underlie plateaus in learning curves may also underlie the stages that are characteristic of cognitive development (Piaget, 1953). Certainly there is recent consideration of the possibility that developmental stages are not entirely genetically determined in the sense that there is a biological program of development, but that the acquisition of high-level cognitive skills is influenced by environmental constraints, such as may be determined by cultural and educational factors (Thelen, 1988; Thelen et al., 1987). In addition, there is evidence that developmental changes are associated with increases in working memory capacity and rate of information processing (Case, 1978, 1985) and that these may be related more to effects of practice than biological maturation (Chi, 1978; Kail, 1988; Kail and Park, 1990).

One corollary of our explanation of plateaus in learning is that it also may provide an explanation for why some high-level skills are notoriously difficult for even highly capable people to acquire. An obvious example from Psychology is learning to perform and interpret inferential statistical tests, such as t-tests and the analysis of variance. Undergraduate students typically have great difficulty in mastering these tasks, and even when they manage to do well in assignments and examinations on these subjects, their understanding of the logic underlying these techniques could be described as sketchy at best. The usual experience is that only those who go on to teach the subject have a clear understanding and this is acquired, not through their original education, but through preparing to teach. Our view on this matter is that, presented as a whole, the topic of inferential statistics is such an alien concept to most undergraduate students, that it overwhelms the mental resources of these students. Without a firm grasp of probability, and its relevance to sampling and measurement, students will not appreciate the logic of using a null hypothesis to generate an expected value for a statistic against which to compare an observed value. Further, students will struggle to learn the processes involved in making such a comparison if they have not mastered the relationship between sampling distributions and probability. In other words, if students cannot deal with issues relating to sampling distributions and probability automatically, they are unlikely to have sufficient mental capacity available to tackle problems, such as whether or not to reject a null hypothesis when the probability of a test statistic is below some critical value. It is our contention that the typical statistical education does not involve sufficient practice at dealing with the basic building blocks of inferential statistics before exposing students to the complete task of statistical hypothesis testing. Students need to practice making decisions about distributions and probability to the point where it is almost second nature. These decisions will then not require mental resources that are needed for tackling the next stage of evaluating statistical hypotheses. We would also suggest that the general lack of understanding of the logic of inferential statistics among Psychology graduates has probably contributed to the widespread misuse of these techniques that has caused the recent backlash against this form of analysis (Cohen, 1994; Hammond, 1996; Wilkinson and Task Force on Statistical Inference, 1999).

A further implication of the Component Theory of Skill Acquisition concerns the nature of the resources that constrain whether or not a particular task can be performed with the current level of skills. The theory has been presented along the lines of a traditional cognitive theory where the major limitation is the amount of information that can be processed by a fixed-capacity working memory. This treatment implies that working memory has structural limits, possibly related to the biological nature of the system. This type of working memory is a bit like the RAM of a computer that limits the size of the software program that can be processed by the computer. Our theory, however, does not rely on the existence of such a fixed structure, or indeed on the idea that mental resources equate to something concrete, such as the information processing capacity of neurons or the volume of blood flowing to areas of the brain. Mental resources in our theory can be interpreted as component processes relevant to the performance of a particular task. If a person is able to complete a task in the requisite time, this means that they have the necessary component processes for performing the task. Thus having sufficient mental capacity to attempt a task means having appropriate component processes available that can be applied quickly enough to satisfy the time constraints associated with the task. Mental resource limitations can then be viewed in procedural terms rather than structural. A similar proposal has been suggested by Carlson (1997, p. 150).

One other major implication of our view of skill acquisition is that it potentially provides an explanation for behaviour that looks as if it relies on processing systems that are comprised of discrete modules. The case for modules comes from research that associates damage to particular regions of the brain with specific processing deficits (e.g. Humphreys and Riddoch, 1987; Morton and Patterson, 1980; Newcombe and Young, 1989), the implication being that the damaged areas must have been responsible for the particular forms of processing observed to be affected, with other areas responsible for other forms of processing. In other words, the brain is organized into discrete processing modules, each with their own peculiar set of stimuli to which they are sensitive, processing roles, and other modules to which they pass on information. Fodor (1983) characterized modules as being innate and hardwired (i.e. subject to developmental maturation but not subject to change with practice), informationally encapsulated (i.e. the processing that goes on in a module is not affected by processing that occurs in modules prior to or following the operation of the particular module), ballistic in nature (i.e. once modules commence processing they run on to completion), and domain specific (i.e. modules will only process a specific type of information and produce a particular form of output).

The field of Cognitive Psychology is full of models of cognition that possess the modularity feature. Many models of complex skills invoke the idea of several modules, each with their own task to perform, operating in concert to achieve the overall task. Coltheart's (Coltheart *et al.*, 1993; Rastle and Coltheart, 1999) DRC model of reading aloud is an example of a model that makes explicit use of these types of modules. Figure 4.3 is a visual representation of the various modules involved in reading letter strings aloud. Each of the boxes represents a processing module, in which a discrete part of the process of decoding letter strings and converting them into a phonemic code is carried out. It is not difficult to understand why models, such as this one, are often referred to disparagingly as 'boxes-in-the-head' models.

According to our conceptualization of skills, automatic component processes possess many of the same properties as modules, although they

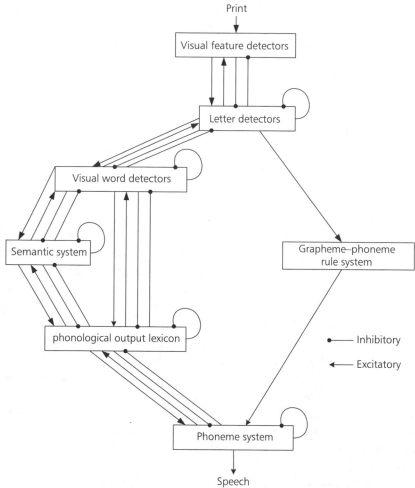

Fig. 4.3 Outline of the dual-route cascaded model: a computational version of the dual-route model of reading (from Coltheart *et al.*, 1993).

differ with respect to their origin. The acquisition of component processes is influenced by the type of practice experienced, whereas modules develop according to an innate trajectory triggered by encounters with the environment. In our view, then, these 'boxes-in-the-head' models of complex behaviours are really descriptions of the final skill that has developed over a lifetime of practice, rather than a description of brain structure or function. The 'boxes' or modules in the adult system are really highly practiced component processes. Being so highly practiced, these component processes have become automatic and so appear to be a fixed feature of the system, just like an encapsulated module.

Furthermore, practice in a particular domain will lead to domain specific skills. Complex skills are acquired in response to some challenge in the environment. Hence, a word-recognition module will be acquired in response to the necessity to develop word-recognition skills. Similarly, a face recognition module will be acquired when it is necessary to recognize faces. These two modules will be independent of each other because these tasks are rarely if ever performed in the same context. Thus, these two modules will appear to be completely separate entities, but, according to our proposal, their development will follow similar principles, and so the functioning of these modules should show similar properties. For instance, in addition to the general features of modules, they should also exhibit priming because it is an example of learning (e.g. word priming: Roediger, 1990; face priming: Cabeza *et al.*, 1997; Johnston *et al.*, 1996), transfer gradients (e.g. words: Kirsner *et al.*, 1983; faces: Jemel *et al.*, 1999), and automaticity (e.g. words: MacLeod, 1992; faces: Renault *et al.*, 1989). Thus, our proposal regarding cognitive modules implies that if we look closely at behaviour that has been explained in terms of modular systems, or look at children's behaviour, we should see skill acquisition type phenomena as outlined in the five principles described earlier. In particular, we should observe evidence of individual differences in 'modules' that are related to the nature of the developmental experience. That is, the nature of the practice received will determine the nature of the resultant skill. This issue of the veracity of modules in cognition will be considered in greater detail in the following chapters.

In this chapter, we have presented five principles of learning that underlie all the known features of skill acquisition and transfer. We have also presented a framework for a theory that is consistent with these principles. The missing element in our presentation of the theory is the mechanisms that support this framework. That is, we have not considered so far questions such as: What is it about repeated performance of a task (i.e. practice) that leads to faster performance? What does strengthening actually mean and why does it lead to faster performance? Why does practice lead to improvement functions that are negatively accelerated? We postpone presentation of our views on these mechanisms until after the next chapter in which we evaluate the theory's framework against the Behaviour Phenomena Criterion for suitability as a theory of skill acquisition. In Chapter 5, we consider the extent to which the theory can apply to a field of research in which skill acquisition explanations are not traditionally considered. This application of the theory to the study of the mental lexicon leads us to a set of proposals regarding the mechanisms that underlie skill acquisition and these are described in Chapter 6.

Chapter 5

The lexicon

Learning is not like a coin, which remains physically whole even through the most infamous transactions; it is, rather, like a very handsome dress, which is worn out through use and ostentation.

Umberto Eco ('The Name of the Rose')

The purpose of this chapter is to test the Component Theory of Skill Acquisition against the Behaviour Phenomena Criterion we introduced in Chapter 1. That is, can the theory account for phenomena in a domain that is seemingly unrelated to the domain of skill acquisition, or in which skill acquisition explanations of behaviour are rarely considered. In this chapter, we test the notion that phenomena concerning the mental lexicon can be accounted for by a skill acquisition explanation. Accordingly, the test of our theory against the Behaviour Phenomena Criterion does not constitute a test of the theory against other skill acquisition theories. Rather, we explore the possibility that a skill acquisition explanation of lexical phenomena is superior to the types of theories that are normally proposed in that domain. Our approach in this chapter is to first present a review of research and theory on the nature of the mental lexicon. We then consider the extent to which lexical data reveal the principles of learning we enunciated in the previous chapter. We pay particular attention to Principles 1 and 5. That is, we examine the extent to which lexical performance reveals: (1) negatively accelerated improvements related to practice; and (2) the influence of component processes of varying practice histories. We conclude that a skill acquisition explanation does provide an illuminating account of lexical phenomena, and this leads us to consider the implications of a mental lexicon that has its character determined by interaction with the linguistic environment. Our argument detailing the relationship between the lexicon and the environment highlights a number of connections between lexical phenomena and the characteristics of complex adaptive systems. Discussion of these issues then leads into the final chapter of the book in which we outline mechanisms that underlie the Component Theory of Skill Acquisition.

5.1 **Repetition priming: Data and paradigms**

The primary purpose of this chapter is to examine the application of our frame of reference to the 'mental lexicon'. This term is often used interchangeably with the 'mental dictionary', and the central assumption is that we each possess and exploit a memory system that includes all of the words in our individual vocabularies. It is also assumed that the number of entries will vary from individual to individual, and that an individual with an exceptionally large vocabulary might have as many as 75,000 words in his or her lexicon (Oldfield, 1966). It has also been suggested that multilingual speakers have two or more lexical systems, and that distinct systems are required for reception and production, and for speech, print, and object recognition. Needless to say, the lexicon of each individual should reflect the experience of that individual. Strangely, though, this obvious point is not implicit in descriptions of the structure and operation of the lexicon. Descriptions of the lexicon typically attempt to describe how the lexicon operates *now* and make little reference to how the lexicon got to this point. The argument we will be making in this chapter is that the development of the lexicon is central to its current operation, and both reflect the effects of practice.

Figure 5.1 was prepared to depict the architectural implications for a Japanese–English bilingual, with two spoken languages, three modalities (i.e. speech, print, and 'objects'), and four writing systems (i.e. English, Kanji, Hiragana, and Katakana). The figure does not include provision for language production, the contrasts between handwriting, typing, and printing, the contrasts between different writing styles and type fonts, the contrast between upper and lower case for the Roman alphabet, or for the contrasts between the voices of different speakers. Furthermore, at a lower and finer level of analysis, it is possible that a comparable provision should be made for the contrast between irregular and regular words, a contrast that involves both linguistic (Kirby and Hurford, 2002) and cognitive (Coltheart, 1978) distinctions, and even for the vast array of linguistic paradigms defined by morphology, involving /TERROR/, /TERRIFIED/, /TERRORIZED/, /TERRORIST/ and even /TERRIBLE/ and /TERRIFIC/, for example. Now if we combine each of the divisions implied by the foregoing summary, the potential for an expanded cathedral involving a more or less unlimited array of chapels is obvious. The figure incidentally encompasses different ways in which the term module has been used. Some authors write about language as a module, an even bigger umbrella than the lexicon. But others write about modules as if they operate for the individual testing paradigms (Levy, 1996).

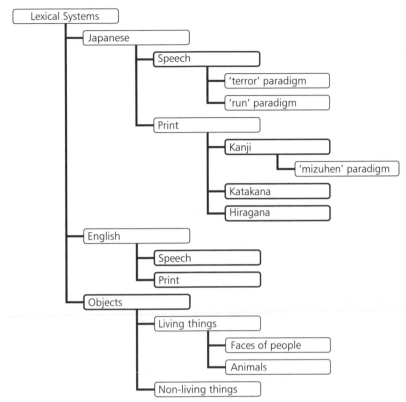

Fig. 5.1 Hypothetical lexical system for reception for Japanese–English bilingual.

Figure 5.1 represents one hypothesis about the structure of the lexicon for the particular person mentioned above. The aim of lexical research is often to test hypotheses like this one. Table 5.1 depicts the design typical of research in this area. The experiment involves the lexical decision task (LD), although many other tasks yield essentially the same pattern of results. The participants have to classify each letter sequence as a 'genuine' (English) word or a false (English) word. The experiment comprises two phases. The first phase includes presentation of say 100 words, the BAKER words in Table 5.1. These words might be drawn from a variety of word frequency bands, and they might be presented in lower or upper case. They are typically presented one word at a time at an interstimulus interval of about 3 s. The second phase might include presentation of 200 words. This set would include the old or repeated words from the first part of the experiment (i.e. the 100 BAKER words), together with 100 new words, the APPLE words not presented during the first part of the experiment. The difference between mean reaction time for the old and

Table 5.1 Repetition priming paradigm

Phase	Words ('genuine')				Non-words ('false')			
	New	**LD**	**Old**	**LD**	**New**	**LD**	**Old**	**LD**
1			BAKER	720			BILP	820
2	APPLE	700	BAKER	600	ALIG	800	BILP	700

Note: LD = RT(ms) on a lexical decision task (illustrative data).

new words presented in the second part of the experiment is referred to as a repetition priming effect. The relevant value in this experiment is 100 ms. Simply because they were presented and classified earlier in the day, lexical decision time for these words is significantly faster than would otherwise be the case.

Table 5.1 also includes illustrative data for general or item-independent practice. Whereas mean lexical decision for the BAKER words in Phase 1 was 720 ms, mean lexical decision time for the APPLE words is 700 ms. Each of these word sets was new when it was first presented. But the mere experience of working in the laboratory on a lexical decision task during the first phase of the experiment has produced a 20 ms reduction in mean lexical decision time. This would probably not be the case if the task involved something that the participants did every day. With familiar tasks there is not much room left for general practice effects. But with unfamiliar tasks, and lexical decision is an unfamiliar task for most of us, there is still room for improvement during a short session, and that improvement is illustrated in Table 5.1.

For expository reasons this chapter has been written around a single task, lexical decision. It could have been written around any one of five or six tasks. Naming latency is another task that we could have used, for words or pictures. Naming latency is a measure of the period from onset of the test stimulus—be it a word or a picture—to the commencement of an oral naming response by the participant. Repetition priming is assessed by reference to the difference in naming latency (in milliseconds) between treatments that involve OLD and NEW words.

Yet another task involves stimulus identification. In this case, the test stimulus is presented under threshold or near threshold conditions, and some property of the display is manipulated systematically until the participant can identify the stimulus. In some of our early work we used oscilloscopes involving word displays of 20–30 ms followed by presentation of a visual mask comprising letter fragments for a further 50 or so ms (e.g. Kirsner *et al.*, 1983). The dependent variable in this case involved the interval between the onset of the test stimulus and the mask, an interval that we could manipulate in 1 ms steps to obtain a precise estimate of the threshold—the period of un-masked presentation required by each participant for stimulus identification. Repetition priming under these conditions involves the difference in stimulus duration between OLD and NEW words, with priming being revealed by OLD words requiring a smaller duration than NEW words to be identified.

Two other tasks involve stem and fragment completion. In the case of stem completion, the participants see complete words during the priming phase of the experiment whereas, in the test phase, they are presented with the stems of both new and old words, and invited to complete each display. For example, the study and test phases of an experiment might include the letter strings COMPOST and COM, respectively, and repetition priming would be determined by the impact of repetition on the probability of giving COM-POST as the response to COM. Fragment completion is identical except that the test stimulus might involve C-MP-S- rather than COM. In both cases, priming is indicated by an increased probability of OLD words being used to complete the stem or fragment.

This group of tasks can be thought of as a paradigm. While the test procedures differ in detail, the procedures all involve presentation of isolated stimuli—letter strings, pictures, or spoken words—that are more or less devoid of context. In broad terms, they all produce similar results under repetition priming conditions. Intriguingly they have been used to support rather different types of enterprises. Whereas the latency and threshold procedures have usually been used to explore questions about the lexicon, the stem and fragment completion tasks have usually been used to explore the contrast between implicit and explicit memory.

5.2 **Theory**

The repetition priming paradigm has attracted the attention of two distinct traditions in Cognitive Psychology. The first of these concerned representation—how is knowledge of words represented mentally? Representation is critical to all discussions about the mental lexicon. Questions about representation are of course present in discussions about other types of skill, involving chess (Chase and Simon, 1973) and medical decision-making (Patel and Groen, 1991), for example. However, the focus in these domains typically involves 'reasoning' and 'knowledge' rather than representation. Representation is central to the lexicon, however. Morton (1969) established the benchmark for lexical representation, with the idea of a 'logogen'. According to Morton's account, word identification depends on reference to signal detection units, or logogens, where each unit has a resting level of activation, and a threshold, and where specific words become available when input to the unit concerned drives activation for that unit above the threshold. Information from the receptors is distributed to the logogens in parallel, and they act as passive detectors. In principle, practice effects could exert their influence through an increase in the resting levels of the signal detection units, or adjustment in the thresholds (the position adopted by Morton), or both. Significantly, Morton eventually expanded his account to cater for the performance changes associated with practice or, more narrowly, repetition priming.

Repetition priming has been used extensively to explore structural questions about the mental lexicon. Indeed repetition effects have been used to partition the mental lexicon. The basic assumption is that transfer effects between alternative forms of the same word can be used to define the boundaries of lexical units or, perhaps, lexical systems. If repetition priming is similar for OLD words presented in Different Forms (e.g. /TERRIBLE/ and /terrible/) and OLD words presented in the Same Forms (e.g. /TERRIBLE/ and /TERRIBLE/), it may be inferred that they involved reference to the same lexical representation in, presumably, the same lexical system. But if repetition of two forms of a word, /WHALE/ and /BALEINE/, for example, fail to yield repetition priming it may be inferred that they are being referred to different lexical representations. The paradigm and a hypothetical set of results are illustrated in Table 5.2.

The experimental illustration comprises two phases with a lexical decision task in each phase. The words in the /APPLE/ word set are not presented at all in the first phase; the /BAKER/ word set is presented in lower case in the first phase, and the /COTTON/ word set is presented in upper case in the first phase. The entire set of 300 words, 100 per set, is presented in upper case in the second phase of the experiment. The words are presented one at a time, and the participants are expected to press GENUINE WORD and FALSE WORD buttons as quickly and as accurately as possible as each letter string is presented. The critical comparisons involve the Old—Different Form set. Specifically, does performance on this set match performance on the Old—Same Form set, or the New set, or does it fall somewhere between these extremes? In the hypothetical result depicted in Table 5.2, repetition priming for the Old—Different Form set is close to that observed for the Old—Same

Table 5.2 Transfer effects in repetition priming

Phase	New words	LD	Old words—Different Form	LD	Old words—Same Form	LD
1			baker	720	COTTON	720
2	APPLE	700	BAKER	605	COTTON	600

Note: LD = RT(ms) on a lexical decision task (illustrative data).

Form set. Thus, despite the fact that words in the first and second phases in the Old—Different Form set differ in regard to case, the result indicates that there is virtually no cost associated with this manipulation. It is tempting to infer that the two forms depend on reference to the same representation. The effect of this type of manipulation can be quantified, as relative priming (RP), where,

$$RP = (LD_{New} - LD_{OldDifferent}) / (LD_{New} - LD_{OldSame}) \qquad (5.1)$$

Thus, if lexical decision time is 600, 650, and 700 ms under Print → Print (words presented in print during the study and test phases), Speech → Print (words presented in speech and print in the study and test phases, respectively), and New Print conditions, where the words are presented for the first time, in print, during the test phase, Relative Priming is calculated as follows:

$$\text{Relative Priming (RP)} = (LDT_{NewPrint} - LDT_{Speech \to Print})$$
$$/ (LDT_{NewPrint} - LDT_{Print \to Print})$$
$$= (700 - 650) / (700 - 600) = 0.5$$

The RP value for the attribute change illustrated in Table 5.2 is 0.95. This general approach has been applied to a wide range of stimulus transformations, some of which are discussed later in the chapter. Perhaps the simplest approach to this general class of result was offered by the late Paul Kolers (1979b) although he did not use RP. According to our interpretation of Kolers's argument, the RP value simply reflects the extent to which the information processing procedures associated with the critical treatments are unique or shared; where RP = 1.0, sharing is assumed to be complete, but where RP = 0.0, sharing is absent and the two forms depend on non-intersecting procedures. The RP values for translations, such as BAKERY and PANADERIA approach 0.0 (Cristoffanini *et al.*, 1986) and are consistent with the assumption that different lexical representations are involved in these cases.

The role of morphology adds a layer of complexity to the mental lexicon. What is a word, for example, and where do we draw the line between words that share morphological, orthographic, or phonemic features? Does recognition of MORPHOLOGY and MORPHOLOGICAL depend on reference to the same mental representation, or do they depend on unique and independent representations? And what about PUBLICITY and PUBLICIDAD, where the difference between the stems involves pronunciation rather than orthography? What about CAR and CART? They are orthographically similar, but do they depend on reference to the same representation or procedures? And what about MARRY, MARRIES, MARRYING, MARRIED, MARRIAGE, and

MARIAGE, the French translation of MARRIAGE? And what about words that are distinguishable only by their context, as in the contrast between BANK when it is preceded by reference to MONEY, FLYING, or RIVER?

The second research tradition to which repetition priming effects have been applied was to a large extent created by Graf and Schacter (Graf and Schacter, 1985; Schacter, 1987). Whereas Morton assumed that repetition priming was an essentially 'perceptual' phenomenon, and other people writing at that time ignored the taxonomic question (e.g. Kirsner and Smith, 1974), Graf and Schacter treated repetition priming as a memory phenomenon but drew a sharp line between repetition priming on the one hand, and recognition memory and other explicit memory tasks on the other. Graf and Schacter used the instructions to the experimental participants to distinguish the tasks and, by extension, systems. If the instructions required the participant to answer the question by reference to the original experience or 'study' event, performance was attributed to explicit memory. But if the task made no reference to the study event, performance was attributed to implicit memory.

Examples of implicit memory tasks include lexical decision and fragment completion, where participants might be provided with strings of letters and dashes, and invited to complete the string as a word, as in ASSASSIN for 'SS–S–N'. The 'memory' effect in the implicit memory or repetition priming paradigm would be the difference between performance on the new and old treatments. In Table 5.1, for example, this difference is 100 ms for the word treatment. By contrast, a participant in an explicit memory treatment might be shown ASSASSIN in the study phase, and then, in the test phase, asked to indicate whether or not he or she had seen ASSASSIN during the study phase. With reference to the BAKER word set in Table 5.1, for example, it would be possible to simply change the classification question to convert the lexical decision task into a recognition memory task. Word selection and stimulus presentation would follow the pattern described above exactly. But instead of asking the participants to classify each letter string as a 'word' or 'non-word', they could be asked to classify each word as 'old' or 'new' with reference to the words presented in the first phase of the experiment. Thus, instead of classifying the words in the APPLE and BAKER sets as 'genuine' English words (because they both involve genuine English words), participants should say 'old' and 'new' to the BAKER and APPLE word sets, respectively. Performance could of course be measured in terms of accuracy or speed in either task.

The theoretical distinction between these procedures relied on more than the difference between the tasks of course. The most treasured inferential procedure in both Cognitive Psychology and neuro-psychology, dissociation, was usually employed as the critical test. Dissociations are used to infer the existence of separate mental processes. There are two main types, single and double. Let *A* and *B* be two tasks and let *a* and *b* be two experimental or clinical manipulations. A single dissociation is observed if manipulation *a* affects performance on *A* but not on *B*. A double dissociation is observed if, in addition, manipulation *b* affects performance on *B* but not on *A*. In cognitive neuro-psychology, a manipulation usually consists of a comparison between different patients. Both single and double dissociations are used to advance the claim that *A* and *B* depend on distinct mental functions if not modules. Dissociation has been extensively used to support the distinction between implicit and explicit memory, for example. Some of the variables involved include depth of processing (selective impact on explicit memory), surface differences between the study and test conditions (selective impact on implicit memory), delay (selective or at least greater impact on explicit memory) and amnesia (selective impact on explicit memory).

5.3 Challenges

We see several challenges to the inferences that have been made on the basis of repetition priming effects about separate memory systems and separate modules within the mental lexicon. In particular, we question the logic of dissociation. We also express some disquiet over the particular tasks used to reveal repetition priming and thus query the sorts of inferences that are possible from priming results.

5.3.1 Double dissociation

When one of us first became interested in double dissociation (Dunn and Kirsner, 1988) our interest was piqued by some research published by Larry Jacoby (Jacoby, 1983). Jacoby had found that when word generation is used as an 'encoding' variable (e.g. what is the opposite of COLD?), it increased accuracy in recognition memory for the word HOT (relative to the use of a simpler reading condition involving presentation of HOT) while decreasing the magnitude of repetition priming on a fragment completion task for the same word. According to the argument advanced by Jacoby, this involved a 'crossover interaction', and provided compelling evidence that the two tasks—recognition memory (i.e. old/new judgements) and repetition priming (under lexical decision conditions)—involved different processes.

However, when we plotted the data for this and other studies, we kept seeing negative associations, as if the two tasks used the same data although, because they used that data in different ways, performance on the two tasks was negatively associated. The results in question involved the relationship between: (1) transfer effects in repetition priming; and (2) memory for attributes (Cristoffanini *et al.*, 1986; Downie *et al.*, 1985; Kirsner and Dunn, 1985). We have already discussed repetition priming, a measure that can be obtained from performance on a variety of tasks including lexical decision. Transfer effects (as measured by Relative Priming (RP)—see Equation 5.1) generally approach 1.0 when the change in stimulus form involves surface variables, such as type font and voice, fall midway between 0.0 and 1.0 for variables, such as mode (i.e. transfer between pictures to words) and modality (i.e. transfer between speech and print), and approach 0.0 when there is no surface or structural relationship between the two forms (e.g. /fromage/ and /cheese/). Memory for attributes is measured under similar but not identical conditions. Conditions for the study list would usually be identical, with a mixed list of spoken and printed words, for example. But the test procedure might involve presentation of an old word coupled with an instruction to the participant to indicate whether that word was presented in spoken or printed form during the study phase. Attribute memory is high (c.0.8, where chance = 0.5) for variables that yield little transfer, involving translations, for example, intermediate for variables that yield intermediate levels of transfer, modality, for example (c.0.7), and low for variables that yield maximum transfer, case or speaker's voice for instance (c.0.6).

The relationship is illustrated in Figure 5.2. The figure includes the results from two experiments, involving English–Spanish translations and cognates (Cristoffanini *et al.*, 1986), and English inflections and derivations (Downie *et al.*, 1985). In the experiment involving Spanish–English translations and cognates, the dependent variables involved attribute memory (was this word presented in English or Spanish during the study phase?) and Relative Priming in lexical decision, and the points represent translation types that differ systematically in regard to orthographic and phonemic similarity, ranging from 'bakery ≈ panaderia' to 'publicity ≈ publicidad'. In the experiment involving the English inflections and derivations, the dependent variables involved attribute memory (was this word presented in the same form in the study phase or not?) and Relative Priming in word identification (masked words presented at individually tailored thresholds), and the points represent word forms that differ systematically in regard to orthography and phonology.

The above analysis challenges two assumptions. The first of these involves interpretation of crossover interactions. Crossover interactions are actually consistent with the assumption that the tasks in question are influenced by a common or shared resource. But the second point concerns the assumption that lexical and memory processes can be treated as if they belong to distinct

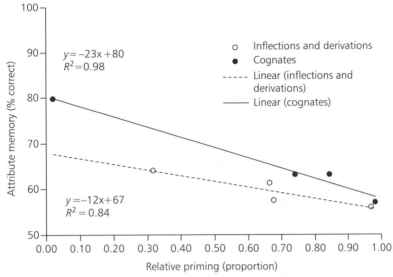

Fig. 5.2 Relationship between transfer in repetition priming and attribute memory.

domains or 'grand' modules (Levy, 1996). It is not our claim that they do not involve some unique processes. Recognition memory and lexical decision must involve some process differences, involving recruitment, retrieval, or decision-making, for example. But the stronger assumption, that they belong to different cognitive domains, is hard to reconcile with the data we have cited.

Our observation about crossover interactions forced us to turn to more general questions about the origin and logic of dissociations, an inferential procedure that has played an increasing and central role in arguments about component processes in general and modularity in particular (Coltheart, 1985; Crowder, 1972; Shallice, 1988; Teuber, 1955; Tulving, 1983; Vallar, 1999). Perhaps the most popular application of dissociation actually involves the distinction between repetition priming and implicit memory, on the one hand, and recognition memory and explicit memory on the other. The distinction is based on innumerable dissociations involving variables, such as stimulus form, study-test delay, neurological classification, and depth-of-processing, for example. Our caution about this body of work has been influenced by concerns about the inferential status of dissociations (e.g. Dunn and Kirsner, 1988, 2003).

The theoretical position that we have adopted is in some respects akin to that adopted by Mayes *et al.* (1997). For us, the critical assumption is that different memory tests will, usually if not invariably, draw on shared informational resources to some extent, and that they will also rely on retrieval and decision processes that are also unique, to some extent, a combination of assumptions which means that associations and dissociations cannot alone play a decisive role. Intriguingly, Willingham and Preuss (1995), in an article entitled, 'The Death of Implicit Memory', adopted an even more challenging position. A critical part of the argument advanced by them is that the set of tasks used to sample implicit memory is not held together by a unifying variable or neurological analysis; and that it does not therefore form a category. If unity involves reference to one shared resource in a mixed portfolio of shared and unique resources, however, the issue is more complex. All of the so-called 'implicit memory' tasks could depend in part on reference to a single resource (such as that which supports the similarity function depicted in Figure 5.2) and yet be dissociable under a wide variety of conditions because each and every task also depends on reference to at least one and possibly several unique resources. This is in a sense obvious.

Consider, for example, naming latency, lexical decision, and fragment completion. Lexical decision we have already dealt with. Naming latency involves the same display conditions but participants are asked to name letter strings instead of classifying them as genuine words or false words. Fragment completion can be used with the same priming conditions as lexical decision— presentation of a list of words including, for example, ASSASSIN—followed by presentation of fragmented test stimuli. Under these conditions the probability of completing -SS–S-N as ASSASSIN is increased by prior presentation of this word during the study phase. The repetition effects involving each of these tasks are consistent with the proposition that they reflect a common resource or, even more generally, principle. But it is also obvious that each task involves processing problems that are unique to it, and that dissociation is therefore of no interest.

5.3.2 Task purity and modularity

In the foregoing analysis, we have expressed doubts about the practice of treating questions about lexical access and memory as if they are inhabited by scientists from different worlds. Each of these worlds has of course been dominated by the assumption that performance must be explained in terms of modules (Fodor, 1983), modules that can be defined by reference to specific criteria, including encapsulation, for example (Coltheart, 1999).

One by-product of the modular approach involves the presence of friction at the boundaries between disciplines and domains. Is lexical decision a pure test of the cognitive processes involved in reading, or is it influenced or even dominated by episodic processes (de Groot and Nas, 1991; Forster and Davis,

1984, 1991), for example? This challenge received added impetus from an accompanying claim that masked repetition priming (a procedure where test stimuli are followed by masked primes) does not reflect episodic effects and is therefore the pure measure of lexical processes. We find it astonishing that the absence of learning effects should be employed to advance the claim that the task in question is a pure measure of lexical processing. How, one might ask, is the lexicon installed?! Is it supplied with enrolment kits to students as they enter their first year at university and, if so, who does the surgery? Evidence that performance on masked repetition priming is insensitive to word frequency is certainly interesting of course, because even primitive visual processes, such as vernier acuity are sensitive to practice (e.g. Li and Levi, 2002; Weiss *et al.*, 1993), but the claim that this can or should be a defining feature for inferences about the lexicon must be justified.

Fortunately, however, relief is in sight, for there is a growing body of evidence that masked repetition priming is under attack from other quarters. There is evidence, for example, that masked repetition priming operates at a sub-lexical level, to facilitate orthographic encoding (Bodner and Masson, 1997), and that the effects are dissipated in less than 0.5 s (Ferrand, 1996). However, none of the foregoing amounts to an argument that masked repetition priming is an instrument that does not reflect 'lexical' processes; only that it has no claim to pre-eminence. We would not quarrel with a weaker claim that one or more of the many component processes in reading is relatively insensitive to word frequency. This would not be surprising because the practice levels achieved for features would in many cases be higher than those achieved for the individual letters. In upper case English, for example, there are no fewer than 15 vertical lines distributed over 13 letters, and the relevant practice levels will probably be an order of magnitude higher for features than they are for letters. Extreme practice levels are generally associated with minimal residual practice effects, and the finding that masked repetition priming is insensitive to practice is therefore consistent with the hypothesis that this task reflects very early and very highly practiced component processes in reading. But the extension of this argument to the claim that frequency exclusively involves 'post lexical' processes (Forster and Davis, 1984) is courageous.

Thus far, in this section, we have expanded our potential brief, to include not only the lexicon, but memory as well. We have developed this position in part because the tools that Cognitive Psychology has traditionally used—task purity and process dissociation—are simply not up to the job; they yield findings that are consistent with claims that the relevant systems consist of specialized and independent modules. But they do not demand this inference; they are also consistent with other types of organization.

5.3.3 **Modularity and stability**

Much of the case for a modular view of cognition rests on neuro-psychological evidence about memory and communication deficits. However, while evidence from these domains can and often does provide support for dissociations and double dissociations, this evidence rarely includes systematic attempts to determine the stability of the putative deficit. And yet, evidence of this type is critical. If brain damage simply reduced overall information processing capacity—and this argument has been put for aphasia (e.g. McNeil *et al.*, 1991; Murray *et al.*, 1997), evidence for dissociations could still be found, but it might vary from day to day or week to week as the cognitive system struggled to come to terms with the reduction or distortion in overall resources.

The diagnostic procedures used to assess patients following stroke usually involve a single test session. The Boston Diagnostic Aphasia Examination (BDAE) fits this general characterization (Goodglass and Caplan, 1972). The participants may be tested for an hour or more, and they may be asked to work on new tasks on subsequent occasions. But it is rare that the full BDAE is implemented for a single patient on multiple sessions, a procedure that would of necessity involve multiple clinicians, and a double-blind procedure owing to the subjective nature of many of the scales in the BDAE.

The presumably implicit assumption underlying the single session approach is that brain damage in general, and stroke in particular, establish stable and long-lasting changes in cognition, and that multiple test sessions would not clarify or modify clinical assessment. It is of course widely recognized that performance changes following stroke are unstable during the acute phase, and it is for that reason that clinical assessment and research applications are generally restricted to chronic patients—although this picture is changing as clinicians and scientists have come to suspect that cognitive change is most likely during the acute as distinct from chronic phase.

In a recent study, one of our students, Natalie Ciccone (Ciccone *et al.*, 2000), attempted to determine the stability of performance on lexical decision over a two-week-period during the chronic phase of aphasia. The stimulus lists included words and non-words, and repeated and new stimuli during each session. There were 13 non-brain damaged and 8 brain-damaged participants.

The results are summarized in Figure 5.3. The results shown in that figure show z values for three of the aphasics, where each value is defined by its position relative to the means and standard deviations for the non-brain-damaged participants. Thus, given a mean and standard deviation of 1000 and 100 ms, respectively, a z value of 10.0 implies that the mean for that participant was 2000 ms. The data for the aphasics depicted in Figure 5.3 do not reveal dramatic changes from session-to-session apart from the fact that mean lexical

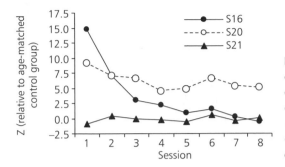

Fig. 5.3 The impact of stroke on lexical decision for three cases. The values for each case are shown in z units relative to an age-matched control group (from Ciccone *et al.* 2000).

decision for one aphasic, S16, commences 15 standard deviations above the mean for the control group but ends up at the same level as the control group in the eighth session. The patterns for the other two aphasics are relatively stable, within two standard deviations of the mean for the normal group for all eight sessions for S21 and improving gradually in the range 5–10 standard deviations above the mean for the control group, for S20. Clearly then, diagnostic procedures that involve data from a single session are insecure, as are inferences about cognitive architecture that are based on such data.

5.3.4 Dynamic hypotheses

Debate on these vexing issues is unfolding in two, related arenas. At a general level, it is reflected in a debate about the dynamic hypothesis (Bechtel, 2002; van Gelder, 1998). The argument advanced by van Gelder includes two points that are of interest; first, the claim that 'coordination is an emergent property of a non-linear dynamical system', a claim that focusses on transitions as distinct from structures (p. 616); and, second, the claim that the changes associated with system variables actually depend on changes in other systems external to the system of interest as well as the system itself. Together, these assumptions impose a burden on cognitive modelling that has barely been attempted for even 'slow' changing domains, such as skill acquisition, let alone fast changing ones, such as speaking.

The second arena involves questions about timing in communication. According to the modal model of language processing, the critical description involves a complex structure that consists of tiers of modules, each of which is dedicated to solving a specific problem without intervention from other modules and systems (e.g. Coltheart, 1999). However, as may be inferred from arguments advanced by Port and Leary (2002), this class of description depends on the validity of the assumption that the translation of conceptual, semantic, and phonological information into speech distributed in real time can be deferred to another and later stage of analysis. Port and Leary actually developed their argument in opposition to what they referred to as 'descriptive linguistics', but the view advanced here is that it applies to any system that depends on structural as distinct from dynamic premises. Coltheart (1999) explicitly limits the application of the modular paradigm to the analysis of single words, but that only underlines the problem.

The fact that the tasks that form particular paradigms usually involve presentation of de-contextualized stimuli can be thought of as an advantage or a disadvantage. It is an advantage in so far as the tasks can be used to measure supposedly pure processes. However, it is a disadvantage, if not a barrier, if the processes in question normally form part of a complex dynamic system, and are simply not open to meaningful measurement as isolated components. Thus, if the predominant cognitive challenge actually involves situations where learning and communication unfold in real time, the construction of models involving components formed, tested, and refined under de-contextualized conditions may provide us with lots of information about information processing components that are more or less irrelevant to the components that operate under routine conditions.

Essentially the same point has been made by Bechtel (2002). The problem is a bit like the old computer joke about, 'garbage in, garbage out'. Tasks that sample static and de-contextualized operating conditions can only provide information about static and de-contextualized operating conditions. If the real task that is of interest is dynamic, as is the case for reading and speaking, for example, the products and measurements produced by static and de-contextualized tasks will by definition fail to tap into the dynamic heart of the domain.

It is hard to avoid analogies. Neville Hennessey, for example, recently suggested that the lexical decision paradigm involved assumptions comparable to those that would arise if we were to use a 'reversing paradigm' to study cognition under highway driving conditions. The psychological gulf between the mass of de-contextualized paradigms and the real issue (e.g. comprehension of textual material) is so vast that it behooves us to ask ourselves about the nature of the endgame. How did we think that we would skip from the products of de-contextualized tasks to an operational world replete with dynamic problems? Was it our corporate assumption that once we have identified the component processes—a goal that could in principle be achieved by the discovery of tasks that are so pure that they each sample specific processes—it would simply be a matter of drawing arrows between the components, setting a lever to 'reading', 'speaking', or 'writing', and turning a handle marked 'clockwise only'?

5.4 **The lexicon and skill acquisition are seen as unrelated**

Research into language has established a modular view of the brain, and a paradigm that has created and protected that view. Double dissociation, the main inferential technique, is generally used to support arguments about module and process specialization even though it is widely accepted that evidence of this type does not demand the conclusion of preference (e.g. Dunn and Kirsner, 2003). Cognitive research is dominated by de-contextualized procedures dedicated to the view that this or that paradigm or task is 'the' true measure of lexical processes or of one of the many specialized modules that contribute to word recognition or naming or some other hypothetical process. Different levels of processing are often structured as if they need to be treated by people with different specialisms, in phonology, or orthography, or lexical processes, or discourse structure. It is rare in this corner of science to see any attempt at integration or synthesis. We think it is time, though, for integration, and we propose that the principles of learning we have identified can provide the link between the seemingly disparate elements of the modular view. But why has it taken so long for learning, and in particular skill acquisition, to be considered seriously in lexical issues?

It is a matter of curiosity that books and articles on skill acquisition do not in general explore questions about the mental lexicon (e.g. Anderson, 1983a; Proctor and Dutta, 1995a; Welford, 1968). In part, this omission stems from the very particular way in which the term 'skill' evolved in psychological research. Many, and perhaps all, of the early studies involving skill or skill acquisition were restricted to specific problems in applied science or industry, where the questions were treated as a set, as if they involved a principle or principles (e.g. Bartlett, 1948; Book, 1925; Bryan and Harter, 1899). This no doubt implicit segregation of early work in the area declined with increasing awareness of the power law of learning, and development of models that catered for learning data from the laboratory as well as industrial environments (Anderson, 1982; Newell and Rosenbloom, 1981).

A second and perhaps more interesting form of segregation involved that between the mental lexicon and language development. Here, too, the segregation is or has been implicit, and driven mainly by the constraints and demands of laboratory-based science. There is, however, an explicit justification for the distinction between language development in children on the one hand, and research into the mental lexicon and industrial skills on the other. Where industrial skills are concerned, the claim that they depend on innate processes—for cigar-rolling, for example—has not to the best of our knowledge been advanced. Where language acquisition is concerned, however, the last 30–40 years have been influenced if not dominated by the claim that language development cannot be explained solely or even primarily by reference to children's experience of language. The developmental literature has been dominated by an alternative paradigm, involving the role of innate processes or, more specifically, an innate 'language acquisition device' (Chomsky, 1975; Pinker, 1989). The critical argument is that 'children possess grammatical knowledge from the onset of language development, as part of an innate language facility' (Bloom, 2000, p. 23). However, the general principle has also been extended to the mental lexicon, where it has involved the notional role of 'primitives' in the establishment of word meanings (Fodor, 1979).

In addition to 'positive' claims about the importance and contribution of innate processes in grammatical and lexical development, 'negative' claims have also been advanced. The negative claim is that we simply do not have sufficient exposure to language, and, more particularly, to instances involving appropriate feedback, to explain the variety of language forms that we use routinely and more or less successfully (Juffs, 1996; Pinker, 1989). According to this argument then, an innate explanation is essential because the amount and type of practice provided by the social environment is not sufficient to account for critical aspects of our communication skills. The validity of the innate claim is not critical to the present argument. Our point is simply that the presence and widespread acceptance of the innate claim has acted as a barrier between not only language development and skill acquisition but also, more surprisingly perhaps, between language acquisition and research into the mental lexicon. In our own articles as well as those of many of our contemporaries in this area, the issues examined in research involving the mental lexicon would be no different if the lexicon in the typical college student was a product of a simple operation carried out by the local Department of Computer Science, involving installation of an exceptionally sophisticated chip.

We will return to questions about the impact of experience on lexical performance, but it is appropriate to note in passing that the jury is still out on central questions about the impact of experience and feedback on the acquisition of lexical expertise. Two types of argument have been introduced to counter the nativist claim. The first of these involves the impact of knowledge about the world on communication (Searle, 2002). The second and perhaps more topical argument involves the impact of decomposition and its corollary, generalization, on lexical performance (Kirby, 2001). The safest assumption at this point in time is that the 'negative' claim is 'not proven'; and that some combination of regularity in the cultural lexicon and decomposition and generalization in the mental lexicon might yet account for language development including development of the mental lexicon.

5.5 Can skill acquisition explain lexical data?

Several years ago, we were drawn to the operational similarity between the repetition priming and skill acquisition paradigms (e.g. Kirsner and Speelman, 1996). Consider Table 5.3, for example. It depicts a simple extension of the traditional repetition priming paradigm in order to examine practice effects involving multiple blocks of trials. Most natural learning tasks involving either language or non-verbal problems involve multiple opportunities for practice, and Table 5.3 illustrates the typical pattern for performance under these conditions. The results reflect two forms of practice. The lexical decision times shown in the new column (LD_{new}) illustrate item-independent practice; that is, the extent to which performance improves as a result of practice on the task even when the sequence does not include repetition of the individual words. Given comparisons that involve new sets of words for each session, it can be seen that performance improves by 20, 5, 4, and 3 ms on these new word sets on sessions 2, 3, 4, and 5, respectively. Item-specific practice is illustrated by the changes in the LD_{old} column. The /APPLE/ words are repeated once each in all five phases of the experiment, and the improvement can therefore be associated with repetition of the individual items. The values shown in the second, third, fourth, and fifth rows in that column indicate the changes that occur for the original word set when they are repeated in the second, third, fourth, and fifth sessions. It is of course impossible to define the repetition priming effect independently of the two practice or skill acquisition effects. There are not enough free parameters. Once the magnitudes of the item-independent and item-specific effects are known, the magnitude of the

Table 5.3 Operational similarity between repetition priming and skill acquisition paradigms

	Words ('genuine')				Non-words ('false')			
Phase	New	LD_{new}	Old	LD_{old}	New	LD	Old	LD
1	APPLE	720	(APPLE)	(720)	ALIG	820	(ALIG)	(820)
2	BAKER	700	APPLE	600	BALF	800	ALIG	700
3	COTTON	695	APPLE	595	CIDEL	795	ALIG	695
4	DINGO	691	APPLE	591	DOKE	791	ALIG	691
5	EAGLE	688	APPLE	588	ERLO	788	ALIG	688

Note: LD = RT(ms) on a lexical decision task (illustrative data).

repetition priming effect is also known. The values presented in this table imply that the item and task practice effects are additive, but this need not be the case.

5.5.1 Item and task practice effects

The hypothetical set of results provided in Table 5.3 illustrates the first principle of learning we identified in Chapter 4. Practice leads to faster performance and, significantly, to improvement that is negatively accelerated. Because of the different ways in which practice can have an influence in this paradigm, this pattern can be detected in four or possibly five distinct ways, each of which could have different implications for skill acquisition. The first and second of the means by which practice can influence performance in this paradigm were introduced above. They involved experimental practice effects. The first aspect of the design that reflected practice effects was the repetition priming effect itself; the improvement associated with repetition of specific items during an experiment. The pattern of improvement in reaction times in this situation has been observed to follow power functions (Kirsner and Speelman, 1996; Logan, 1990). The second aspect of the design that reflected the influence of practice involved the task; the general improvement associated with repeated practice involving a single task but different items. This improvement has also been found to conform to a power function (Kirsner and Speelman, 1996). Already, then, we have evidence that performing the lexical decision task over multiple repetitions results in negatively accelerated improvements in performance time. This suggests that the traditional repetition priming effect—faster responses to an item that has been responded to previously—may simply be a sample from the range of possible practice-related improvements that can be detected with longer-term observations. There are, however, complications to the story that nevertheless illustrate the universality of practice as an influence and also illustrate the role of skill acquisition in the development of the lexicon.

5.5.2 Word frequency and age of acquisition effects

The third and fourth of the means by which the multiple presentation design can reflect the influence of practice involve a mixture of 'natural' and laboratory procedures. That is, final performance is measured in the laboratory although the actual practice manipulation involves variation in the distribution of events in the natural as distinct from the laboratory world. Thus, the frequency of occurrence of a word (word frequency) and the age at which a word entered a person's vocabulary (age of acquisition) could arguably represent measures of the degree of practice with a word prior to entering the laboratory. Word frequency has traditionally been extracted from careful counts of the frequency of occurrence of individual words in various types of text. The methodology is of course changing rapidly with the use of computer databases and search engines, but the major collations involved laborious manual work (Kucera and Francis, 1967; Thorndike and Lorge, 1944), and a tradition that can be traced back to the seventeenth century in French analyses that involved words from a variety of scientific and literary traditions in the various editions of the *Dictionnaire de l'Académie française*.

When words from different word frequency bands are included in an experiment of this type, the initial and final results are different for words from different bands. Thus, as illustrated in Table 5.4, initial lexical decision time is different for words from different word frequency bands, a finding that implies that practice in the real world can be detected in laboratory tasks, as it should be if the procedure is valid. Table 5.4 also illustrates the fact that practice effects are not the same for words from different word frequency bands. The high frequency words are of course near some hypothetical floor before commencement of the experiment, and they receive correspondingly less benefit from further practice (see Kirsner and Speelman, 1996, for real data along these lines).

Word frequency effects on lexical decision are similar to age of acquisition effects. Words that are acquired early in life are responded to faster than words that are acquired later in life. With experimental repetition, however, performance with late-acquired words improves by a greater amount than with early-acquired words. The similarity of the effects of word frequency and age of acquisition on repetition priming suggests the possibility of a relationship between the two factors.

Table 5.4 Lexical decision RT(ms) (illustrative data) for repeated words from three-word frequency bands

| Session | Word frequency (occurrences per million words) | | |
	High (100/million)	Medium (10/million)	Low (1/million)
1	500	600	700
2	485	570	640
3	478	555	610
4	474	548	595
5	472	544	588

One of the most interesting issues in recent research into the cognitive lexicon involves the relative contributions of word frequency and age of acquisition to performance on lexical decision and naming tasks. The two variables arguably involve different aspects of practice or even just different ways of measuring practice. Age of acquisition carries a frequency assumption because words that are learned early are, in all probability, words that occur more frequently during childhood, over the first decade or so. Word frequency also carries a frequency assumption of course, but in this case, it usually involves adult experience, involving frequency of occurrence in adult texts of various types. Despite the complex interaction between these variables in the real world, research on this topic tends to have a black and white flavour, as if the variables can be disentangled if we try hard enough. We are not convinced that the conditions have been met. We are not even sure that they can be met.

The critical research programs have been designed to determine whether or not word frequency effects can be detected when age of acquisition is controlled, age of acquisition effects can be detected when word frequency is controlled, and whether or not the complex pattern of results observed for these variables actually reflect a further conditionality, involving the distinction between speech and print. The results of this body of research support three broad findings; first, that age of acquisition effects are usually, although not always, observed when word frequency is controlled; second, word frequency effects are usually, although not always, observed when age of acquisition is controlled, and, third, that the interaction between age of acquisition and word frequency is conditional on modality, with word frequency effects being limited to visual presentation in some cases (Baumgaertner and Tompkins, 1998; Brysbaert et al., 2000; Morrison and Ellis, 1995, 2000; Turner et al., 1998).

This body of research involves some daunting methodological considerations, however. Word frequency, for example, is usually obtained from word frequency counts involving newspapers, books, and other public materials, measures that do not of course include provision for developmental patterns of vocabulary size and, by extension, that aspect of word frequency. Word frequency counts for very young children will be distorted in a number of ways, some of which may impact on early frequency in quite dramatic ways. One of these involves adoption of a selective vocabulary by parents, involving the deliberate use of forms that are both easy, and critical to parent–child communication during infancy (see Fernald, 2000). In addition, parents tend to adopt an exaggerated prosodic variation—in regard to fundamental frequency, amplitude, and articulation rate (Fernald, 2000)—a class of manipulation that probably fades with advances in the language skills of the child. However, this twist is only a precursor to a second and more dramatic source of distortion. At some point in a child's life it is safe to assume that she has a vocabulary of only one word, where this is followed by short periods where she has two, and then three, and then four words, and so on. A critical and unknown if not unknowable question concerns the way in which these words are used while they occupy a sparsely populated lexicon. Should the 'first' word be 're-used' and 'tested' dozens or even hundreds of times, cumulative frequency for that word might reach levels that later experience involving a more densely populated lexicon would never approach. Words such as MUM, DAD, MILK, PUSS have high absolute frequencies in early childhood.

The actual extent of the distortion is unclear and may be incommensurate, however, MUM might account for 50% or more of a child's genuine reception and expression for a period during the first or second year of his or her life, for example. In contrast, while we probably did not hear, read, or write the word COGNITION at any time before we were 20 or so years of age, it has probably been one of the most frequent words in our vocabularies from that point on. Nonetheless, it would never enjoy the type of privileged status that MUM enjoyed during the second year of life because it would have shared its representational world with another 50,000 or so words.

Words are like cells

Another way in which word frequency counts could be distorted by early experience could follow the model of cell division, where words divide, but continue to inherit cumulative frequency values based on the experience of their ancestors as well as the root form. Thus, for Tyko, the first word was 'bir'. Tyko used bir to refer to one bird or many birds, and she repeated it dozens if not hundreds of times but we do not know whether or not her second word ('du', used with reference to Gus, our Airedale Terrier) was a product of dividing 'bir' into a completely new form.

The extent to which changes in vocabulary size impact on cumulative frequency is unknown. But consider the data summarized in Figure 5.4 (from Nation, 1990, p. 12), for example. In broad terms, the figure indicates that children commence the second year of their lives with a vocabulary size of approximately 100 words.[1] A critical question concerns frequency of use of

---

[1] Estimates of vocabulary size at 1 year of age vary considerably (see Bloom, 2000, 2002). We have used Nation (1990) because his sources examined vocabulary size over a wide age range, enabling us to plot a vocabulary acquisition function.

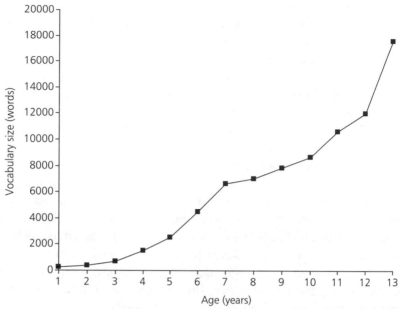

Fig. 5.4 A vocabulary acquisition function (from Nation, 1990).

these words by their carers, and by themselves, values that will impact on their cumulative reception and production rates, respectively. There are unknown variables of course. We do not know how many words children utter per hour or per day during this period, although recent research suggests that it can be as high as 20 words per minute at 14 months of age (Sumargi, 2001). The point of our argument is that the actual practice rates for early words could be orders of magnitude greater than would be predicted from simple age of acquisition and word frequency assumptions. During the early years of vocabulary acquisition, 'early' words could accumulate ultra-high frequency rates, and reach values that will not be reversed by any imbalance in subsequent experience or speaking.

It is our suspicion that the age of acquisition and word frequency studies are not in fact measuring the critical parameter, practice, and its obvious companion, recency. It is possible, for example, that a simple practice count could explain a variety of interactions between word frequency and age of acquisition although it would probably be necessary to measure practice for both printed and spoken language. Thus, over and above the fact that words that are experienced early in life might involve the formation of representations that are experienced later in life, early words receive extraordinary amounts of practice. It is of course possible to model the practice effects that will accrue for the first word for the period that it is a singleton, and for the first and second words while they share the lexical theatre in their turn, and so on. It is now possible to identify the most parsimonious question that bears on this issue. Are the observed word frequency and age of acquisition effects in performance explicable by reference to practice alone, or must we give specific and separate consideration to word frequency and age of acquisition? It would of course be necessary to make provision for recency and decay but these variables might be treated as parameters rather than independent variables. Although we have no data that could convincingly demonstrate that word frequency and age of acquisition effects reduce completely to practice effects, it is certainly our argument that both reflect practice and thus an explanation of these effects based on practice is more parsimonious than separate explanations for each set of effects. In other words, we claim that practice history is the major determiner of the structure of the lexicon, and word frequency and age of acquisition represent different instantiations of practice.

5.5.3 Functional equivalence of practice and repetition priming

The fifth way in which the multiple presentation design depicted in Tables 5.3 and 5.4 can reflect the influences of practice is closely related to word frequency and age of acquisition. In a recent paper, we assessed the relationship between pre-experimental practice (e.g. word frequency), experimental practice (e.g. session), and repetition priming (Kirsner and Speelman, 1996). The experiment involved seven sessions. The sessions constituted the experimental practice manipulation, the low-, medium-, and high-frequency word sets defined the pre-experimental practice manipulation, and repetition priming involved the contrast between words that had and had not been presented earlier in the experiment. If simple assumptions about word frequency are granted, it is possible to place the data on a practice continuum that depicts the effects of the pre-experimental and experimental practice side-by-side. Specifically, if it is assumed that people read or hear 25,000 words per day, and that consideration is restricted to 20-year-olds, and that modality, chronological age, age of acquisition, and morphology are irrelevant, it follows that a word in the '1 occurrence per million words' frequency band will have been experienced about 10 times per annum, or 200 times over a period of 20 years. Similarly, a word in the '10 occurrences per million' frequency band will have been experienced about 2000 times over a period of 20 years and a word in the '100 occurrences per million' frequency band will have been experienced around 20,000 times over a period of 20 years. In Figure 5.5 the word frequency values are translated into practice values, and

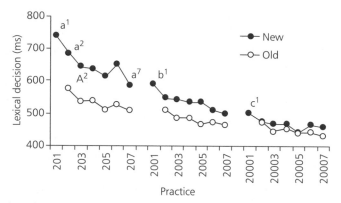

Fig. 5.5 The relationship between pre-experimental practice (i.e. a^1 to b^1, b^1 to c^1), task practice (i.e. a^1 to a^2), and repetition priming (a^2 to A^2) in a multi-session lexical decision task (from Kirsner and Speelman, 1996).

treated accordingly. The first point in each group of seven represents the starting point for words from each of these word frequency bands, the closed and open circles depict performance for new and repeated words, respectively, and the three seven point sequences of filled circles depict the effect of practice at the task on performance. The results indicate that there are actually three practice effects, the gradual change associated with pre-experimental practice (i.e. word frequency), the dramatic change in lexical decision time following the first experimental presentation of a word (i.e. repetition priming), and the task practice effect (i.e. the session effect involving new words). The pre-experimental practice effects are reflected in the differences between a^1 and b^1, and between b^1 and c^1. The task practice effect is reflected in the difference between a^1 and a^2, and the overall experimental practice effect is reflected in the differences between a^1 and A^2. Repetition priming represents the benefits of repeating a word over and above repeating a task, and this is reflected in the difference between a^2 and A^2.

Do these functions require separate explanations, or can they be modelled as two or even one process? If the pre-experimental and the experimental practice effects are quantitatively equivalent, for example, repetition priming effects could be predicted by changes in the pre-experimental or word frequency function. Indeed, it would be expected that the repetition effect would fall on the pre-experimental practice function. But it is not, of course. Pre-experimental practice produces a reduction of about 150 ms over 1800 trials (from a^1 to b^1 or the 201st to 2001st trial), and a further reduction of less than 100 ms over the next 18,000 trials (from b1 to c1). But repetition priming yields an immediate improvement of nearly 200 ms (i.e. A^2 compared with a^2), and it is evident therefore, that experimental and pre-experimental practice are not quantitatively equivalent. Indeed, these results suggest that practice in the 'real' world of work, study, novels, and conversation has a small impact relative to laboratory experience. Given an improvement of 150 ms from 1800 encounters in the real world, and 150 ms from a single encounter in the laboratory, it may be inferred that the quantitative impact of laboratory experience is between 100 and 1000 times greater than natural experience.

Can repetition priming never the less be used as a 'bio-assay' technique, to assess practice? Presumably, the answer to this question is 'yes', provided that the full set of potential variables is known, and the effects of each variable are predictable, and qualitatively comparable under pre-experimental and experimental practice conditions. According to this view, then, the difference in magnitude between the two effects is explicable in terms of operational differences between the procedures, and the relative impact of variables that influence experimental practice (repetition priming) will be maintained when they are examined under pre-experimental practice conditions. Several procedural variables merit consideration.

One of the most obvious differences involves differences between the semantic equivalence of repeated words under natural and laboratory conditions. Under natural conditions it is probably appropriate to assume that no two occurrences of a word ever involve exactly the same meaning. Thus, the 'bank' in 'get your money out of the bank immediately' and the 'bank' in 'you can bank on it' involve different readings or interpretations even though the words are identical. The central point here is that repetition of words under contextualized or natural conditions and de-contextualized or isolated conditions involve different semantic equations. The representational products of contextualized presentation will be coloured by the context as well as the word of interest, whereas the products of isolated presentation will be coloured only by the citation sense of the word, and this may remain more or less stable from presentation to presentation, even if we cannot determine which reading a particular viewer is adopting. Thus, if an individual's preferred reading for the word 'bank' presented in isolation involves the riverine or aeronautical readings, the chosen reading will in all probability be used every time the word is presented under de-contextualized conditions, an assumption that more or less removes semantic variability from the equation. If the foregoing argument is granted, it follows that it will be difficult to detect repetition priming under natural or contextualized conditions, because meaning changes from event to event, and changes in meaning compromise repetition priming. Speelman, Simpson, and Kirsner (2002), for example, examined the impact of one or more repetitions of selected words from Milan

Kundera's novel, 'The Unbearable Lightness of Being' on lexical decision time under isolated conditions—a contrast that involves transfer from contextually constrained to contextually unconstrained conditions—and found very small priming effects. Pre-experimental practice will of course involve many variations apart from meaning, involving type font, speaker's voice, and modality.

Another manipulation that distinguishes pre-experimental (practice) and experimental (repetition priming) conditions involves the interval between the study and test events. Under natural conditions, the typical interrepetition intervals for 1 occurrence per 1,000,000 words and 100 occurrences per 1,000,000 words will be about 40 days and 0.4 days (given 25,000 word encounters per day). But the typical interval in a repetition priming experiment is in the vicinity of 60 min, a value that does not provide comparable conditions for low frequency and high frequency words. Interactions between word frequency and the repetition priming treatments are probably critical. Records involving high frequency words will be far down the learning curve, and they will be correspondingly indifferent to additional practice. Thus, manipulations which involve word sets at different practice levels can yield spurious dissociations because repetition priming effects will be harder to detect for high frequency words than low frequency words.

Things, actions, words, gestures, and emotions

We have tabled the idea that word frequency counts, and the relationship between word frequency and age of acquisition, are both likely to be distorted by the exceptional practice opportunities enjoyed by early words. Most if not all of this advantage will of course involve spoken words rather than written words, and the distortion is therefore likely to be stronger for spoken language than printed language.

However, this form of distortion does not exhaust the way in which early experience can generate practice patterns not reflected in adult word frequency patterns. Another problem concerns the extent to which the representations of printed and spoken language are correlated. If the representations associated with alternative word forms depend on reference to a common representation to some extent, then, to that extent, each form will enjoy the benefit of experience or practice involving the other modality. But what about things like objects, pictures, and actions? Even if we adopt a conservative approach to these counts, and assume, for example, that a child only sees her plate once per meal, it follows that she will have seen her plate for one thousand or more times before she can utter even one word.

The type of distortion introduced above will compromise frequency counts to the extent that the additional practice actually influences one or more of the component processes that are eventually brought together to understand the words in question. A crucial question therefore concerns the extent to which processes that are developed to solve recognition problems in one modality are also required to solve recognition problems in other modalities. If the processes concerned are specific to each modality, the amount of practice that accrues for a particular concept presented in a particular form in one modality will not influence performance when the same concept is presented in an alternative modality. Under this assumption then, the spoken and printed forms of words do not share component processes, experience and practice will be modality-specific, and there will be no transfer from modality to modality.

But if one or more modalities depend on access to a common or shared resource, even if this only applies to a fraction of the component processes involved, specifying the amount of practice for each modality becomes a critical and complex task, for we cannot predict the impact of word frequency or any other variable unless we know both the amount of practice associated with each modality and the extent to which practice in each modality produces a resource that can be used by other modalities.

We will return to this issue when we move on to transfer and repetition priming. But there is one study that touches on this issue directly. Gallivan (1987) discovered that the order of acquisition of motion verbs in 4-year-old children is predicted by the order and the frequency of occurrence of the actions denoted. This correlation can of course be explained in a number of ways. One possibility is that the relationship simply reflects the order and frequency of occurrence of the relevant set of actions in the world, as determined by the carers of the children in question. A second possibility is that it is only the actions that are constrained by the carers. But that acquisition of the representations of the actions establishes a platform for acquisition of the words, and that this, rather than lexical exposure and training, determine the order and frequency of occurrence of the words. And it is of course possible that both of these propositions are valid, and that the representational platform simply reflects patterns of covariation that exist in the world. From this platform it is but a small step to the proposition advanced by McNeil and Duncan (2000) to explain covariation between speech and gesture during speaking. The central idea is that speech and gesture are 'co-expressive'; they 'express the same underlying idea unit but (they) do not necessarily express identical aspects of it' (McNeill and Duncan, 2000, pp. 142–143). McNeill and Duncan illustrated this point by reference to 'rising up', a concept with obvious gestural and vocal concomitants. If it is assumed that these components were integrated at some remote point in vocabulary acquisition, or even that their manifestations reflect activation of some supramodal concept during expression, the potential for transfer across the surface forms associated with this representation is apparent.

Given these arguments, the ontological and evolutionary relationship between the components of a lexical paradigm, involving the various ways of representing 'rising up', for example, could determine the extent of transfer between those forms. Thus, if the gestural version of 'rising up' preceded exposure to and recognition of 'up', the representation of 'up' could inherit the practice values associated with 'rising up', practice values that might both precede the first presentation of 'up' and occur after that time. Another and closely related issue concerns the extent to which our hypothetical representations are loaded, emotionally, a consideration that is likely to be particularly important for early words. This form of modulation could transform the representational status of socially and biologically important representations, a proposition that is consistent with the extent to which learning (and therefore language acquisition) and emotion involve the mid-brain including the limbic system (Pulvermuller and Schumann, 1994). The special relationship between emotion and language continues into adulthood, where aphasics sometimes speak with comparative ease when they are in a heightened emotional state (involving swear words, for example, Broca, 1861, as cited in Harrington, 1987).

We were unable to discover evidence that bears on these questions at the item level, but the idea has been applied to the relationships between the systems. For example, there is evidence of a strong relationship between gesture and emotion (Buck and Duffy, 1980), and several studies have found a positive correlation between the use of gesture and language development (Goodwyn et al., 2000). Children who produce large amounts of gesture are also advanced in language development, for example, and children who are encouraged to gesture in their second year have faster verbal language development than children who are not so encouraged. The changes in question tend to involve increasing synchronization between modalities, a finding that Iverson and Thelen (1999) attributed to the theory of activation. According to their analysis, speech development requires cognitive energy; the release of this energy involves activation, activation which spills over into other systems including the gestural system. Whether or not the spillover involves specific gestures and verbal forms is unclear, and the role of this argument for transfer is correspondingly unclear. A number of studies suggest that spillover effects occur throughout development when children are faced with tasks that involve high cognitive loads (Alibali and Goldin-Meadow, 1993). Consider a child learning to count, for example. Children often use fingers to aid them in counting. But then, as counting becomes easier, gesture is reduced accordingly. Alibali and Goldin-Meadow (1993) have described children who can demonstrate an understanding of scientific concepts via gesture when they are unable to express this through spoken language.

In conclusion, notwithstanding the complications, an explanation of repetition priming effects that sees them as just another example of the effects of practice on performance seems to us to provide a parsimonious account. This implies that skill acquisition and repetition priming involve the same principle; that performance improves as a negatively accelerated function of practice (Principle 1). In the next section we demonstrate how this conclusion is further supported by repetition priming effects that can be accounted for by an analysis that assumes that performance is determined by the transfer of component skills.

Transfer and repetition priming

When a monolingual English speaker is suddenly exposed to French, will twenty years of exposure to /MARRIAGE/ provide her with a representation that she can use immediately to recognize /MARIAGE/, or must that word be treated as a completely new word in a new lexical system? And what about /FIN/: will the emotional associations provoked by /FIN/ on an Australian beach overwhelm her ability to respond appropriately to the term that routinely signals the end of French films?

There is extensive evidence to show that exposure to the stem or root form of a word changes access to inflections, derivations, and even the cognates of that word. We explore this issue in detail below, but in broad terms the evidence indicates that exposure to morphological components of words facilitates performance for other words that share the practiced component. The effect appears to depend on the 'similarity' between the forms, although similarity may take any one of several forms. It probably depends in addition on the relative frequency of the two forms. As depicted in Table 5.4, the benefits of item-specific practice are much less for high frequency words than low frequency words (at 28 ms versus 112 ms across 5 practice trials in this illustration), a characteristic that could reflect a reduction in the opportunity available for further improvement in an empirical or procedural sense. But the same problem applies to transfer between morphologically related words. While a low frequency word will benefit dramatically from the existence of a high frequency relative in the same morphological paradigm or cluster, high frequency words will be more or less untouched by the presence of other high frequency words let alone low frequency words from the same cluster.

According to Principle 5, mastery in a domain involves application of an array of component processes. As we suggested in Chapter 4, word recognition may be a situation where some words are recognized directly (i.e. through the operation of processes specific to a word) and other words are recognized through the operation of processes that recognize parts of a word but work in concert to recognize the whole word. Thus, there will be some words for which recognition occurs through a process of decomposition into parts of the word that can be recognized directly by component processes. As a result, some words will be recognized by shared component processes. This implies that recognition of a word could influence the later recognition of another word with which it shares component processes. That is, recognition of a word could result in priming of a different but related word. The magnitude of transfer will be sensitive to many variables of course; transfer may be difficult to detect and measure under a variety of conditions, and it could even be negative under a limited set of conditions. And, of course, this principle is not restricted to words. Thus, it is our expectation that decomposition and transfer will be observed for signs and pictures as well as words, and that they will also be found for lower levels of representation, including letters and characters (e.g. radicals in Kanji) and for higher levels of representation, including possibly sentences and discourse. Below we examine transfer effects in repetition priming that can be related to stimulus similarities and this leads us to the conclusion that the mental lexicon is consistent with Principle 5.

Practice in the real world

Practice effects with language can be measured in a variety of ways. The effect of word frequency and age of acquisition on performance on tasks, such as naming latency and lexical decision, involves one general approach. Numerous experiments have demonstrated that lexical decision time, for example, is sensitive to word frequency and age of acquisition. A variant on this paradigm involves the measurement of transfer effects between words which share one or more constituents. This paradigm involves an interesting combination of natural practice conditions on the one hand and an artificial or experimental test procedure on the other. The practice manipulation involves the contrast between two word types where the examples enjoy the same surface frequency value but quite different cluster frequency values. Consider 'inducement' and 'atonement', for example. Although the surface forms displayed in the preceding sentence enjoy similar word frequency values, the clusters which they belong to involve very different values. If decomposition is occurring during word recognition, lexical decision time for the word from the high frequency cluster will be shorter than lexical decision time for the word from the low frequency cluster (Bradley, 1979). This paradigm can be exploited in various ways of course, involving words with similar cluster frequency values but different surface frequency values, to determine the role of whole-word analysis.

The results for experiments involving this general procedure can be used to support a variety of different arguments, most but not all of which invoke morphological analysis and decomposition. Bradley (1979), for example, found that lexical decision time reflected word cluster frequency for most but not all forms of suffixation, and she also found only weak effects for surface or 'whole-word' frequency. Similarly, Cole *et al.* (1989) found that cumulative root frequency for French words influences lexical decision time, although this pattern was restricted to suffixes. They considered the hypothesis that different processes could be required for suffixed and prefixed words. But there is evidence that surface frequency also exerts an influence on lexical decision time. Gordon and Alegre (1999) for example, found that whole-word frequency influences performance when cluster frequency is held constant, although the effect was not significant at low frequency values, under 6 per million, and Gurel (1999) found evidence of whole-word effects in Turkish, an agglutinative language, indicating that decomposition may not be present under all circumstances. Not surprisingly perhaps, the complexity of the performance patterns involving this paradigm has led the combatants to develop a compromise, involving the hypothesis that word recognition routinely involves parallel contributions from both whole-word and morphological or analytic processes (Carlisle and Fleming, 2003), although there is some suggestion that contributions from the analytic arm are restricted to low frequency words (Meunier and Segui, 1999).

But debate concerning the relative importance of the whole-word and morphological processes is complicated by several other issues. The first of these concerns the contrast between type and token frequency. There is evidence that type frequency rather than token frequency influences performance (Schreuder and Baayen, 1997), a shift of argument which leaves the decomposition hypothesis intact while compromising arguments about the nature of the underlying process. If type frequency is critical, then simple accumulation of frequency across all occurrences of a stem or root does not provide a sufficient explanation of the observed effects.

A second complication concerns the null hypothesis. This is of course a 'chestnut' that we have learned to tolerate and even ignore for decades. However, as dissociation is critical to this body of work, and dissociation is routinely used to justify dual process interpretations of interactions between morphological effects (Gordon and Alegre, 1999), the question is critical. The dissociative argument depends in this context on the co-occurrence of (1) a significant difference between two word types for one frequency band or range and (2) the absence of a significant difference between the same two word types for a different frequency band or range. The dual process inference depends critically on acceptance of the null hypothesis in (2) above. If the effect is merely masked at this frequency level—by variability, for example,—the dual process interpretation will be insecure.

A study by Pylkkanen, Feintuch, Hopkins, and Marantz (2004) provides an intriguing illustration of this type of masking. Pylkkanen *et al.* examined a word type (nouns) that does not usually exhibit cumulative frequency effects (unlike inflections), and made specific predictions about the impact of morphological frequency on the magneto-encephalographic response component M 350. Their specific predictions were not supported but Pylkkanen *et al.* did find an effect of morphological frequency on the magneto-encephalographic response component. The result indicates that the absence of significant effects for lexical decision for limited word frequency ranges must be treated with caution; in a complex system with multiple processes operating at the same time, the absence of an effect on one parameter or even one class of parameter is not definitive. This is of course a serious problem for inference in Cognitive Psychology and in the brain sciences generally. A closely related issue concerns the extent to which effects which can be detected under de-contextualized conditions—involving single word lexical decision, for example,—are reduced or abolished altogether when the test procedure involves a more naturalistic procedure (Hyönä, Vainio and Laine, 2002). Here too, it might be appropriate to assume that the process is operational, and sensitive to the imputed set variables, but that performance effects cannot be detected under the specific conditions in use at the time.

An additional consideration involves the possibility that performance in this domain is dominated by systematic individual differences (Baayen and Tweedie, 1998), a claim that further compromises the value of double dissociation, and processing inferences based on acceptance of the null hypothesis. If the impact of variables, such as age of acquisition, context, word type, productivity, homonymy, and type and token frequency reflects individual differences in the allocation of attention, for example, the quest for a universal morphological model will not be productive. Similar questions compromise inferences about differences between languages, and between monolinguals and bilinguals. Should we conceptualize the answers to questions about these issues in terms of specialized modules (e.g. Waksler, 1999), or, rather, should we rather conceptualize the problem in terms of one or a few general principles, where the performance patterns reflect the impact of individual, language and cultural differences on the way in which material is segmented and represented? We propose the latter.

Paradigm issues: Environment variables versus laboratory manipulations

If, as we suggest, there is transfer between related words because of shared component processes, then any distinctions between environmental and experimental variables may not be clear. We can, for example, examine interlingual transfer effects under experimental conditions in the laboratory by presenting a Spanish–English bilingual with PUBLICIDAD and PUBLICITY as, say the 100th and 200th words in a lexical decision task where the participants are expected to classify letter strings as words that belong to the English or Spanish corpuses. The words are cognates and the usual finding under these conditions is that performance is faster and/or more accurate when morphologically related words are presented in the relevant language to fluent bilinguals. But we can examine what is at least essentially the same question by comparing lexical decision for two English words that have high and low frequency Spanish or Italian cognates, respectively. For example, ARID and ADORATION have similar word frequency counts in English, at 3 and 1 per million, respectively. But the Italian cognates for these words, ARIDO and ADORAZIONE, are relatively high and relatively low frequency words, respectively, at 31 and 1 per million, respectively, and their relative status in Italian influences lexical decision in English provided of course that the participants are fluent in both languages (Lalor and Kirsner, 2000).

The results involving the laboratory procedure—repetition priming—and the environmental manipulation—interlingual transfer based on frequency counts rather than prior presentation—are logically equivalent; they each involve transfer via a root or stem morpheme that is common to the languages concerned. There are complications of course. Etymologically related languages often have many false friends (e.g. FIN in English and French) as well as cognates or 'true friends', and these can play havoc with transfer effects under both laboratory and environmental conditions as well as second language learning. But that is a detail. Our general point is that environmental and experimental transfers are equivalent, and can be treated as if they reflect the same lexical property.

The equivalence of these two results is important for another reason. One of the many boundary disputes involving repetition priming involved the claim that repetition priming compromised the presence of episodic effects; the implication being that it is not a true lexical effect (Forster and Davis, 1984; de Groot and Nas, 1991). But transfer effects involving word frequency counts from the natural environment are not open to this charge, and the two types of results are equivalent. Here, too, it would be inappropriate to assume that they depend on exactly the same set of component processes; but it would also be inappropriate to assume that they do not involve at least one common or shared process.

Classification problems

Repetition priming can be detected in performance changes that encompass all languages, modalities, and stimulus classes. A review includes evidence involving pictures of objects (Cave, 1997; Winnick and Daniel, 1970), printed words and spoken non-words (Kirsner and Smith, 1974), spoken words and spoken non-words (Kirsner and Smith, 1974), familiar and unfamiliar environmental sounds (Chiu and Schacter, 1995; Cycowicz and Friedman, 1998), French (Kirsner et al., 1984), Hindi (Brown et al., 1984; Kirsner et al., 1980), Urdu (Brown et al., 1984), the Japanese scripts, Hiragana, Katakana, and Kanji (Kirsner et al., 1993), faces (Ellis et al., 1987), and the production of words in spontaneous speech (Robertson and Kirsner, 2000).

The critical issue in repetition priming involves the presence and the magnitude of transfer effects between corresponding concepts from different stimulus classes. Given the assumption that decomposition is universal, and the suite of skill acquisition measures involve essentially the same process, it follows that transfer between stimulus classes should be present for forms that share records or part thereof. But stimulus equivalence is a vexing issue, particularly when we—the experimenters—generally prefer to test our stimuli under static de-contextualized conditions. Even if we take a simple word form like BALL, questions about equivalence are anything but simple. Does BALL on its own refer to a physical object used for sport and play, or does it refer to a specialized type of social activity, or does it refer more loosely to 'having a good time'? In discourse of course, these questions fade away; 'She kicked the ball to her team-mate', 'He caught the foot-ball', 'They arrived at the ball after the Governor-General', and 'she had a ball after the exams', are unambiguous, in Australia at least. In research involving isolated words in lexical decision, for example, these questions have generally been set side, even though we know that 'number of meanings' influences lexical decision time (Jastrzembski, 1981). But there is another problem, particularly if we want to treat repetition as an assay procedure for evaluating skill acquisition.

Stimulus class is of course ambiguous too. What constitutes a stimulus class? Published research suggests that we can and should treat mode (e.g. pictures versus words, faces versus the names of faces), modality (i.e. spoken words versus printed words), language, (e.g. English versus German), case (i.e. upper case versus lower case letters), and sex of speaker (male voices versus female voices) as stimulus classes, and draw inferences about lexical organization from the transfer patterns between these forms. But does this stand up to scrutiny? While we can assume with confidence that modality is a fixed factor, and that each and every experimental stimulus can be classified appropriately, such confidence cannot be extended to the difference between male and female voices (where the populations overlap in regard to fundamental frequency, one of the most obvious sex markers), or even to the difference between upper and lower case letters in English, where 'cos' could (if presented in isolation) be in upper or lower case, and the introduction of type font only underlines the problem. Where then should we draw the line?

Another and comparable set of problems involves language. This is of course straightforward when we are dealing with language differences that also involve script differences like Hindi and Urdu, or English and Chinese. But it is not so easy when language pairs do not involve script differences, as is the case for many pairs of European languages. The equivalence issue is further compromised by the presence of both true and false cognates. Almost any monolingual English speaker who has ever watched a French language film knows that FIN in French is anything but equivalent to FIN in English, a word that has iconic status for Australian speakers of English because of our more or less pathological fear of sharks. But there are also many genuine cognates between pairs of European languages, including ANIMAL in English and Spanish, for example. Thus, even the boundaries between languages are fuzzy, like the voices of male and female speakers, and cannot be used to define stimulus class with confidence. But there are other problems involving meaning. Even if it is agreed that ANIMAL is the best Spanish translation of the English word, does it mean exactly the same thing, and if it does not, does that mean that transfer will be compromised? Consider CHEESE, for example. For most English-first language people in English-speaking countries CHEESE is wrapped in plastic, and kept in a refrigerator. But, traditionally at least, this is not the case for FROMAGE or FORMAGGIO, the most obvious French and Italian translations, and these forms are usually accompanied by olfactory as well as visual cues.

In the following review of transfer effects, we have adopted a conventional approach to stimulus class. However, the presence of fuzzy boundaries between several stimulus class pairs poses a significant problem for scientists who use that variable to define boxes, bins (e.g. Forster, 1976), modules, and systems specific to one language or category (Kirsner et al., 1983). In one foray into this arena we explored the hypothesis that lexical organization is based on morphologically as distinct from language defined classes (Lalor and Kirsner, 2000). It was our assumption that lexical paradigms would either be lost or survive as a set so that the interlingual boundary line for aphasics would be jagged, with some lexical paradigms surviving as sets, and some paradigms being lost as sets. The results were inconclusive, but the question remains.

Measurement issues

Because of the volume and complexity of the transfer research, and the variety of paradigms that have been used, Kirsner and Dunn (1985) adopted Relative Priming (RP) as a transfer measure. The measure calculates transfer under cross-form conditions as a proportion of repetition priming under intra-form conditions (see Equation 5.1). The measure has face validity. RP values range from zero to one, with a range of intermediate values from studies involving planned, multi-treatment experiments as well as meta-analyses of independent studies. The procedure is not without its limitations, however. One of these stems from the fact that RP is sensitive to not only the position of the transfer value in the range between zero (no transfer, as observed for morphologically unrelated translations) and unity or near unity (complete transfer, as observed for small surface differences involving speaker's voice and case). RP values are in addition sensitive to the value of the denominator; that is, differences between the old and new treatments, involving word frequency, for example. This problem is not of course specific to RP. It is comparable to problems mentioned earlier involving the null hypothesis in experiments that compare priming for high frequency and low frequency words, and fail to find significant differences for the former, an outcome that could reflect the presence of a ceiling effect under high frequency word testing conditions or a dissociation. The difference between OLD and NEW word treatments is usually very small for high frequency words, and the RP values are correspondingly vulnerable.

Meta-analysis

Table 5.5 comprises a meta-analysis based on a sample of empirical studies. The sample includes our own work (e.g. Cristoffanini *et al.*, 1986; Downie *et al.*, 1985; Kirsner and Smith, 1974; Kirsner *et al.*, 1980, 1984, 1993; Brown *et al.*, 1984) as well as that of Roediger and Blaxton (1987).

The table was designed to summarize the observed patterns of transfer effects. The second column provides a general label for each treatment. The third and fourth columns specify the mode or form of presentation of the study phase and test phase stimuli, respectively. The fifth columns indicates the range of RP values observed for each group of treatments. The sixth and final columns involves reference to four hypothetical variables of interest, each of which appears to influence RP in one or more of the 13 groups identified in column 1. The variables of interest are: Semantic Equivalence, Structural Correspondence (Transparent) (where the correspondence is given, as in the relationship between printed and spoken words), Structural Correspondence (Opaque) (where the correspondence must be derived, as in the relationship between a picture and a name associated with

Table 5.5 Summary of transfer effects in repetition priming

G[1]	Label	Study phase	Test phase	RP[2]	Similarity Analysis[3]
1.1	Translations[4]	BALEINE (French)	WHALE (English)	≈ 0.0	Semantic Equivalence is not alone *sufficient* for partial or full RP
1.2	Synonyms	LARGE	BIG		
2.1	Homo-graphs	River (before) BANK	money (before) BANK	≈ 0.0	Transparent Structural Correspondence and Surface Similarity are not together *sufficient* for partial or full RP
2.2	False cognates	FIN (French context)	FIN (English context)		
3.1	Modality	'whale' (speech)	WHALE (print)	0.3–0.7	Semantic Equivalence and Transparent Structural Correspondence are together *sufficient* for partial but not full RP
3.2	Script	केला Hindi[5] script for 'kela'[6]	کیلا Urdu script for 'kela'[6]		
4.1	Mode	Picture of a whale	WHALE (print)	0.3–0.7	Semantic Equivalence and Opaque Structural Correspondence are together *sufficient* for partial but not full RP
4.2	Generation	BALEINE—participants specify 'number of letters' in translation	WHALE (print)		
5.1	Inflections	DOGS	DOG	0.5–0.8	Semantic Equivalence and Transparent Structural Correspondence are together *sufficient* for partial but not full RP
5.2	Derivations	COURAGEOUS	COURAGE		
5.3	True cognates	MARIAGE (French)	MARRIAGE (English)		
6.1	Speaker's voice	'banana' uttered by Maggie	'banana' uttered by Tyko	0.7–1.0	Combination of Semantic Equivalence, Transparent Structural Correspondence and Surface Similarity are together *necessary* for full RP
6.2	Type font or case	BANANA, banana, BANANA, etc.	BANANA		

Note: [1] Group

[2] RP = Relative priming

[3] Transparent similarity is used for cases where the relationship can be recognized via analysis of the sub-lexical constituents; this applies to the relationship between Hindi and Urdu. Opaque similarity is used to refer to cases where the relationship cannot be recognized via analysis of sub-lexical constituents, involving pictures and words, for example.

[4] Morphologically unrelated translations as distinct from cognates

[5] Devanagari script used for Hindi

[6] kela = banana

that picture), and Surface Similarity (where the study and test stimuli are physical transformations of each other). For these variables read SE, SC(T), SC(O), and SS, respectively.

Table 5.6 depicts the logic states that characterize transfer effects in repetition priming. Arguably, they apply to transfer effects in skill acquisition and transfer effects in the real world as well. The analysis in these cases will of course be compromised by variation in the nature of practice events.

We propose that transfer effects are contingent on the co-occurrence of Semantic Equivalence and Structural Congruence. Beyond that, the extent of transfer or RP reflects the extent of Structural Correspondence and the extent of Surface Similarity. We propose furthermore that this argument is valid for both opaque and transparent forms of structural correspondence; that is, whether congruence involves derivation (where correspondence between the letters or sounds is more or less obvious), modality (where correspondence between the phonemes and graphemes is clear even though the mapping relationship is not 1:1, for English in particular), mode (where the correspondence between a picture and word depends on activation of lexical codes for the picture), and cases where structural equivalence is absent but the participants are invited to generate the structure and elements of the target words, as in the example involving morphologically related translations. It should be noted that this analysis says nothing about the order of processing; it simply specifies the logical conditions that control Relative Priming.

We will illustrate the proportional argument from studies conducted by Stanners *et al.* (1979) and Cristoffanini *et al.* (1986). The experiment implemented by Stanners *et al.* included four comparisons of interest, involving (1) number of letters added to inflections, (2) the number of letters changed in irregular verbs, the extent of the change in adjectival stems, and the extent of the change in verb stems, and Relative Priming was invariably smaller in the

Table 5.6 Logic states for magnitude of relative priming

Case	Semantic Equivalence	Structural Correspondence	Relative Priming
1	0	0	0
2	1	0	0
3	0	1	0
4	1	1	$RP \propto SC_{range\,=\,0.3-0.7}$ $+ SS_{range\,=\,0.0-0.3}$

Notes: SC = Structural Correspondence
     SS = Structural Similarity

treatments subject to greater change. In a somewhat similar study involving translations, Cristoffanini *et al.* found a similar pattern for English–Spanish cognates, and they also found that memory for language was associated negatively with Relative Priming, as if similarity, or 'discriminability' is a critical variable influencing both tasks. It is proposed therefore that the extent of structural correspondence between the study and test forms determines Relative Priming. We are not aware of any studies that have manipulated structural correspondence and surface similarity but we suspect that these variables are additive, as suggested in Table 5.6, and that while high levels of structural correspondence will yield high levels of RP, these levels will be less than unity unless surface similarity is also very high.

Our analysis is in some respects similar to that of Shepard (1987). It is different in that we have treated Semantic Equivalence as a pre-condition for transfer, as if semantic similarity is either present or absent, and transfer is present or absent accordingly. Beyond that, where structural correspondence and surface similarity are concerned, transfer or Relative Priming will reflect the similarity of the study and test forms. It may be hypothesized, further-more, that the underlying dimensions reflect the universal principle defined by Shepard (1987), and that degree of similarity is a direct determinant of the extent of transfer, provided that the pre-condition is met. According to Shepard, the likelihood of obtaining the same response to two stimuli decreases exponentially with their separation in a psychological space, as defined by multidimensional scaling, for example. In our case of course, we are dealing with study test relationships that involve not only three partially correlated dimensions, but also a situation where the second and third dimen-sions apply only when the first dimension has passed a threshold or criterion level. The similarity argument has precedents of course. It was present in Kolers's early work (Kolers, 1979b), where he asserted that practice effects reflect the extent to which the practice and test operations involved the same procedures, and it is a concept that we too have drawn on in the past, with ref-erence to the role of perceptual records in word recognition and attribute memory (Kirsner and Dunn, 1985). Of course, the similarity argument is also a reflection of Principle 5, and the fact that it describes well transfer effects in repetition priming supports a skill acquisition account of the lexicon. Given that repetition priming effects also reveal evidence of Principle 1, we conclude that repetition priming effects are just practice effects, and that the lexicon can be understood as the product of years of skill acquisition. Before we deal with some of the implications of this conclusion, we deal finally with old views of the lexicon.

5.6 **Revisiting old theories**

5.6.1 **Modularity: doubts and uncertainties**

Table 5.6 could be seen as a platform for a model involving stages or modules. Our analysis provides a platform for the assumption that three types of information are involved in repetition priming, and transfer. One type, involving meaning, does not appear to involve domain-specific processes, and, following the argument advanced by Coltheart (1999), it can therefore be inferred that this source of processing does not involve a module. However, the second and third forms do appear to involve domain-specific processes, and a modular interpretation can therefore be advanced. The second form involves treatments that yield Relative Priming values that are typically although not invariably greater than zero and less than unity. Transfer from speech to print and from pictures to print are obvious examples. It is a plausible inference that transfer is present for a processing level that is modality-*independent*, involving phonological form, for example, whereas the modality-specific components are handled by domain-specific and therefore modular processes. Some neuro-psychological evidence provides further support for this interpretation (Carlesimo *et al.*, 1994; Joyce *et al.*, 1999), providing evidence that particular forms of brain damage influence the modality-specific and modality-independent contributions to transfer.

But there are some tantalizing twists in this story. One of these involves the extraordinary variety of RP values observed for different degrees and forms of structural or morphological similarity between the study and test forms. In our own work, for example, we have found RP values that range from slightly greater than zero to slightly less than unity for inflections, derivations, and cognates. Similar variability is present in studies that involve transfer between speech and printed words and between pictures and printed words. Transfer between pictures and words involves a particularly interesting issue. Domain- or modality-specific analyses of these forms do not involve any form of similarity until and unless morphological or phonological analyses reveal codes in a common dimension. But by the time analysis reaches this level, we are clearly outside the domain-specific argument, and performance involves codes that are not domain-specific. It is evident therefore that structural correspondence involves opaque as well as transparent dimensions, and that because these dimensions are not present in the actual stimulus, interpretation does not lend itself to modular arguments involving the domain-specific assumption.

But variability poses even greater problems when we turn to surface form. It is possible to manipulate a host of surface variables, including type font, case, size, and colour in printed words, and fundamental frequency, volume, gender, accent, and emotion in spoken words, and, arguably, all of these manipulations will yield similarity continua in RP, as if similarity is a continuous as distinct from a categorical variable. Perhaps similarity-based processing is synonymous with the operation of domain-specific contributions to RP. However, the fact that repetition priming is only observed when the old and current stimuli involve reference to the same basic sense or meaning *implies that similarity has its effect subsequent to interpretation*, hardly a solid platform for a linear account that commences with modality- or domain-specific processes, and ends up with meaning. But similarity functions involving surface form are an important part of repetition priming. When both the semantic and structural criteria are met, RP generally increases as a function of increasing surface similarity, involving type font, speaker's voice and other variables. But how can this be the case if we are dealing with cognitive work that follows rather than precedes interpretation? An alternative approach to this question involves the assumption that analyses involving old records and current stimuli actually involve the entire record where this includes surface and structural form as well as meaning. Each record must therefore include at least approximate information about all aspects of each episode or event.

5.6.2 Dissociation: doubts and uncertainties

Debates about stores, systems, and modules have driven cognitive research for much of the last 40 years. The most significant divisions comprise short-term memory versus long-term memory (Crowder, 1972), episodic memory versus semantic memory (Tulving, 1983), explicit memory versus implicit memory (Graf and Schacter, 1985), and procedural versus declarative processes or knowledge (Anderson, 1983a). The third and fourth of these divisions are of particular interest to us, as is evidence for and against a further division between the perceptual and conceptual sub-systems of implicit memory.

But the evidence that is being used to support the presence of these components or sub-systems is far from convincing. In recent reviews, one of us outlined the doubts about dissociation hypotheses (Dunn and Kirsner, 1988, 2003). A short list of the problems included: (1) confusion over terminology, (2) disagreement over the inferential status of different types of dissociation, (3) reliance on acceptance of null hypotheses, (4) the extent to which modular interpretations are demanded by even double dissociations, (5) argument that dissociation tells us only that there are two processes (at best) without enabling us to characterize the processes in question, and (6) the extent to which many of the tasks that underpin particular theoretical constructs—and implicit memory in particular—are themselves subject to dissociation leading to the suspicion that more or less everything can be dissociated from everything else, an outcome that is light on charm. The second of the review articles, an editorial, attracted some 20 or so commentaries, the vast majority of which either endorsed the arguments presented by Dunn and Kirsner (2003), or added new doubts to the security of inferences based on dissociation.

We have participated in the campaign to demonstrate that the pattern of transfer effects in repetition priming reflects contributions from a suite of separate systems or modules (e.g. Kirsner and Smith, 1974; Kirsner et al., 1983). This campaign has yielded evidence that inter-modal and intra-modal effects reflect conceptually driven or top-down processes, and data-driven and bottom-up processes, respectively. Our approach to this issue was driven by the hypothesis that the intra- and inter-modality components were insensitive and sensitive to word frequency effects, respectively. In experiments involving transfer between speech and print and pictures and print we found support for this hypothesis (Kirsner et al., 1983; Stumpfl and Kirsner, 1986). However, although the RP values for transfer between speech and print and for pictures and print, for English, are relatively if not absolutely insensitive to word frequency, and this pattern is duplicated for Hiragana and Katakana, the syllabic scripts used for Japanese, the pattern changes dramatically when Kanji is used (Kirsner et al., 1993). The intra-modal component of repetition priming is far larger for Kanji than the inter-modal component, and it is this compo- nent which shows far greater sensitivity to Kanji frequency. The reason is obvi- ous, *in retrospect*. There are 1945 Kanji characters, and their average occurrence rates in written language are correspondingly lower than it is for English characters, while their sensitivity to one more exposure, under lexical decision conditions, is correspondingly greater. Even when consideration is restricted to the 200 or so radicals that under-pin Kanji, the radical frequency values are an order of magnitude lower than their English counterparts. Thus, word frequency effects are not limited to the domain-independent component of word recognition, and it may be inferred that the same principle is involved in practice effects involving both domain-specific and domain-independent manipulations.

In summary, research in our area of interest has focussed on differentiation and fragmentation. Scientists working with skill acquisition rarely work with repetition priming or even morphological practice effects. Researchers tend to specialize in faces, or objects, or voices, or printed words or spoken words, but not in all of them, and they or rather 'we' tend to develop arguments and models specific to each stimulus class. We also tend to specialize in particular procedures, and dependent variables, and, inevitably, each procedure has its adherents and detractors. The enterprise can of course be defended, and it can be argued that we must understand each paradigm before we can develop an over-arching model. However, we have adopted a rather different point of view. It is our claim that all stimulus classes and all transfer effects reflect the operation of the same small set of principles, as we have outlined as underlying skill acquisition.

5.6.3 Language production: the heart of the problem

Natural speaking consists of alternating bursts of speech and silence. The silent periods in speaking are usually referred to as pauses. For more than 40 years, language scientists have ignored pauses under about 250 ms, and treated both pause duration and speech segment duration as if they are normally distributed, an interpretation based on the fact they have measured and averaged pause duration in real time (cf. Jaffe and Feldstein, 1970). Pause and speech segment duration distributions are not normal. They are massively skewed, and they are at a first approximation log-normal (Campione and Veronis, 2002; Kirsner *et al.*, 2002). Now this particular distribution has significant ramifications for the way in which we theorize about language production. While scientists were assuming that pause duration distributions were normal, they could adopt the additional assumption that the relevant processes or modules were independent and additive. But once it is assumed that pause duration distributions are log-normal, it is necessary to move to an entirely different class of model. This new class of model involves multiplicative interaction among the mass of variables that influence pause duration. In fact there are two log-normal pause duration distributions in natural speaking, with means of about 4.2 nl (60 ms) and 6.3 nl (700 ms) and standard deviations of approximately 0.5–1.0 nl, and the speech segment duration distributions are also approximately log-normal. Now consider the variables that, arguably, influence the longer of the two pause duration distribution values. A short list includes conceptualization, monitoring, planning, communicative intent, lexical retrieval, and syntactic construction. If performance as distinct from competence in natural speaking involves multiplication among these and other variables, is it not likely that input or reading processes involve a similar form of integration, and that models which presuppose that reading including word recognition depends on an array of encapsulated and domain-specific modules are insecure?

5.7 The lexicon reflects the environment

Once we assume that the lexicon is a product of years of skill acquisition, and that repetition priming just reflects continued practice with language, it then becomes obvious that a person's lexicon should reflect the particular experience they have had with language, both in terms of producing speech and listening to others speak, as well as reading and writing. In this section, we consider the evidence in support of this claim, as well as some of the implications of such a conclusion.

There are many signs that practice plays a critical role in the shape of the mental lexicon. Word frequency and age of acquisition are only the most obvious variables. Gardner *et al.* (1987), for example, found that lexical decision among adults is sensitive to the professional experience of the individual participant. Adults with backgrounds in engineering, nursing, and law tend to respond more rapidly to words associated with their individual professions than control words or words associated with the other professions. Lexical decision is also sensitive to educational experience. Tainturier *et al.* (1992) found that the slope of the function relating lexical decision time to word frequency is steeper for people with less education, as if the participants concerned had lower than 'normal' frequency values for low frequency words. The general principle advanced here is that the shape and content of the mental lexicon can only be defined by reference to the shape and content of the external world, the way in which we interact with that world during and beyond childhood, by an appreciation of covariation among alternative forms of presentation, particularly during the early stages of language acquisition, and, finally, by understanding practice and priming effects on representation.

5.7.1 Distributional characteristics of the external world

The idea that mental representations conform to the distributional characteristics of the external world is by no means new. Essentially the same idea was advanced by Anderson and Schooler (1991). According to Anderson and Schooler, the probability that a specific word will be required on a given day is closely related to the historical record for that word; the frequency, recency, and pattern of prior exposures predict the probability that that word will be needed on a future occasion. Anderson and Schooler also demonstrated that the quantitative forms of the practice and retention functions are consistent with equivalent environmental parameters. It is a matter of particular interest that Anderson and Schooler developed their account to explain memory effects, and explicit memory effects at that. Their analysis was advanced without reference to the lexicon even though their data actually involves words, and could have been put side by side with word frequency and other lexical parameters.

Questions about decomposition and transfer can be considered with reference to two lexical worlds, involving the 'internal' and 'external' representations, respectively (Chomsky, 1986). The internal lexical world involves mental representations, and so concerns the way in which words are represented in the mind, or in memory. In a now classical article entitled, 'Things, words and the brain', Oldfield (1966) identified and discussed most of the questions about lexical organization and retrieval that have attracted so much attention in the ensuing decades.

The external lexical world involves the way in which 'words' and 'things' are distributed in the environment, in newspapers, books, magazines, conversations, and so on. We have already introduced the external world, by reference to word frequency. Measures of word frequency were developed to provide an index of frequency in the external world. Historically they have been based on counts involving books and newspapers (e.g. Kucera and Francis, 1967), or a variety of cultural, scientific, and literary sources as in the case of the work in the *Dictionnaire de l'Académie française*. But the Internet now provides a far more accessible medium for reference and measurement purposes. Inferences about states and processes in the internal world are often based on evidence about the relationships between performance measures on the one hand and distributional measures involving the external world on the other.

It is a matter of some interest that while these worlds provide grist for each other's mills, they are rarely honoured as two faces of a single problem or question. Is the internal world simply a 'pale' reflection of the external world, an internal system that reflects the statistical properties of the external system, or does the internal system depend on layers of specialized modules, each of which has a defined role at a specifiable level in word recognition or word production? Our suspicion that this question has not been honoured can be justified by reference to recent work on the relationship between word frequency and age of acquisition. One of the first issues to be considered in this arena involves the statistical relationship between these variables, where studies have been implemented to determine whether they influence independent information processing stages. The question is appropriate from a purely cognitive perspective of course. But when the internal and external worlds and the relationships between these concepts are considered as part of the same problem, the topography of the external world takes on a new significance.

While it is possible to measure word frequency, and to estimate or even perhaps measure age of acquisition (Baumgaertner and Tompkins, 1998), some of the early contingencies between word frequency and age of acquisition may be incommensurable. The point that we wish to make is based in part on the distinction between input and intake (Bloom, 2000, p. 90). Simply counting the word types and tokens that are used in front of a child or even addressed to a child is not sufficient. The child might not understand half of them, and might elect to ignore 50% of the balance, particularly in the early stages of vocabulary acquisition. Production will also play a part. The child may elect to repeat a selected word to herself or himself, and apply it repeatedly to selected objects, for minutes or even hours on end. The quantitative implications of these questions are difficult to assess. It is likely, however, that word frequency values will be distorted dramatically for words that are learned early and repeated often by children either overtly or covertly. Yet, another factor that will influence this equation involves the fact that our spoken language, and particularly that directed toward children (Fernald, 2000), involves a selected and small vocabulary, thereby adding an additional source of distortion to word frequency. The simplest assumption is that practice—the incommensurable variable in early language experience—will explain the full pattern of word frequency and age of acquisition effects without the need to treat these variables as independent.

However, practice alone cannot account for all of the published findings. It is probably useful to think in terms of a pool of words. The size of the pool is more or less stable. But the relative position of the individual words in the pool is in a constant state of flux. Some words are singletons, used just once and then discarded. Other words are used repeatedly again in a wide variety of slightly different contexts. Decay and recency play a critical role. The front or operating end of the system is limited by the fact that the eyes, the ears, the hands, and the mouth can only recognize or express one word at a time, and that a decision to use one word is also a decision not to use tens of thousands of other words. Thus, word representations that are not used are subject to decay until they are used again, and restored to something approaching their previous state. A hint that the overall pool may be a stable resource comes from evidence that word frequency effects are relatively if not absolutely indifferent to age (Allen *et al.*, 1993; Tainturier *et al.*, 1989). It is as if the quantitative relationship between word frequency and performance is stable even though the representations of the individual words are in a state of turmoil.

Information about speaking rate and volume are not well documented, and there is little published data about word recognition and production rates in young children. But the central issue is clear; arguments about the structure of the internal lexicon should be informed by information about the topography of the external lexical world as well as performance, and the external world must be treated as a dynamic system where developmental experience is concerned.

Simon Kirby

Simon Kirby (Kirby, 2001) has provided an elegant analysis of one aspect of the external world. In an approach which assumes from the outset that the internal and external worlds are both adaptive and interactive, he has described and modelled language change including the emergence of established contingencies involving regularity, frequency, and length. Perhaps the most intriguing argument advanced by Kirby involves the proposition that it is the language rather than the language user that adapts to improve its own survival. Thus, given pressure on language, and reference to a Zipfian (see below) surface (see Figure 5.6), the high frequency range is dominated by short and irregular past tense forms, such as BE, HAVE, DO, SAY, MAKE, GO, TAKE, COME, SEE, and GET whereas the low frequency range is dominated by decomposable forms that are long and regular.

Kirby's explanation for this distribution involves reference to what he refers to as the human 'bottleneck'. The central assumption is that the distribution of words in the external world is a by-product of transactions involving the internal and external worlds, and that limitations in human information processing capacity place constraints on the survival, growth, and decline of different types of words in the external world. His model also involves an assumption that humans tend to process words in one of two ways. The first mode is 'non-compositional' and involves storage of holistic and idiosyncratic

	a0	a1	a2	a3	a4
b0	g	s	kf	jf	uhif
b1	y	jgi	ki	ji	uhli
b2	yq	jgq	kq	jq	uhlq
b3	ybq	jgbq	kbq	jbq	uhlbq
b4	yuqeg	jguqeg	kuqeg	juqeg	uhluqeg

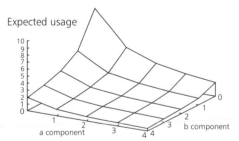

Fig. 5.6 Illustration depicting strings from adult agents of an artificial language at 256 generations when run with non-uniform distribution over meanings based on a Zipfian surface. The short, irregular, high frequency forms occupy low values on variables a and b (from Kirby, 2001).

representations of whole words. The second mode is compositional, and depends on the application of general rules involving decomposition. This contrast implies that the internal system has a limited capacity to form idiosyncratic representations of words, and that it can do so or does so only for words that are in frequent use.

Kirby's analysis is consistent with our fourth principle, that skill acquisition is dominated by resource issues, and the fifth principle that implies that decomposition and generalization play a central role in the mental economy. The beauty of Kirby's argument is that it points towards the source of the limitation. It involves a limitation in the number of representations that can be maintained at a level of activation sufficient for easy access. Kirby's argument suggests that we cannot store an infinite number of holistic representations or that, if we can, we cannot access them efficiently under real-time processing conditions.

George Zipf

Zipf's Law is central to Kirby's argument (Kirby, 2001). Zipf's Law currently occupies an interesting space between cognition, linguistics, and mathematics. According to Adamic (2000), Zipf's Law refers to the size of occurrence of an event relative to its rank i. The law asserts that the size of the i'th largest occurrence of an event is inversely proportional to its rank, and that this relationship is a power function. In English, or any other language for that matter, it follows that the terms with the highest frequency will occupy the smallest sets, whereas the terms with the lowest frequency will occupy the largest sets. Quantitatively, the law asserts that

$$P_i = P_1 i^{-\alpha} \qquad (5.2)$$

where $\alpha \approx 1$, and P_1 is the probability of the most frequent word. The relationship can also be expressed in terms of the number of words in each word frequency band. Thus, for English, there might be just 1 word in the range 1000–10,000 occurrences per million, but 50,000 words in the range 1 per million.

We will use Japanese to develop our ideas about the importance of Zipf's law for lexical science. Japanese is particularly interesting because it is possible to discern regularity at a variety of points in what is by any standards a complex and 'irregular' system.

Printed Japanese involves three separate scripts, Kanji, Hiragana, and Katakana. Modern Japanese is generally restricted to an administratively defined set of 1945 Kanji, and this set makes up approximately 80% of printed Japanese, the balance being depicted in either one of two syllabic scripts,

Hiragana (for native words) or Katakana (for loan words). Although Kanji is often referred to as pictographic (derived from the shape of objects), this sub-category makes up only 13% of the total set of Kanji (Tamaoka *et al.*, 2002), and the balance involves ideographic, semantic, or phonetic constituents.

Figure 5.7 shows 29 Kanji. These Kanji form a cluster or paradigm (in the linguistic sense). The paradigm is defined by the presence of one particular radical embedded in each Kanji. For a rough equivalent involving English and French one might think of a paradigm, such as /MARRY/, a paradigm that includes /MARRIAGE/, /MARRIED/, and /MARRYING/. The radical in this case is MIZUHEN (see large font), and its English translation is WATER. This radical is embedded in some form in all except three of the Kanji in the figure. The items in the set also bear a more or less obvious semantic or functional relationship to MIZUHEN. The three Kanji that do not include MIZUHEN do not enjoy a semantic relationship with this radical.

The spatial distribution of the Kanji in Figure 5.7 is the product of a multidimensional scaling analysis. In broad terms, variation along the y-axis appears to involve the transition from water to things that can be done with water, including extinguishing and pouring, for example, whereas variation along the x-axis appears to involve the transition from things that

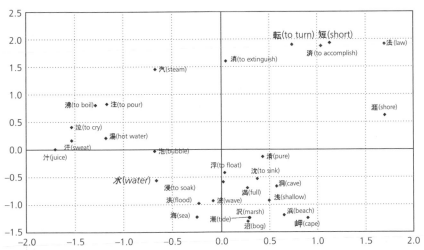

Fig. 5.7 Multidimensional scaling solution for 29 Kanji from a cluster that is based on the radical for /mizuhen/ or 'water'.

Notes: Semantic categorization of kanji with the radical 'water' (Mizuhen) The large character 水 in italics is the kanji for 'water'. Large characters, 岬, 短 and 転 are kanji with no 'water' radical.

actually involve water in some form to things that are merely associated with water.

Overall, the entire set of 1945 Kanji are based on just 199 radicals where there are between 1 and 103 Kanji per radical. Although the individual Kanji operate as Japanese words, they also operate in combination with other Kanji to form thousands of other Japanese words. The spoken forms of these words often involve the spoken forms for each of the individual Kanji that make up the word, but they sometimes involve a completely new spoken form, as in the case of the Tekujikun word set.

Using the Sydney Morning Herald Database (Dennis, 1995), we prepared Zipf functions for data sets from English. The functions for English are depicted in Figure 5.8(a). The functions involve token counts for English words and letters, respectively. The English word frequency values were derived from the Sydney Morning Herald Database, and the English letter frequency values were derived from the word set. The database comprised 97,031 different words. As shown in Figure 5.8(a), the relationship between English word frequency and ensemble size, and the relationship between English letter frequency and ensemble size approach but do not precisely conform to Zipf's law. That is, a power function is observed for the high frequency items, with an exponent close to one, but for lower frequency items, the slope of the line takes a sharp drop away from unity.

The functions depicted in Figure 5.8(b) involve the Kanji characters and radicals. The Kanji values were derived from column 9 of the Database of Characteristics of the 1945 Basic Japanese Kanji (Tamaoka et al., 2002). The analysis involved 1945 Kanji types, 248 radical types, and 24,280,450 Kanji tokens. Figure 5.8(b) involves the number of *tokens* associated with each Kanji. The radical values are the sums of the frequency values for each radical, where frequency for each radical was determined by summing the frequency values associated with each of the Kanji associated with each of the individual radicals. The radical analysis is, therefore, a *token* analysis too; it involves the number of *tokens* associated with each radical. As shown in Figure 5.8(b), the relationship between ensemble size and Kanji character frequency, and the relationship between ensemble size and radical frequency, approach but do not precisely conform to Zipf's law.

However, these analyses do not exhaust the way in which the argument introduced by Zipf can be discerned in the Japanese script. It is also possible to examine the relationship between the radicals and Kanji. The radicals are constituents of Kanji but as there are only 248 approximate radicals and 1945 Kanji, many of the radicals are present in more than one Kanji, as illustrated in Figure 5.7 where a single radical serves more than 20 Kanji. On average of

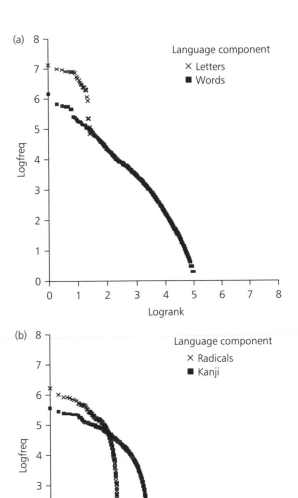

Fig. 5.8 Frequency rank distributions of (a) English letters and words and (b) Japanese Kanji and radicals.

course, we might expect about eight Kanji per radical. But the data yield yet another Zipf function. The most popular radical is present in 103 Kanji but there is only one radical in this class. The least popular radicals are present in just one Kanji but there are no fewer than 77 radicals in this class; that is, there are 77 radicals and Kanji with a 1 : 1 mapping.

The examples depicted above suggest that Zipf-like functions are universal, while recognizing that the exponent is not in all cases equal to unity. The Zipf function is relevant to the arguments developed in this book for several reasons. First, it provides the platform for the proposition that lexical models should reflect the dynamic properties of both the cultural and cognitive lexica. If the constraints that govern language acquisition are to be inferred from the mathematical characteristics of corpora, it follows that assumptions about the latter are critical to models of lexical development, and lexical change in the individual. The second reason stems from the fact that the Zipf function and even the more recent analyses that involve departures from the original model all involve reference to resource limitations as the critical determinant of Zipf or Zipf-like functions. The third reason involves the proposition that a priori segregation of language by stimulus class is inappropriate, and that all categories or levels, from letters to discourse, should be treated as if they belong to a single system until and unless this assumption is falsified. It is possible, for example, that the relationship between ensemble size and frequency conforms to a single Zipf function straddling all stimulus types.

The exponents of the functions described above approach but do not equal unity. But, if it is assumed that they are characteristics of a dynamic system driven by both internal and external forces, this is to be expected (Halloy, 1998). But let us abandon the 'pre-theoretical' assumption that words and letters must be treated as qualitatively different systems on *linguistic* grounds. The next analysis treats this assumption as a question, and uses Zipf functions to test the relevant hypotheses. If the frequency rank distribution for words and letters fit a single function, we can infer that the two stimulus types belong to a single system. But if the frequency rank distribution involves a discontinuous function, we can infer that they form different systems. Figure 5.9(a) shows the results for words and letters, and it is apparent that the function is discontinuous, as if words and letters occupy distinct regions in the frequency rank distribution space, and do not, therefore, constitute a single system. Figure 5.9(b) shows the results for Kanji and the radicals, and it is apparent that the function is continuous, as if these stimulus types occupy a single region in the frequency rank distribution space, and that they therefore constitute a single system. There is of course an obvious difference between the relationship between words and letters and the relationship between Kanji

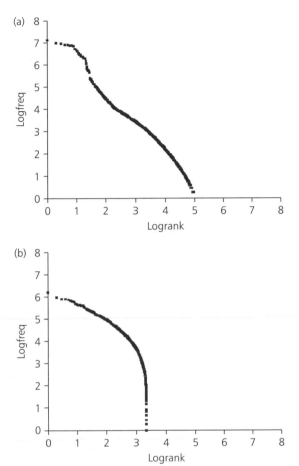

Fig. 5.9 Frequency rank distributions of (a) English letters and words combined and (b) Japanese Kanji and radicals combined.

and radicals; letters do not provide any semantic information about words whereas radicals do provide semantic information about the Kanji.

The results depicted in Figure 5.9 are suggestive. We are using Zipf to provide new leverage on a very old question about *systems* (e.g. Crowder, 1972; Tulving, 1983). The procedure does not involve dissociation. Instead, it involves questions about continuity and discontinuity. It is our contention that discontinuity is consistent with the presence of two systems, whereas continuity is consistent with explanations based on the presence of a single system. The procedure does not rely on dissociation but on tests of mathematical discontinuity involving large datasets. The analysis involves a somewhat different notion of the term *system*, however. Whereas the distinctions between short-term memory and long-term memory, and semantic and episodic memory, involve functional or even engineering principles, the system question that is of interest to us involves set membership; do letters and words behave as if they belong to a single pool, or system, or do they behave as if they belong to two pools or systems?

Caution is of course required. Our argument involves evidence that while the exponent of the function relating rank and frequency approaches unity, substantial departures from this value have been reported (e.g. Cancho and Sole, 2003). It is also evident that the functions tend to depart from unity in the low frequency ranges, as we have found here, as well as in the very high frequency ranges (Kornai, 1999; Powers, 1998). It is also evident that token size influences the relationship, with dramatic effects on both mean word frequency and the proportion of hapaxes, words that occur only once in the database (Kornai, 1999; Sproat and Shih, 1996). Assumptions about these issues have important implications for interpretation. Cancho and Sole (2003), for example, proposed that the Zipf function for English words actually involves two components, where $\alpha_1 \approx -1$ and $\alpha_2 \approx -2$, respectively. Kornai (1999) has advanced a comparable point of view based on evidence that the lexicon comprises two 'urns' one for high frequency function words, and the other for content words from mid-range and low frequency words.

The case for treating the lexicon as if it is a dynamic system does not depend solely on arguments about the extent to which it conforms to Zipf. There are compelling and independent reasons why the lexicon should be conceptualized in this way. The problem is in some respects comparable to that faced by oceanographers when they predict the movement of flotsam 100 km off the coast of Western Australia. Movement in this realm involves a liquid mass that is touched by a host of variables, as well as interactions among these variables. It is also of interest that some of these variables involve low velocities, vast areas, and slow moment-to-moment fluctuations in direction, whereas other variables involve high velocities, localized movement, and high rates of change. The relevant list of variables ranges from oceanic drift, a process that moves slowly and involves slow rates of change, to leeway and wind driven current, variables that involve high velocities and rapid changes in velocity and direction. Thus, oceanic drift involves a general anticlockwise movement of water around the Indian Ocean. Two hundred kilometres off the coast of Western Australia, it might involve a regional movement of 5–10 km per day, to the north. Inshore, another current runs in the opposite direction, from north to south, and at a velocity that varies from season-to-season and year-to-year. Where these currents meet, turbulence including vast nebulae is common, and the water movements are variable and unpredictable. Over and above these processes, the wind induces movement in the surface layer of the water, and a 15–20 knot wind from the south-east might move an object at 1 km per hour or more to the north-west. And over and above these variables, if the flotsam is light, and includes an above-water component, the wind will act directly on the exposed surface, and produce a leeway movement. But even this is not all. Vast oceanic highs roll in from the west. They involve changes in the height of the water of less than 50 cm but as flotsam usually go around them rather than over them, *and they can be up to 50 km in diameter*, their impact on the movement of flotsam can be dramatic.

Now let us turn back to the lexicon. One of the slowest moving variables involves the drift that occurs between dialects or languages when a single cultural and linguistic group is divided by migration. Swadesh (1952, see Kruskal *et al.*, 1971) determined that the rate at which word substitution occurred for words from 371 pairs of Malayo-Polynesian languages is approximately 20% per millennium. This type of change might or might not occur in the mind of the individual, but it is a consideration if we wish to embrace the cultural lexicon as well as the cognitive lexicon.

A second variable involves the unknown but implied relationship between type and token frequency within the vocabulary of the individual. It must change with experience and therefore age. But how does it change? What does the relationship between type functions look like for a 2-year-old child? Does the function conform to the relationship observed for adults? A *possible* relationship is depicted in Figure 5.10. The abscissa involves accumulated practice rather than word frequency because word frequency will change as a function of age. The figure depicts one way in which the relationship might develop with chronological age. It shows a simple quantitative change; the practice and

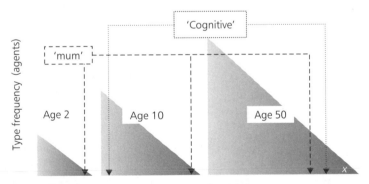

Fig. 5.10 Hypothetical relationship between type frequency and practice at 2, 10, and 50 years of age. Speculative trajectories for 'Mum' (dashed arrows) and 'Cognitive' (dotted arrows) are implied by the arrows. The density gradient is used to indicate changes in particles per agent. Thus, at x, the ratio of particles to Agents will be high.

therefore the token values increase with age (on the abscissa), the number of word types increases with age (on the ordinate), and the slope describing the relationship between type and token frequency is a constant. The figure highlights a point we made earlier, concerning the scale of the difference in total practice between early words and late words. Whereas late words are practiced in the context of thousands or even tens of thousands of word types, early words are practiced in the context of ten or fewer words; and their practice values will be orders of magnitude higher than the levels reached by later words. This issue has not yet touched the debate concerning the relative effects of word frequency and age of acquisition.

A third variable involves the trajectories for the individual items in the lexicon. Consider Figure 5.10 again. The figure includes two cases, cases that could be applied to the authors. The first case involves MUM. The figure implies that MUM is the most practiced word in the lexicon at ages 2 and 10 but that it falls away thereafter, to a mid-frequency range by age 50. COGNITIVE has a completely different history, however. It was not present in the production lexicon at age 2, and it had barely entered that lexicon by age 10 but by age 50, it has one of the highest practice counts of any word. We could not discover any data involving cases such as these, yet, the effects must be there, and an effective model of lexical function will need to consider them.

A fourth variable involves homography, which involves words with more than one meaning, BANK being an obvious example. Baayen and Tweedie (1998) detected small departures from linearity in Zipf-like functions, and then used translation equivalents to show how the departures reflected separate contributions from each of the potential meanings. They reported evidence that the observed frequency standings of homographs reflect contributions from component frequencies that are specific to each meaning. Thus, the position of BANK in word frequency counts should reflect the sum of the frequency values for the WET, MONETARY, and AERONAUTICAL senses of the term, and the overall distribution will be distorted accordingly. The assumption that the cognitive lexicon is sense-specific is supported by evidence that repetition priming is context-sensitive, and therefore specific to meaning, and that the individual senses or meanings of words can be primed as if they involve separate representations (Bainbridge et al., 1993). Thus, sequential presentation of DOLLAR and then BANK in the priming phase of an experiment will yield priming for BANK during a subsequent test presentation if and only if it is preceded by a monetary term, such as FINANCE; sequential presentation of RIVER and then BANK during the test phase will not yield repetition priming. Thus, analysis of the cultural lexicon arguably involves countless questions concerning sense and nuance, and the impact of these issues on the frequency counts for each type.

Another source of change involves what Clarke and Nerlich (1991) referred to as 'word waves'. According to their analysis, not only do words change their meanings, but meanings change their words as well. 'Gay' is an interesting and familiar example. Fifty years ago, 'gay' referred to a familiar and unremarkable name, or a happy and frivolous mood. But it has acquired a new and very different meaning in the intervening decades. Clarke and Nerlich considered the idea that changes in the relationships between words and meanings actually follow a regular pattern, as novelty and boredom produce regular changes in word usage.

The issues discussed above suggest a change in granularity. In particular, they suggest that a full understanding of Zipf functions will only be attained when we understand the dynamics of a mass of specific word classes or even individual words. The relevant list of word classes may eventually reflect the following distinctions and variables: orthographic regularity, open and closed class words, content and function words, word frequency, age of acquisition, grammatical class, imagery and sense, nuance and homography, for example.

In summary then, there are compelling reasons to adopt the assumption that the lexicon is a dynamic system, and that we should model it accordingly. The critical factor probably involves interaction. If these and many other variables interact with each other in the lexicon, adoption of a dynamic hypothesis may be unavoidable.

5.7.2 Principles requiring review and explanation

Our argument differs from other approaches involving decomposition. We specifically stand aside from the proposition that every stimulus type and level requires its own paradigms, module, and model. Instead, it is our assumption that a single over-arching explanation is required, and that synthesis rather than analysis is critical. Our argument also differs from many other arguments about 'things, words and the brain' (Oldfield, 1966) in that it presupposes the operation of a 'dumb' system, a system that does not depend on genetically programmed modules, and a system that treats all perceptual events or objects in essentially the same way.

The argument advanced here is that all transfer effects in repetition priming and skill acquisition reflect the operation of a single principle. It is our contention that this principle is honoured in operations that occur at each of many levels of stimulus analysis for both 'perceptual' and 'symbolic' objects. We have used the term honoured deliberately. It is not our assumption that the principles are present in the form of rules or algorithms in the relevant neurological structures. Rather, it is that each structure is shaped by the same biological and evolutionary pressures, and that they have evolved essentially the same procedures for dealing with the same set of problems.

If a single principle (i.e. Principle 1) governs performance improvements associated with learning including repetition priming, it follows that frequency of occurrence will have qualitatively or even quantitatively comparable effects on all stimulus classes. This is of course an extension of our assumption about the negatively accelerated feature of learning. It is that residual improvement— the amount of benefit that will flow from one additional presentation—will be inversely related to practice. Evaluation of this hypothesis is complicated by several considerations, however.

One such consideration involves the fact that residual improvement arguably involves stimulus components as well as the whole stimulus. Thus, residual improvement for a complex word, such as PUBLICITY will be influenced by the amount of prior practice on the whole word, PUBLICITY, the morphological components of that word, PUBLIC and ITY, the cross-modal forms of that word, 'publicity', 'public', and 'ity', and, under some circumstances at least, the cross-language forms, as for PUBLIC for Spanish–English bilinguals. It is also possible that even finer components will function as records, if they are repeated under functionally equivalent conditions. As stated in Principle 5, the array of representations that contribute to the processing of a word will reflect experience with the word and the family of words to which it belongs.

Principle 5 actually involves a suite of related assumptions. The first and most general of these arguments involves the concept of *decomposition*. It is our claim that the system deals with all types of stimuli in essentially the same way. Decomposition is therefore relevant to many *levels of analysis*—from discourse to letter analysis, for example—and to all stimulus forms including speech, print, signs, sounds, and the pictorial world. Decomposition involves a number of subsidiary arguments.

The first of these involves *discovery*. Discovery involves an attempt to find structures or constituents of the current stimulus over which experience has been accumulated. Thus, in a word, such as publicity, decomposition will involve an attempt to discover established constituents, where PUBLIC and ITY constitute obvious examples for PUBLICITY. The second subsidiary argument involves *accumulation*. Constituent representations are defined and protected solely by success. Constituent representations are not established unless they are re-used during interpretation or communication. Constituents or elements that are not repeated with essentially the same meaning or value in other stimuli and other contexts do not become established. The third subsidiary argument involves *re-description* (Kirsner and Dunn, 1985). Discovery and accumulation are not restricted to surface form. They can also, we claim, involve contact between the product of re-descriptions of the current stimulus and the products of re-descriptions of past stimuli, a claim that provides a bridge between the spoken and printed forms of words. Discovery, accumulation, and re-description each imply reference to the fourth of our subsidiary arguments, involving what we will refer to as *records* (Kirsner and Dunn, 1985). Records are created as by-products of perceptual, discovery, and generative processes, and they therefore reflect the many ways in which perceptual objects can be decomposed, re-described, and transformed. The fifth subsidiary argument involves the concept of *resource competition*, the idea that all other things being equal, re-descriptions that involve accumulation over large sets of tokens or types will triumph over re-descriptions that involve small sets of tokens and types. The sixth subsidiary argument involves the concept of *self-similarity*. Although this chapter is primarily concerned with words, it is our assumption that the system characteristics under the microscope are present at all levels of analysis, from discourse to letters. This means, for example, that Zipf-like relationships should be present at all levels of system description, from discourse to letter recognition. But there is an important caveat. Although levels provide an obvious basis for system analysis and description, it should not in our opinion be assumed that each of the obvious levels is represented *as such* in either the cognitive or neurological system. A more parsimonious assumption is available. It is that the levels of language that have formed the basis of psycho-linguistic analysis for decades are not recognized as such at the cognitive or neurological levels. The system is in this sense, dumb; it looks for representations that correspond to any part or the whole of a stimulus array, and the representations themselves are not specifically organized in terms of letters or other constituents. Clearly, the Zipf law must be present in some form, but that form could involve all possible levels of analysis.

The notion of levels is critical. Are we dealing with levels in the systematic sense associated with psycho-linguistic analysis, for example? Should we regard discourse, sentences, phrases, words, and letters as qualitatively distinct domains, requiring unique and specific principles? Or should we rather assume that these 'levels' are mere artifacts of a single complex system, a system where self-resemblance is critical, and the entire system follows a single set of principles? Essentially the same question can be posed with reference to morphology, mode, and modality, and to transfer of practice and repetition priming effects across these forms. Do each of the many forms and operations implied by these terms involve separate levels of process, or do they too reflect the operation of a single set of principles?

The argument that we would like to advance is functional. If a particular constituent belongs to a collection or system that comprises repeatable elements, that collection of constituents will conform to the same basic principles regardless of questions about level, granularity, and stimulus type. It will be valid for graphemes, letter bigrams, morphologically defined stems, lemmas, words, and many other constituent types, and it will be valid for constituents in all language types, including Japanese and Chinese, and the various sign systems. Our approach dispenses entirely with the notion of modules, and deals instead with component processes that are created by the repeated presentation and use of constituents, regardless of mode, modality, and language.

The foregoing analysis raises the question of 'self-similarity'. We have claimed that essentially the same principles can be applied to all stimulus classes and to all forms of transfer. Should we expect qualitatively comparable priming and transfer effects at different levels of granularity as well? More specifically, should transfer conform to the same principle for letters and discourse as well as words? Our provisional answer to this question is 'yes'. If self-similarity applies to letters, words, and discourse, for example, we would expect repetition priming to operate at each of these levels, as it does (e.g. Rueckl, 1995, for letters, and Levy and Kirsner, 1990, for text). The patterns of transfer relationships between levels are less clear, and prediction is in any case problematic. Speelman *et al.* (2002), for example, found small levels of transfer when students were exposed to test words that they had previously encountered to different extents in a set text, but Rueckl (1995) found little or no transfer from the word to letter level.

The Sierpinski triangle (Figure 5.11) is often used to illustrate the concept of self-similarity as it has been applied to fractals. The critical feature in our analogy is that objects remain the same even when they are zoomed through an infinite number of levels. Approximate self-similarity is achieved when the observed pattern looks recognizably similar but not identical at all levels of zoom. For us, of course, the analogy involves inferred *patterns of representation* rather than objects. Is decomposition a universal feature for all stimulus types? Is it present in qualitatively comparable ways as we move from discourse, to sentences, to words, letters, scenes, and faces? For example, can the priming effects observed for morphologically related words be discerned in transfer effects involving other stimulus types? Are the effects of decomposition sensitive to practice in qualitatively comparable ways as we move across the various levels and stimulus types?

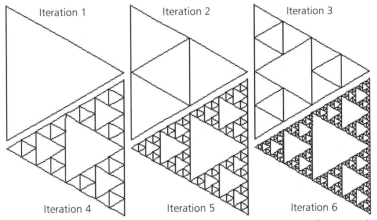

Fig. 5.11 Illustration of self-similarity involving the Sierpinski gasket (from Bourke, 1993).

In summary then, although this chapter is primarily concerned with words, it is our assumption that the system characteristics of interest are present at all levels of granularity, from discourse to letter features, for example, and in all types of stimulus classes, from words to signs and objects. The importance of putting Kanji on the table in addition to English is that it undermines arguments that assume that the representation levels associated with psycho-linguistic analysis of English are *necessary*.

5.8 **Distributions and mechanisms**

The major conclusion of this chapter is that a skill acquisition account provides a satisfactory explanation of the mental lexicon. In particular, lexical data reveals patterns that are wholly consistent with the operation of the Learning Principles 1 and 5 identified in Chapter 4. This conclusion led us to propose that a person's mental lexicon is therefore a product of that person's language experience. As a result, the lexicon should reflect the structure of the cultural lexicon and a person's interaction with it. The missing elements in our argument, however, are the same elements missing from the Component Theory of Skill Acquisition described in Chapter 4. As yet, we have not proposed any mechanisms that could underlie the theory and therefore have not indicated how a lexicon might work. In the remainder of the chapter, we start with the intimate relationship that we posit exists between cognitive and cultural lexica, and end with some pointers to what these mechanisms could be. Full details of these mechanisms are presented in Chapter 6.

We have made much of the fact that distributions of words in lexica are at least in part consistent with Zipf's law. Zipf-like functions have been reported for a variety of inanimate as well as animate phenomena. An illustrative list includes the size of earthquakes, the scale of forest fires, and the height of sandhills. Zipf-like functions have also been reported for complex social phenomena, such as city size, the distribution of professions, and the magnitude of stock market crashes. In addition, if consideration is extended to Pareto's law, a close relative of the power law (i.e. Zipf's law), the list can be extended to include income distribution and visitors to Internet sites. The ubiquity of these functions introduces a particularly challenging question. Do they reflect some artifactual process involving the law of probabilities, or do they reflect an as yet unidentified principle that stands above the distinctions between the organization of animate, inanimate, and social systems? The most parsimonious approach to this problem involves the assumption that several descriptive and modelling levels must be involved, and that convergence can be expected at only the highest level, if at all. Consider, for example, recent work on genomic properties. Luscombe *et al.* (2002) noted that frequency of occurrence of the generalized molecular parts associated with genomes followed the power law with a few parts occurring many times and most parts occurring only a few times. Luscombe *et al.* attributed these patterns to a DNA duplication process as genomes evolved to their present state. It might be appropriate to hypothesize that while this explanation involves the same general principle as that which applies to the Zipf-like functions for words, the relevant explanations must involve different physical material. They involve different domains, and the critical question concerns the presence or otherwise of a single over-arching principle, a principle that could be applied to both the animate and inanimate domains while protecting the assumption that they enjoy distinct physical mechanisms.

Halloy advanced a model that reflects this point of view (Halloy, 1998). Halloy's argument includes reference to evidence involving the evolution of both animate and inanimate systems, and employs an over-arching principle to account for the ubiquity of Zipf-like functions. Complex adaptive systems, according to Halloy, consist of agents that are made up of particles. Agents compete with each other for resources. Particles are the basic unit of resource for which agents compete. Agents can grow in size because they have been able to attract more particles, or they can split to create two or more smaller agents. According to Halloy (1998, p. 5), 'The abundance distributions of agents tends to a power function with increasing slope towards the right in a log–log rank abundance relation or a log-normal'. However, the term 'tend' is critical. Halloy adopts the further assumption that 'natural systems will approximate to log-normal models when left to their internal mechanisms, while distancing themselves from the log-normal when pressured by external forces'

(Halloy, 1998, p. 3), an assumption that 'circumvents the debate on the appropriate mathematical distributions to fit to natural systems' (Halloy, 1998, p. 3). Nonetheless, the log-normal distribution in a frequency-abundance context is '... a signature of complex systems'. (Halloy, 1998, p. 2).

Halloy's analysis raises a novel issue for the lexical world. Let us assume that Halloy's analysis can be applied to at least three levels in the reading world, a lexical level, a sub-lexical level, involving letters and other orthographic features, and a supra-lexical level involving phrases, sentences, or even concepts, and that, at the lexical level, the distinction between particles and agents in Halloy's account mirrors that between types and tokens in the lexical world. If this is granted, it follows that diversification and speciation occur when a particular type (e.g. 'mum') reaches a size (number of particles) that is not sustainable within the infrastructure, and a split involving the creation of a sibling or child occurs. This might involve the distinction between MOM and MUM, for example, where the former refers to MOTHER while the latter refers to the need to remain silent about a topic. But a particularly interesting question concerns vocabulary development. Is it possible, for example, that vocabulary development depends directly on differentiation where the step from a one word vocabulary to a two word vocabulary as well as all subsequent steps involves division in the evolutionary sense? The implications of this approach for both the cultural and cognitive lexica are challenging.

The axis labels in Figure 5.10 reflect two perspectives, one empirical and one theoretical. The empirical perspective involves Types and Tokens. Type refers to number of different *word types*, a variable that will fluctuate with age, education, and experience. Token refers to *total encounters* for each word type. Although *total encounters* can only remain stable or increase, the possibility that word types will die in the absence of use cannot be discounted. As depicted, the number of *word types* is the inverse of *total encounters*; there are many word types with low encounter counts, and very few word types with high encounter counts. Thus, for a corpus of 1 million words, there might be only one word type with a total encounter count of 10,000 whereas there might be 10,000 words with a total encounter count of 1. The second perspective is theoretical, and it involves the parallel between word types and agents on the one hand, and total encounters and particles on the other. Our argument follows Halloy's analysis of abundance distributions (Halloy and Whigham, 2004). Halloy's model was originally advanced to explain changes in the behaviour of crop species. Agents and particles are substituted for types and tokens, respectively. In Halloy's account, a small number of agents acquire a large number of particles, and a large number of agents acquire very small numbers of particles. But Halloy has added an interesting twist to the conventional account. According to Halloy, the agents compete with one another for resources, and success is measured in terms of the acquisition of large numbers of particles, an outcome that involves only a small number of agents. Now let us return to the lexicon. Each word type is an agent, and each occurrence is a token. Each agent or word type *wins* if it can increase its range of application, although, if it wins too big, and causes confusion, it runs the risk of splitting into two or more word types. Zipf's Law, or more generally, a log-normal distribution, will therefore be a by-product of this process; showing the relationship between number of word types and token encounters at any one moment.

If, as we are suggesting, lexica, including both cognitive and cultural types, are complex adaptive systems, then one would expect that abundance distributions of words, and related stimuli, should conform to the log-normal. The drop-off on the right side of the functions in Figure 5.8 is consistent with this suggestion, as this pattern is characteristic of the log-normal (Halloy and Whigham, 2004). A more explicit test of this proposition is possible, however. Figure 5.12 presents a test of whether the distributions of words and letters depicted in Figure 5.8 conform to the log-normal, either individually, or together. Figure 5.13 represents the same sort of test with the Kanji and radicals data of Figure 5.8. Figure 5.12 shows that when words and letters are considered as one set, the log-normal does not provide a very good fit to the distribution, but the distribution of words considered alone is described well by the log-normal. Letters on their own also appear to approximate the log-normal, although even within letters there appears to be a distinction between the high frequency letters and a handful of low frequency letters. Figure 5.13 presents quite a different picture. Although the radicals and the Kanji, when considered individually, do approximate the log-normal, when they are considered together, the log-normal provides a far closer fit to the distribution than in either of the individual cases.

The analysis of whether the log-normal describes the abundance distributions of the letter/words Kanji/radicals is revealing on several fronts. First, the fact that the log-normal fits the distributions so closely is consistent with the proposition that we are observing complex adaptive systems. In the case of the Japanese characters, it would appear that despite the linguistic distinction that is often invoked with respect to Kanji and radicals, this analysis suggests they operate as part of the same system. In contrast, the analysis suggests that letters and words do indeed function as part of separate systems. Second, the different results for Japanese and English appear to match what is known about 'systems' within these languages. For instance, although each Kanji has a specific meaning, the radicals that make up each Kanji also have their own

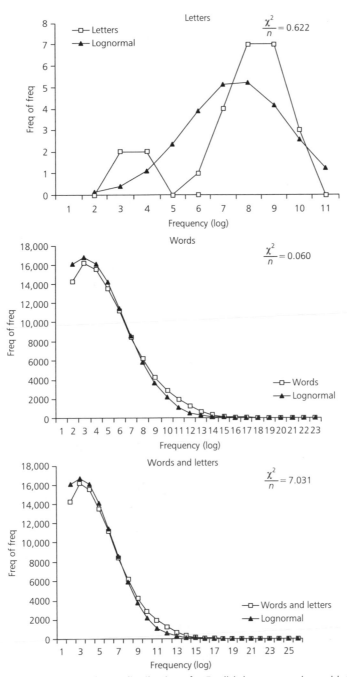

Fig. 5.12 Frequency abundance distributions for English letters, words, and letters and words combined, and log-normal distribution fits.

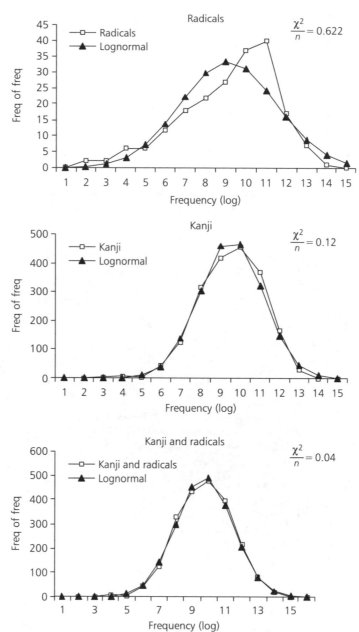

Fig. 5.13 Frequency abundance distributions for Japanese radicals, Kanji, and radicals and Kanji combined, and log-normal distribution fits.

meaning, and so can have a linguistic 'life' of their own. That is, radicals can function as Kanji on their own. Therefore, in one sense, Kanji and radicals are all meaning units and probably compete with each other to be used in communication. In contrast, although words comprise letters, the algorithms that determine which letters go into which words are not based on meaning, but on sound. Hence, the function of words in language is quite different to that of letters, and so it should not be surprising that they would appear to operate as two separate systems.

The closeness with which the notion of complex adaptive systems fits the abundance distributions within English and Japanese leads us to propose that these systems may have wider applicability within cognition. In the final chapter of the book, we explore this idea by adopting Halloy's characterization of complex systems as inspiration for a set of mechanisms to underlie the Component Theory of Skill Acquisition.

Chapter 6

A new view

The art of being wise is the art of knowing what to overlook.

William James

In coming to consider complex systems ... history is important.

Mark Buchanan

The failure of applied statisticians and social scientists to heed Zipf helps account for the striking backwardness of their fields.

Benoit Mandelbrot

In Chapter 1, we identified a problem with the field of Cognitive Psychology. The Problem is that most explanations of cognitive phenomena involve the proposal of systems without any consideration for the origins of these systems. As such, we consider such attempts at explanations merely re-descriptions of the phenomena. We also stated in Chapter 1 a solution to the Problem, which was that the origins of systems should always be considered, with learning playing a central role in the development of cognitive systems. Consideration of the learning origins of systems could lead to greater insight into the operations of those systems.

A further claim made in Chapter 1 was that our argument regarding the central role of learning in cognitive development should be tested against several criteria. We proposed several levels of criteria for determining whether a theory of skill acquisition could also serve as an explanation of more general cognitive phenomena. The Skill Acquisition Phenomena Criterion concerned the ability of a theory to account for the 'basic facts' of skill acquisition. As our argument progressed throughout the book, the basic facts were summarized as the five Principles of Learning. In Chapters 2 and 3, we evaluated the extent to which existing theories of skill acquisition could account for these principles and associated data. We concluded that none of the theories could account for all of the data. The major area of failure concerned the way in which transfer affected the shape of learning curves.

In Chapter 4, we presented the Component Theory of Skill Acquisition as our attempt to make-up the shortfall left behind by earlier theories. In some respects, this theory can be considered as inheriting many of the successful elements of the previous theories while overcoming the limitations of those theories. In particular, the Component Theory was developed to provide an account of the effects of transfer on the shape of learning curves.

In Chapter 5, we considered whether a theory of skill acquisition, such as the Component Theory could meet the Behaviour Phenomena Criterion identified in Chapter 1. That is, could the theory account for phenomena in an area where skill acquisition accounts are not traditionally considered? We demonstrated that commonly observed phenomena in research examining the mental lexicon—namely repetition priming and how the extent of priming is determined by the similarity of repeated presentations of a word—are amenable to a skill acquisition explanation.

Having concluded that the Component Theory of Skill Acquisition meets the Skill Acquisition Phenomena and Behaviour Phenomena Criteria, it is now necessary to test the theory against the Biology, Evolution, and Explanation Criteria. The first two of these criteria relate to whether a theory fits with non-Psychological data. That is, is the theory compatible with known principles of brain function and evolution? The third criterion concerns the extent to which the theory provides an explanation of phenomena rather than just a re-description. In particular, can the theory provide an account of the learning principles without building those principles into the theory? To evaluate the theory against these criteria requires that the mechanisms underlying the theory be described. The purpose of this chapter, then, is to describe these mechanisms and then complete the evaluation of the theory. At the end of the chapter, we also consider whether learning could be central to all cognitive phenomena and the implications this holds for Cognitive Psychology in particular and Psychology in general.

In Chapter 5, it was noted that features of distributions of words in lexica were consistent with abundance distributions associated with the operation of complex adaptive systems. In addition, we highlighted several characteristics of the behaviour of words that were similar to the behaviour of entities in complex systems (Halloy, 1998; Halloy and Whigham, 2004). As a result, we have been inspired to suggest that the human mind is a complex system and to develop the Component Theory as a human instantiation of Halloy's theory. Thus, the mechanisms underlying our theory honour Halloy's description of the behaviour of agents and particles in complex systems. In the next section we describe Halloy's theory in detail, and then follow this with a presentation of The Component Theory of Skill Acquisition that assumes the mind is a complex system.

6.1 Halloy's theory of complex systems

According to Halloy, all complex systems possess a range of character-istics that give rise to similar statistical relationships. Four important concepts in Halloy's theory are those of resources, particles, agents, and boundaries.

> *Resources* (are) anything for which agents may compete...*Particles* are the minimum units of resources. From an agent's viewpoint they are discrete packages of resources of variable size or 'mass'. Particles are analogous to individuals in a biological population, to quanta of light or space in a plant community, to particles of dust in the cosmos, or to economic elements....*Agents* arise when an initial undifferentiated mass of particles breaks up or coalesces (i.e. boundaries are formed) into a number of parts. Each agent contains or controls a number of particles. Agents are analogous to species or companies....*Boundaries* are formed where interactions are proportionally more important between the particles inside the agent than they are between them and particles outside. The same applies for boundaries between systems at a higher level. Boundaries fluctuate and have a certain degree of permeability.
>
> (Halloy, 1998, p. 3, italics added)

> Complex adaptive systems have been characterized as systems made up of interacting agents which use rules to maximize their survival....A unifying feature of such systems is that agents are 'greedy', i.e. they attract resources, as much resources as they can grab. However, in evolved systems this attraction may become remarkably subtle, with time delays and complicated strategic decisions to forego a resource here and now for one in the future and somewhere else. Since agents are greedy, they necessarily compete for resources. Hence possibly the primal feature of complex systems is greed (or more euphemistically, resource attraction) and competition as its secondary outcome. It is this resource attraction and competition which in turn determines the primary interactions between agents, as well as the adaptive nature of agents changing rules to outcompete others.
>
> (Halloy and Whigham, 2004, p. 4)

The competition for resources between agents in a complex system can result in the development of clusters of agents into larger agents or the splitting of large agents into smaller ones. The conditions under which these two outcomes occur are determined, in part, by the level of attraction between and among agents and particles in the system. This attraction is proportional to the existing resources of the agents (i.e. larger agents are more 'attractive'), and inversely proportional to the difficulty in obtaining resources (i.e. agents are more likely to attract particles or to combine with other agents when this will make obtaining resources easier).

Two important outcomes of the competition for resources that Halloy (Halloy and Whigham, 2004) highlights are differentiation and adaptation of agents.

> (A)ll agents eventually reach a size where their growth is not practical within their infrastructure. At this point they split...into sibling or parent and offspring agents (e.g. bacteria splitting, plants sprouting new shoots...). Initially, as they are informationally almost identical, these siblings may be considered part of the growing

agent. However, this split has set the stage for the drifting of information which leads to *differentiation* and diversification. As differentiation (inevitably) proceeds, the siblings become different agents separated by informational barriers and competing with each other. In biology this is known as speciation.

(p. 5, italics added)

(E)volving agents typically explore new pathways and opportunities to attract resources. This is a consequence of resource attraction as modified by differentiation. As they explore new state space and rules, some agents find more efficient ways to capture resources and survive, while others die off. This is the process of evolution and *adaptation*.

(p. 6, italics added)

Halloy (1998) has demonstrated that complex systems with the features described above can evolve into systems with abundance distributions that are log-normal (i.e. a class of distributions of which Zipf's law is a subset). That is, complex systems possess a small number of large agents, a large number of small agents, and a smooth transition between these two extremes.

Log-normal abundance distributions have been observed throughout nature and indeed throughout a range of human affairs. For instance, Halloy and Whigham (2004) report that such distributions exist in 'planet sizes, earthquakes, animal and plant sizes and abundances, sizes of firms, behaviour of the stock market, (and) traffic congestion'. (p. 7). They have even been observed in the size of potato fragments that occur when a frozen potato is smashed into pieces (see box below). All of the situations in which such distributions have been observed constitute 'networks of interacting things under non-equilibrium conditions' (Buchanan, 2000, p. 16), and such systems are known as complex systems. Halloy's theory represents an explanation for how such systems evolve, and is general to all complex systems. Below we extend this ubiquity to human cognition and thereby suggest that the functioning of the mind follows universal laws of nature.

Frozen potatoes

If you throw a frozen potato against a wall with sufficient force, it will shatter into many pieces. These pieces will typically vary in size. If you smash several such potatoes in this manner, and then compare the sizes of the resulting fragments, you will notice a simple relationship between fragment size and the frequency of occurrence of particular fragment sizes. For instance, you could group the pieces into 10 piles of ascending size, with the pile of smallest pieces being one gram (ignore pieces smaller than this for the moment). You will notice that there will be many more pieces in the small sized pile, and this

Frozen potatoes (*continued*)

number will get smaller as the fragment size of a pile gets larger. In other words, small pieces are far more common than large pieces. The relationship is actually a systematic one—with each doubling of the weight of a fragment, the number of fragments of that size will be reduced by a factor of six. This relationship is a form of power function similar to the Zipf function discussed in Chapter 5. Furthermore, this relationship does not just exist in fragments down to 1 gm. Many fragments smaller than 1 gm would be created by the smashing of several frozen potatoes. If you repeated the above procedure of dividing these small fragments into 10 piles that vary according to size, you would observe exactly the same relationship between the number of fragments in a pile and the weight of those fragments. In other words, the power function relationship that exists for one range of mass values also exists for another range of values. It turns out that this relationship exists for all ranges of mass values up to the pre-smash mass of each potato and theoretically down to the mass of an atom, although practical limits occur at low masses due to cohesion. This example reflects a characteristic feature of complex systems known as scale invariance or *self-similarity*—a property of a system that is observed at one level of a system can be observed at other levels of the system. In frozen potatoes, it is the relationship between the size of fragments and frequency of occurrence of fragments, in earthquakes it is the relationship between the magnitude of an earthquake and its relative likelihood of occurrence, and in humans it is the relationship between task performance speed and amount of practice. In all these cases, the mathematical relationship observed at one level of the system is observed at all levels of the system.

(adapted in part from Buchanan, 2000, ch. 3)

6.2 The Component Theory of Skill Acquisition: the mind as a complex system

The basic unit in the Component Theory of Skill Acquisition has, until now, been the component process. We have not been precise about the nature of these processes, but it has been sufficient to simply consider these as properties of the brain that carry out some form of information processing. Ultimately these component processes must be related to the functioning of neurons in the brain, which essentially are processors of information. In order to develop a theory of skill acquisition that honours Halloy's specification of a complex system we will define our component processes as consisting of agents. Certainly, this is not a precise specification of component processes, but this lack of specificity actually reflects part of our argument, that the specification of component processes will depend on the level of analysis (more on this later).

Our proposal is that the human brain and therefore the human mind is a complex system. The agents in this complex system receive, process, and transmit information. Depending on the level of analysis, these agents may be individual neurons, or networks of neurons, or even networks of networks. The degree to which consideration of these agents as networks of neurons will assist in understanding their function will also depend on the level of analysis. For example, developing an understanding of the processing of lines and edges in visual stimuli may rely on a focus on the performance of individual neurons, however, it may be more sensible to explain the comprehension of written text by recourse to higher order agents that correspond to networks of neurons. Ultimately, though, an agent will only have utility by virtue of its input and output connections—that is, an agent must receive information and then pass it on once it has been processed. Thus, all agents exist in networks with other agents. Furthermore, an agent will incorporate feedback mechanisms whereby the success or otherwise of the agent's processing will determine the likelihood of that agent performing that processing in the future. Details of these feedback mechanisms are provided below.

For the brain to be considered a complex system, its agents must compete for some resource. In our view, this resource is information, because it is a *sine qua non* for adaptation to the world. The fundamental drive of agents in the mind is to be used to process information. This feature of our theory mimics that of neural systems where the survival of connections between neurons depends upon regular activation (Bruer and Greenough, 2001; Lathom-Radocy and Radocy, 1996). In our model, agents compete to process information. If the outcome that results from the operation of an agent leads to success in achieving some goal, then the agent will be likely to be recruited for processing in the future. Thus, success can lead to an increased potential for further success for an agent and hence continued survival. Failure, however, will lead to a reduced potential to be used in future, and so possibly the demise of the agent.

Agents live or die on the basis of their usefulness. First, they have to compete to be used. Second, if the result of their processing is successful, this then increases the chance of continued survival for the winning agent. This principle, then, suggests some fundamental drives of the mind. Early in life these drives will relate to survival. For example, if the products of an agent's functioning in a particular situation lead to food, water, or warmth, then the feedback associated with these rewards ensures that the agent is used again in future when a similar situation is encountered, and alternative agents are less likely to be recruited. Thus an infant can learn the utility of crying, calling for 'mum', and saying 'drink'. Similarly, social rewards can act as drivers for learning (e.g. if a particular facial feature leads to positive attention from people, repeat it; if uttering a certain sound leads to food, a toy, or affection, repeat it).

The *raison d'être* of an agent is simply to be used. A reasonable question, though, is what is the point? One response to this is that being used means survival. One might wonder, then, what is the point of an agent's survival? Clearly, it is to engage in information processing that might increase the opportunities for further processing in the future. The circularity of this state of affairs should be obvious. This should not, however, detract from the usefulness of this idea as a description of the mind. After all, this cycle is similar to many life cycles:

Why does X hunt for food?
To eat and so maintain energy reserves.
Why does X need to maintain energy reserves?
In order to be able to hunt.

In complex systems, agents are usually referred to as growing in some sense as they attract further resources. The sense of growing, however, is dependent on the situation in which a complex system is being considered. In our complex system version of the mind, agents 'grow' with use in the sense that, with success agents come to be recruited more often to perform a particular task and so they come to dominate processing. Agents will increase their chances of being recruited to perform a task through a number of mechanisms, including performing the task more efficiently than competing agents (see below), or forging connections with other agents. In other words, there will be an increase in the number of situations in which an agent is useful. There will be limits, however, on the extent to which forging connections with other agents leads to an increased usefulness—some connections will prove to be fruitless because the processing that the agents can do is not relevant for some tasks (e.g. for some infants, every animal is a 'dog', until that response regularly attracts no reinforcement). Thus, the nature of the environmental demands will shape the usefulness of an agent.

In addition to the success or otherwise of an agent's actions, the competition between agents for the right to process information is decided by the speed with which the agents complete processing. In a similar vein to Logan's (1988, 1990) Instance theory, the agent that completes the necessary processing in the shortest time will be the winner of the competition. That is, the fastest agent is most likely to be used in future. The products of the fastest agent are used, and hence, that agent receives 'success' feedback. This feedback has the effect of making this agent more likely to be used in similar situations when they occur in the future.

The competition to be used that agents engage in can result in the combination of agents to form larger sized agents and also the splitting of large agents into smaller, more specific agents. The conditions under which these events occur will be associated with the particular task presented to the complex system. The system will try to respond to any challenge that the environment presents, and so the resulting agents will be a match for the environmental demands. If a challenge can be met by combining agents, then this will occur. If a particular environmental niche is detected that requires a more specific processing task than an existing general agent can complete, then a more specific agent may 'break away' from the parent to exploit this opportunity to be used. Following Halloy and Whigham (2004), the competition to be used among agents results in a log-normal distribution of agents such that there will be a large number of small agents that have very specific purposes, a small number of general purpose agents, and an inverse non-linear relationship between frequency and size for those agents between these extremes.

A concrete example of this type of system comes from issues surrounding word recognition that were discussed in Chapter 5. A general feature of skilled performance (Principle 5) is that sometimes it is useful to have skills that can solve problems in many situations, and other times a more specific set of skills will be necessary. This feature is obvious in language skills. For instance, some English words are used in a broad range of situations (e.g. the), and others have a far more limited range of usefulness (e.g. hydrogen). That is, the word 'the' can be used as the definite article for just about every noun in English and so is likely to appear in the majority of English sentences. The word 'hydrogen', in contrast, is likely to appear in sentences relating to chemical contexts. Thus, the agent for processing 'the' is used in more situations than the agent responsible for processing 'hydrogen'. The 'the' situations are not all going to be common—the situations in which 'the' will occur are as varied as the topics of discourse, whereas the 'hydrogen' situations are far more likely to have a common feature—that is, they will concern the element called hydrogen. The 'the' agent is thus an extremely general agent that can be invoked in a number of situations whereas the 'hydrogen' agent is only likely to be used in a small number of quite specific situations. There are very few words that are as ubiquitous as 'the' ('a' and 'I' are other examples), but there are thousands of words like 'hydrogen' that appear in restricted contexts. In other words, there tend to be many more low frequency words than high frequency words. This distribution of words of course corresponds to Zipf's law, which is a member of the log-normal family of abundance distributions.

There are many ways in which agents can improve their competitiveness for resources, or in other words, improve the likelihood of being used. To achieve this, agents must complete their processing in less time than competing agents. In our view, these improvements are the same as those we have highlighted in previous chapters with respect to the effects of practice on performance. That is, practice can lead to faster and more efficient forms of processing. We propose that there are many mechanisms whereby these changes can occur. For instance, agents may process information faster with repeated usage, a reflection of changes to neural function that have been observed to result from practice (Altmann *et al.*, 2004; Barnes, 1979; Bolger and Schneider, 2002; Eccles, 1972). Alternatively, agents may combine with other agents in ways that reduce inefficient forms of processing (e.g. unnecessary processing steps can be skipped). Agents can also split if environmental demands suggest that a smaller agent with a more specific processing function will be more useful. The particular improvement strategy followed will be determined by the nature of the environmental challenge being tackled. Importantly, when a new challenge is encountered, there will be many potential means for improving the competitiveness of agents, and so there will be greater potential for improved processing performance. As the challenge becomes more familiar, though, there will be less potential for improving further the competitiveness of agents, and so performance improvements will be less likely. Thus, performance changes over the course of practice will be negatively accelerated, which is evident in the characteristic shape of learning curves.

A fundamental feature of our theory is that the likelihood of an agent being used in the future depends on the success of its processing. An important question, then, is by what mechanism does current performance affect future likelihood of use? In our theory this occurs as an inherent feature of the feedback process. We adopt the Kirsner and Dunn (1985) idea that every instance of processing results in a record of that processing. We suggest, however, that the record gets stored as part of the agent that performed the original processing, as a means of recording feedback of the results of the agent's processing. When an agent completely fulfils the goals of its processing, a record is created that reflects the operations of the agent. This record then is a bit of information, a particle in Halloy's terms, that is attracted to the agent and is thus stored as part of the agent. The effect of this process is that the agent grows. By growing in this manner, an agent becomes more attractive to future resources. That is, the agent is more likely to be used when faced with the same situation again. It is more likely to be used in future similar situations because its greater mass as a result of successful past performance means it will be faster than other agents. In addition, a history of successful performance in a range of situations will increase the scope of applicability of an agent.

The concept of an agent growing with successful application leading to an increased attractiveness is analogous to gravitational attraction. That is, in a physical system, bodies with large mass possess greater gravitational attractiveness compared to bodies of smaller mass, and so other bodies in the physical vicinity will be more attracted to, and hence, move towards the larger bodies. Similarly, in a complex system, the larger the mass of an agent, the greater the likelihood that it will attract particles in its region. In the mind, particles in the 'region' of an agent represent particles relevant to an agent's processing. Therefore, when a demand is presented to the system, if two agents are of equal relevance to the demand, the agent with the greater mass will be more attractive to the particle that is 'up for grabs'. That is, it will be more likely to complete the necessary processing and hence, will collect the particle that represents the information about that processing episode. This particle will then add to the agent's ability to attract further particles in future.

Although the gravitational analogy is a useful metaphor for understanding the nature of the competition for resources that occurs between agents, we can be more specific about the mechanism underlying the relationship between an agent's successful processing and a subsequent increased likelihood of future recruitment. As stated above, particles in our theory represent processing records. But particles also enable future performance. That is, because they are a record for what worked in the past, they can function as a blueprint for what to do when that previous situation re-occurs. As a result, an agent that has completed a processing task successfully on many occasions will have a collection of particles that represent records of each of these processing episodes. More precisely, an agent is really only a collection of particles, and so this growing collection of particles represents the growing mass of the agent. The mass of an agent is basically a collection of records of what happened in the past when a particular demand occurred. Alternatively, these records can be seen as a series of instructions about what to do should that demand re-occur.

Describing agents as collections of particles raises the question of why a large collection of particles (i.e. an agent with large mass) gives rise to faster performance than a smaller collection of particles (i.e. an agent with smaller mass). To answer this question we again borrow from Logan's (1988, 1990) Instance theory (see Chapter 2). Within an agent, particles will differ in the speed with which they can be utilized as processing instructions. To explain why this is the case, consider Figure 6.1. Both panels of this figure depict a

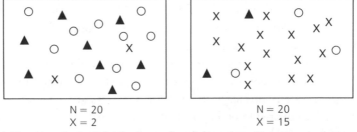

Fig. 6.1 Two hypothetical distributions of particles, where X represents the most relevant particle to the current processing goal.

finite number of particles (N = 20 in both cases). Depending on the current goals, these particles may or may not represent useful forms of processing. Imagine that in both cases the X symbol represents the most relevant particle for the current goal. The other symbols represent particles that are less relevant to the current goal (i.e. solutions that are sub-optimal). In the left panel, there is not as extensive a history of X being useful as in the right panel. That is, there are more Xs on the right. If we then imagine that recruiting one of the particles as a guide for performing the next task is a random search through these spaces, and that the search ends when an X is encountered, there is clearly a greater chance of finding an X in the right panel than in the left panel. Furthermore, an X will be located sooner in the right panel than in the left panel. In general, then, the speed with which a relevant particle can be located is going to be determined by the number of such particles present—the more particles there are, the sooner one can be found and recruited. The speed with which an agent can perform a task, then, will reflect the particle that enabled processing in the shortest time. As in the Instance theory, the distribution of processing speeds among the particles within an agent (i.e. the time to recruit a relevant particle) will be a Weibull (which is also a member of the log-normal family of distributions), and so there will be a power function relationship between the number of particles making up an agent (i.e. the number of successful processing episodes) and the speed of the agent's processing. Thus, an agent is more likely to complete processing before other agents with less mass because it is more likely to have a relevant particle that can enable appropriate processing in a shorter time. Hence, although it might be convenient to think of large agents as attracting a processing episode in their direction, it is more accurate to think of such agents as being the fastest to complete processing. An agent will dominate processing in the sense that it always does the job not so much because at some point it attains privileged status and so demands to do the processing, but more because it is simply the fastest to provide a processing result in a never-ending competition with other agents.

It is important to note that no two situations in the world are ever identical. Even reading the same word on a computer screen in identical formats on two occasions does not represent identical situations because the person reading the word is slightly different from one moment in time to the next. Thus, the human information processing system must be capable of tolerating differences in ostensibly similar stimuli in order to be able to identify them as such. Of course, there must also be limits on this tolerance so that differences can be perceived. Certainly some neural tissue appears to be sensitive to stimulus differences. For example, there are neurons in the visual cortex that appear to be geared to recognizing lines of a particular orientation (e.g. vertical), but which are still active in response to lines that do not match the ideal orientation (i.e. not completely upright). The extent of activation, however, is proportional to the extent to which the lines approximate the ideal orientation (Hubel and Wiesel, 1962). In Halloy's (1998; Halloy and Whigham, 2004) theory, the probability of an agent attracting a resource is inversely related to the distance to the resource. We honour this principle in the cognitive context by proposing that the relevance of an agent to the current goal of processing, or the similarity between the current conditions and the normal conditions processed by the agent, determine the likelihood of the agent being used and thus attracting a particle reflecting success. In other words, similarity determines the likelihood of an agent gaining mass and as a result, the rate of change of performance speed (cf. Shepard, 1987).

For instance, this issue arises when an agent produces results that do not completely match the goals of processing. This could happen, for example, when an agent is used in a slightly different situation to the one in which it was developed. This partial success will nonetheless be stored as a record of the agent's processing. The record of the partial match will be stored with the agent, and this will have two effects. Just as the storing of a record of complete success means an increase in the mass of the agent, a record of partial success will also increase the agent's mass. The increase in mass in this situation, however, will be less than that following complete success. This recognizes the fact that partial matches between old knowledge and new problems can result in partial transfer (Greig and Speelman, 1999; Palmeri, 1997). The mechanism underlying this effect borrows from an idea in Palmeri's (1997) modification to Logan's Instance theory. The speed with which a particle can be utilized in the processing of a new situation will be a function of the similarity between the particle and the processing demand—the greater the similarity, the faster the speed of processing. Thus, the increase in the effective mass of an agent—that is, that characteristic of an agent that reflects the speed with which it will complete processing—that comes from a partial match will be proportional to the degree to which the agent satisfies the environmental demand. The second effect of storing a record of partial success is that information about the different conditions in which the agent was at least partially successful is stored with the agent. This has the effect of expanding the conditions under which the agent is potentially useful. Thus, partial success can increase the potential usefulness of an agent in two ways: it results in increasing the mass of an agent that is associated with faster and more reliable recruitment of the agent, although this will be tempered by the degree of similarity between the experiences embedded in the agent and any new situation, and it also results in an increase in the conditions in which the agent is applicable and so broadens the range of situations in which the agent could be useful.

Dealing with environments in which there is stimulus variability will result in agents that record many instances of complete success in one circumstance and a series of partial successes in another circumstance. As a consequence, such an agent will possess two different types of particles. Under these conditions, there may be sufficient advantage in this heterogeneous agent (i.e. an agent applicable to several situations) splitting so as to create a number of smaller homogeneous agents that are more specific to the particular environmental circumstances. The advantage that will provide the motivation to such a split will be that the more specific agents will more completely satisfy the environmental demands and hence will receive greater increases to their mass than under partial matching conditions. There will, of course, be a trade-off between the extent to which an agent develops to match the environmental demands (i.e. maximum increases to mass), and the frequency with which the specific environmental demands occur. Sometimes an agent that can deal with many situations will remain heterogeneous because the various situations do not occur sufficiently regularly to warrant a splitting to create a more specific agent. That is, the partial increases to the agent's mass that comes from partial matching will justify the continued existence of the agent in its current form, whereas a smaller agent that is specific to the particular situation will not be useful sufficiently often to justify its existence. There will be times, however, when particular situations will occur sufficiently regularly that the increases to the mass of a smaller, more specific agent adapted to that situation will justify its separate existence.

There will also be times when the operations of an agent do not result in success. This can arise when an agent does not win the right to be used (i.e. another agent does the job). Alternatively, the agent does get to complete processing but the result does not constitute a successful outcome. For example, the agent's output does not satisfy the goals of processing. In both cases, the agent would not attract a particle, that is, the record of successful performance. As a result its performance goes unrewarded. In a sense this represents a situation of no change to the mass and hence status of the agent. However, this does not mean that the system remains the same and is unresponsive to failure. Such situations represent opportunities for other agents to prosper. The first situation is one where a competing agent wins the competition to perform because it completes processing faster than the other agent. If this winning agent continues to perform successfully then that agent will become the agent of choice in similar circumstances. In the second situation, where an agent produces a result that is ultimately unsuccessful, a demand on the system remains unsatisfied and so represents an opportunity for new agents to develop. Therefore, as a result of unsuccessful performance, due to performance being too slow or inappropriate, agents can effectively lose their preferred status as more successful agents take over performance of the task. It is important to note that competition between agents can result in successful agents emerging as dominant on the basis of success alone. There is no need to posit an explicit inhibition mechanism (although inhibition may or may not be necessary in neural implementations of a complex system of this sort).

The suggestion that the mass of an agent does not change following unsuccessful performance may explain why, under some circumstances, people persist with inappropriate behaviour beyond the point at which they learn of the inappropriateness of their behaviour. For example, in the Luchins's water jar problem, following the development of a mental set to approach all problems with a particular solution, the majority of people persist with the unnecessarily complex solution after experiencing a problem that could only be solved with a simpler solution (Luchins, 1942). The complex system explanation for this observation is that until an alternative agent is developed that can complete successful processing faster than the original agent can complete its unsuccessful processing, the unsuccessful agent will persist in producing inappropriate behaviour.

An observation about the performance of any task that has been central to this book is that practice typically leads to better performance. Another feature of the relationship between practice and performance that is just as commonly observed is that a lack of practice leads to poorer performance. That is, if someone practices a task for a period of time, performance typically improves in both accuracy and speed, but if the person ceases practice for some time, their performance upon resuming the task is never as good as it was at the end of the previous performance period. Skills seem to suffer a form of decay such that if they are not used, something is lost and this results in poorer performance. Some skill acquisition theories build-in a decay parameter to account for this observation (e.g. Anderson, 1982). In our view there are several reasons why such apparent decay of skills occurs. First, the complex system that is the mind is implemented in a biological system. It will therefore require some form of neural resource to maintain any form of mental representation over time. There may then be a limit on the ability to maintain representations that have not recently been of use. Thus, agents that are currently 'top of the pops' as far as usefulness is concerned grow in mass, and this may occur at the expense of other not currently useful agents. This suggests a principle of conservation of mass whereby a constant mass is shared among all agents, such that any growth in the mass of some agents that reflects current usefulness is matched by a distributed reduction in mass of all other, not currently useful, agents. Another means whereby the apparent decay of skills can come about is associated with the idea that higher level skills require the co-ordination of many agents each performing some sub-component of the task. If a task is not performed for some time, the agents underlying performance of the task may be useful in some other task. So, although the agents themselves may suffer no loss of mass due to inactivity, the connections between the agents that enable their co-ordination to perform the original task may fade with lack of use. For example, a guitarist may work up a solo comprised of various riffs and licks for a particular song. After many years of performing the song, the guitarist gets tired of the song and drops it from his repertoire. Following several years of playing other songs, in which all the riffs and licks from the deleted song appear, but in different orders and across different songs, he receives a request to play the old song. He will find that despite all of the riffs and licks remaining in his repertoire, co-ordinating them smoothly into the solo of the original song will not come easy. The first new performance of this old song is likely to be 'clunky', or at least not as effortless and elegant as the final performance in the original tenure of the song.

Losing language abilities

That agents and their connections to other agents fade over time through lack of use suggests that even well-entrenched skills can be lost. A famous example of the loss of a skill through lack of practice exists in the early history of white settlement in Australia. The original white settlers were primarily soldiers and convicts, with a smattering of pioneer farmers. William Buckley was a convict who escaped from custody around the area of Port Philip Bay in what is now known as the state of Victoria. After some time living on his own in the bush, he encountered a tribe of Aborigines, who mistook him for the reincarnation of a recently deceased member of their tribe. Buckley moved in with the tribe, learning their customs and language, and taking a wife, and fathering a child. After 32 years with this tribe, however, he left and encountered a group of white settlers. This first encounter was marked by his apparent inability to speak or comprehend English. He did, however, point to a tattoo on his arm of the initials W B., in some effort to identify himself. Presumably in 32 years of not speaking or hearing English (at that time, and in that area of Australia, very few Aborigines had encountered white people, let alone learned their language), Buckley's English language skills had very little opportunity to be used and so faded away, and so it appeared as if he had pretty much forgotten his mother tongue. Apparently, though, it did not take Buckley very long to regain his ability to converse in English. He returned to white society and his knowledge of the customs and language of both white and Aboriginal societies enabled him to act as an interpreter in negotiations between the two peoples. His ability to regain his English language skills so quickly suggests that he had not completely forgotten them. Thus, skills probably do not completely disappear through lack of use, but their existence may be difficult to ascertain.

(Source: http://www.cheshiremaazine.com/articles42000/buckley.html, 10 February 2004)

In the Component Theory of Skill Acquisition we described the Fluency Threshold that corresponds to the point at which someone has the ability to attempt a new task. Prior to this point, the component processes necessary to perform the task are not fluent enough to fit within the person's resource constraints. Thus, the demands of the task outweighed the available resources. At the Fluency Threshold, however, the component processes necessary to perform the task have been practiced to the extent that the resources required to perform the task do not exceed those available. In the complex system version of the component model, this Fluency Threshold can be understood in terms of the competition between agents to be used. As described already, agents with greater mass (i.e. more successful experience) have a greater chance of being recruited to perform a task than agents with less mass. There are several reasons for this. If an agent is too slow, another faster agent may win the right to be used (i.e. it produces a solution before the slower agent completes processing). In addition, the complex systems of the human mind exist in a dynamic world, where task demands include time constraints. A slow agent may not complete processing in time for the demands of the task, and so the benefits of successful processing are not realized. As a result, no reinforcement for performance will be received. Thus, such small, 'young' agents are not reliably applied in certain circumstances to enable consistent performance. Reliability of application comes only with sufficient successful past application. When a novice attempts a task that requires the application of several component processes, that is, several agents, they will only be able to complete the overall task successfully when the necessary agents have grown to a sufficient extent that they can do their job reliably. If any agent is insufficiently large to be reliable, then a link in the chain of processing will be inconsistently performed and the overall task will not be completed successfully.

As someone gains experience in a particular domain, the agents responsible for performing components of a task will become faster and more reliable. That is, when necessary, they will more consistently do the required job successfully. Eventually the agents will meet the Fluency Threshold conditions for successful task performance. That is, the person will have sufficient mental resources available, in the form of a set of reliable agents, to attempt the new task.

With further successful practice on this task, the agents responsible for the task components are rewarded for acting in concert by being recruited as a team in future. Indeed, if several agents consistently operate in succession to complete a task, there may come a time when agents that occur later in the chain come to 'anticipate' the point of their own application. Initially agents may only be sensitive to outputs of the agent that immediately precede them in the chain. It is possible, however, that with experience, agents later in a chain can become sensitive to outputs from agents earlier in the chain than those that immediately precede them. Eventually these later agents may become sensitive to the initiating conditions of the task so that these lead directly to the results of the final agents in the chain, and so unnecessary processing steps can be eliminated. This form of learned anticipation is characteristic of all forms of learning, such as chains of associated conditioned stimuli leading to a conditioned response in classical conditioning, or the development of complex behaviour in operant conditioning, and also the chunking of information that facilitates comprehension and memory in domains, such as language. Ultimately, then, a network of agents that enable performance of a particular task could potentially create a new, higher order agent that is adapted for performing this particular task. Furthermore, this higher order agent could then serve as a component agent on some other, even higher order task. Thus, the processes involved at one level of the system occur at all levels of the system.

6.3 Biology, evolution, and explanatory criteria

6.3.1 Is the component theory consistent with biological and evolutionary principles?

Having described the mechanisms underlying the Component Theory of Skill Acquisition, we are now in a position to complete the evaluation of the theory as a candidate explanation for general cognitive phenomena. The final criteria by which we will evaluate the theory are those described as the Biology, Evolution, and Explanation Criteria in Chapter 1. The first two of these criteria concern whether the theory is consistent with biological and evolutionary principles. With respect to biological principles, the most relevant concern brain functions. Already we have alluded to some properties of neurons that are similar to those proposed for agents and particles. That is, both are described as being sensitive to the similarity relationships, either between incoming stimuli and some ideal stimulus characteristic (e.g. neurons sensitive to orientation: Hubel and Weisel, 1962), or between new and old information (i.e. agents). Our theory, however, does not state how the operations of agents and particles are associated with the operation of neurons and their connections. Clearly there must be a relationship. Nonetheless, the fact that we propose that agents and particles exist at many different levels of analysis means that it is not possible to identify the operations of specific agents and particles with specific neural processes. Still, we would claim that competition among agents associated with the acquisition of skills will have detectable physical effects on the cortex. A clear example of this is provided by a recent study reported by Draganski *et al.* (2004). In this study, undergraduates practiced juggling for several months. MRI scans were used to measure the size of various brain areas before and after juggling training, as well as following the cessation of training and any further practice. Draganski *et al.* reported clear expansion of grey matter in cortical regions (left and right mid-temporal area, left posterior intra-parietal sulcus) that was directly correlated with changes in juggling behaviour. That is, directly following juggling practice, the grey matter in these cortical areas was larger in all participants than before the commencement of training or following the cessation of any further practice. Draganski *et al.* stated that it was unclear whether the observed increases in cortical mass were due to the growth of new neurons or increased connections between existing neurons. At the very least, there appears to be an analogous relationship between increases in cortical mass associated with skill acquisition and increases in the mass of agents that we propose underlie this process.

With respect to consistency with evolutionary principles, the Component Theory appears well-equipped. The general principle in our theory of entities competing for survival, with the winners surviving to undertake future competition, and losers dying off, is wholly consistent with natural selection. Indeed this feature of Halloy's (Halloy and Whigham, 2004) theory of complex systems was designed to be consistent with general evolutionary principles. Moreover, our theory appears consistent with the evolutionary picture painted by Plotkin (1993). Plotkin describes three heuristics, involving biological evolution, intelligence, and cultural evolution, and entertains the hypothesis that they reflect different levels within a single, universal, evolutionary tale. The critical issue in his account involves the proposition that they each involve knowledge acquisition, where the shape of that knowledge reflects critical characteristics of the relevant environment, and changes in that environment. Thus, while biological evolution involves inter-generational changes or adaptations in species characteristics, intelligence and changes therein enable intra-generational adaptation in the behaviour of individuals. For our purposes, the critical question concerns the proposition that qualitatively comparable principles support adaptation at each level. The Component Theory of Skill Acquisition explicitly states that skill acquisition involves principles that are qualitatively comparable to those underlying biological evolution. We can thus conclude that the Component theory satisfies both the Biology and the Evolution Criteria.

Finally, as an added bonus, our theory is consistent with physical laws. Certainly, it is the case that log-normal distributions exist throughout nature, and indeed Halloy's (Halloy and Whigham, 2004) theory of complex systems is designed for universal application. That is, he explicitly claims that it provides a description of the processes underlying such diverse phenomena as animal and plant sizes and abundances, earthquakes, sand pile avalanches, and planet sizes. As such Halloy's theory is claimed to represent ubiquitous natural laws. Given that the Component Theory is derived from Halloy's theory, we claim that our theory represents principles that are universal in nature, and that therefore cognitive phenomena reflect these principles.

6.3.2 How the mind as a complex system gives rise to the five principles of skill acquisition

In this section, we consider the extent to which the Component Theory of Skill Acquisition meets the Explanation Criterion. That is, can the theory provide for the five principles of skill acquisition identified in Chapter 4 without explicitly building them into the theory? To answer this question we show how the principles can be explained in terms of the operation of agents and particles. We show too that each principle can be understood as a by-product of the adaptations of the complex system that is the mind. When the system adapts to the environment, it will do so according to the characteristics of a complex system, and the adaptations will then exhibit particular features that are consistent with the five principles. Hence the principles are emergent features of the adaptations of agents.

Principle 1: Practice leads to faster performance

Performance of most measurable behavioural tasks will involve the operation of several agents. Practice on such tasks leads to faster performance for several reasons. One is that individual agents process information faster with practice. As the number of times an agent completes processing increases, more particles representing records of these episodes will be stored with the agent. These particles enable future performance, and so as the collection of particles increases in size, so too does the chance of recruiting a useful particle in less time. As a result, the speed with which an agent can complete its processing can increase with practice and this can lead to faster performance on a task. As mentioned in the previous section, though, the benefit to performance time of increased numbers of relevant particles diminishes as a power function of the number of particles (i.e. practice). Thus, performance improvements on a task will be a negatively accelerated function of practice. In addition, performance of a task that involves the operation of several agents can get faster with practice as a result of changes to the particular agents involved in performing the task. That is, practice can lead to more efficient forms of processing as a result of redundant agents being dropped from processing. The opportunities for such improvements in efficiency are likely to be much greater early in practice compared to later and so improvements in performance time that result from this mechanism will also be a negatively accelerated function of practice.

Principle 2: Practice leads to efficiencies in knowledge access

When completion of a task involves the operation of several agents, practice can lead to the individual agents processing information faster and redundant agents being dropped from processing. As a result, 'super' agents can develop that are responsible for performing the task in fewer steps than the original set of agents. That is, one agent can do the job of several agents. Thus, with reading experience, several agents that are separately responsible for recognizing the individual letters of a word can be superseded by an agent that recognizes the whole word.

Principle 3: Learning leads to less demand on working memory

The idea that there are working memory constraints on the performance of a task is usually invoked when a task is attempted that seems to require more than someone is capable of performing. For instance, a task may require someone to pay attention to more information than is apparently possible. An example of this would be someone who is learning a language and they are required to comprehend a number of sentences that include many unfamiliar words and that are spoken very quickly. Initially their ability to comprehend each word may be non-existent or too slow to enable all of the information about each word to be integrated into some realization of the meaning of each sentence. With growing expertise with the particular language (i.e. they become familiar with more words, and the speed with which they can access their knowledge of these words increases), their ability to process such sentences increases. That is, they can comprehend a sentence soon after it is uttered. In this type of situation, our theory would propose that initially the person does not possess agents for word recognition that are sufficiently reliable and fast as to enable comprehension of the utterances. Words keep being uttered without comprehension keeping up. Thus, each sentence bypasses the listener. With practice, however, agents become very fast and reliable in their processing, and so enable almost instantaneous processing of language. So, rather than a representation of a sentence needing to be retained in working memory for long periods until 'young' agents can process the words, 'old' agents are able to process the sentence quickly and so free up space in working memory.

Principle 4: As expertise increases, fewer mental resources are required to perform a particular task, enabling the development of a hierarchy of skills

Two things can happen when a set of agents is used consistently in the performance of a task: (1) each agent completes its specific task in less time; and (2) some agents may no longer contribute to the overall performance of the task because other agents take over their processing. Thus, as the history of successful performance grows, agents develop in such a way as to perform the task in a faster and more efficient manner. Being able to complete processing quickly is an advantage particularly when performance is in the context of a dynamic task where time constraints exist. These time constraints will include things like the existence of an environmental threat (e.g. an advancing snake) that requires some evasive action be taken in some minimum time, or two people engaged in conversation where boredom could result if the conversation does not proceed at some minimum rate, or a complex task that requires intermediate products of processing be stored (e.g. double digit multiplication) but storage of these products in memory is subject to decay over time. Thus, there is often considerable motivation to perform a task faster, not the least of which is to overcome the constraints of a basic level of performance in the domain. This motivation will provide the impetus to develop agents that are specific to the particular task at hand rather than utilize agents that have been useful in previous contexts. Agents adapted to specific contexts will be more likely to perform a task in fewer steps than agents cobbled together from previous relevant experiences. Ultimately, specific agents may develop to the extent that they enable automatic performance of a task rather than the slow and ponderous performance associated with more general agents. Thus, a certain environmental challenge will trigger an automatic response rather than a chain of processing steps that may or may not produce an appropriate response. Typically, however, there is also motivation to perform at greater than basic level performance. Developing agents that enable fast and automatic performance of the basic task will mean that there may now be time enough available to start attempting more complex forms of the task. Thus, as someone becomes more fluent at evading an environmental threat, such as an advancing snake, then one may be able to attempt another desirable behaviour, such as killing it for food.

Principle 5: Mastery in a domain involves the application of an array of component processes, with varying degrees of specificity to tasks and contexts

Sometimes agents will develop that are specific to a task, and cannot be used in the performance of any other task. At other times, agents will develop that can be recruited in the performance of several tasks. The nature of a domain will determine the relative mix of these types of agents and therefore skills. That is, if a task environment is such that a particular job has to be completed in a particular way, then agents will develop that are highly specialized to perform that task. The existence of such highly specialized agents will be ensured by the continued demand from the environment for such processing. In contrast, a task environment that requires many different performance types in varying contexts demands a flexible set of skills. As a result, agents will develop that are smaller in scope, specific to finer grained details of the task, but be capable of being recruited by other agents in order to complete the overall task. Thus, performance in such a varying domain is unlikely to reach the automatic level of the more constrained environment, but is likely to be more flexible.

Another way to express Principle 5 is that people are sensitive to regularities in a task environment. The skills they develop to perform the task, and their ability to transfer these skills, are a reflection of their adaptation to these regularities. Expressed in terms of the agent theory, this principle arises because the task environment determines the potential for particular types of agents to be used. Agents will develop to exploit opportunities, and will do so in a manner that matches the peculiar requirements of that domain. As a result, the nature of the agents, in terms of whether or not they can be recruited to perform in other task environments will be determined by the nature of the task environment to which they originally adapted.

In sum, we have demonstrated that the five principles of skill acquisition all emerge from the adaptations of agents. Thus, we have not had to build them into the fabric of the system. As a result, the Component theory satisfies the Explanation Criterion. This completes the criteria for appropriateness as a theory of skill acquisition with aspirations of providing explanations in other domains. In other sections we have identified shortcomings of other theories of skill acquisition, mainly with respect to the Skill Acquisition Phenomena Criterion and the Behaviour Phenomena Criterion. Some of these theories also fail on the Explanation Criterion. For example, the ACT family of theories define strengthening as being a power function of practice, thus building in the power law without an explanation for why strengthening and practice have this relationship. In the Component theory, however, power function improvements in performance are observed as a by-product of the process by which agents compete for survival. In conclusion, then, we consider the Component Theory of Skill Acquisition to have satisfied all criteria for consideration as an appropriate theory of skill acquisition in the sense of providing a credible solution to the Problem. We now turn our attention to the implications of such a conclusion.

6.4 Implications

We have outlined here a theory of the mind as a complex system. This theory describes how experience with the world leads to the development of agents that enable performance of tasks necessary for dealing with challenges posed by the world. The theory is not a fully realized theory in the sense that computer simulations are possible based on the details we have sketched above (although Halloy (1998) has developed schematic computer simulations of his model). The development of such a version of the theory is a task we have set ourselves for the future. Our main aim here, though, is to convince others of the importance of this task. As part of this effort we are going to present some of the conclusions we have reached as a result of exposing various aspects of the discipline of Psychology to our new point of view. In essence, the theory we have presented here represents a claim that the contents of the mind are entirely a product of its interactions with the world. If we begin with this assumption, there are some enlightening implications for many areas of Psychology, and for the entire discipline of Psychology. We outline several of these implications in this section.

6.4.1 Skill acquisition

For many years the one great constant about research in skill acquisition was that practice on a task led to performance improvements that followed a power function. This feature of skill acquisition is known as the power law of learning (Newell and Rosenbloom, 1981). As discussed in Chapter 3, however, there has been controversy recently about whether or not learning curves are indeed best described by power functions, and in fact whether or not the power law should actually have the status of a law. One conclusion that seems safe from recent discussions of this issue is that power function learning curves are most often seen in group data, that is, data that is averaged over several individuals. Learning curves tend to be far less smooth in individual data, although there are instances where they do occur as smooth functions (e.g. Speelman, 1991). Therefore, the power law seems only to apply in certain circumstances and hence begs the question about its lawfulness. How then can it be that a generalization applies under some circumstances, but under others it may or may not apply? The Component Theory of Skill Acquisition implies a resolution of this issue. According to the theory, individual learning curves on tasks are a reflection of the improved performance of component processes (agents) throughout practice. Some agents will be newly created for the task and so will probably have a long way to improve. Other agents will be virtual modules in the sense that they are as good as they are ever going to get and so will not contribute to performance improvements on the task. The performance of some agents will improve with practice in a smooth manner, others will improve according to a step function, and there are likely to be many variants in between these extremes. All agents, however, will need to improve to survive, and there will be limits on the extent of improvement possible. Indeed some agents may have reached the extent of improvement (i.e. very old but useful agents) yet, they will still need to continue to be useful to survive. The nature of the particular learning 'curve' for each agent will be largely dependent on the particular processing engaged in. For instance, a task like counting is likely to be associated with a slow incremental improvement in performance that corresponds with a strengthening of number facts in memory (Aunola *et al.*, 2004). In contrast, a task, such as Duncker's Candle Problem would show a dramatic improvement in performance once a workable solution has been provided or is discovered. Thus, different forms of processing involve different potentials for improvement, and will therefore determine the nature of the improvement that can occur. Nonetheless, a task that involves the collaboration of teams of agents will typically show learning improvements that approximate a power function (i.e. are negatively accelerated and monotonic). This is because the averaging of several learning functions to create one omnibus learning function will always result in a power function (Haider and Frensch, 2002; Heathcote *et al.*, 2000; Myung *et al.*, 2000). For the same reasons, smooth power functions will be more likely to be observed in the learning curves of groups of individuals than in individuals' learning curves. Thus, rather than the power law being an all-encompassing law for all occasions, as envisioned by Newell and Rosenbloom (1981, p. 52), the power law only applies in certain circumstances. That is, performance time will be a power function of practice when performance time data represents an averaging of performance times collected from groups of people, or component processes, that each improves individually with practice but not necessarily as a power function. When there is not substantial averaging of separate learning functions, then the power law will not apply. It is important to note, then, that the lawful aspect of the power law comes from the mathematical property of averaging several functions rather than from some property of the brain. This then frees our theory, and any other theory of skill acquisition, from the constraint that it must contain a learning mechanism that not only obeys the power law, but also explains it. Our theory, in fact, can explain why power function learning is observed in some circumstances, and not in others, without in fact having a learning mechanism that follows a power function exclusively.

6.4.2 **Training**

The Component Theory describes how agents are developed as part of the process of adapting to the demands of a task. In addition, agents developed in the context of one task may be utilized to perform a new task to the extent that the existing agents are relevant to the demands of this new task. Thus, a strong message coming from this theory, as well as from other theories of skill acquisition, is that what a person gets out of training is a reflection of what is done in training. That is, agents that are acquired to perform a task represent an adaptation to the constraints of the task. These constraints may or may not exist in another task, and so agents that have adapted to these constraints may not be applicable to a different set of constraints. This suggests that there is little point in practicing some approximation to a target task and hoping that the resultant skill will transfer to the target task. There may or may not be some transfer but there certainly will not be as much transfer as will occur from actually training on the target task. This is not to suggest that there will not be situations where it is necessary to practice a 'cut-down' version of a target task in order to start developing basic skills, without which the target task could never be attempted. Certainly many such situations exist, with pilot training being a classic example, and another being learning to read. Nonetheless, there is always a trade-off between the fidelity of training (i.e. the degree of similarity between training and transfer tasks) and the amount of transfer that results. Sometimes it might be possible for the essential elements of a target task to be captured by an approximation to that task (e.g. see Chapter 3) but generally speaking, as the difference between training and transfer tasks increases, the amount of transfer that occurs diminishes.

The corollary of the relationship between the fidelity of training experiences and the resultant transfer is that it is unreasonable to expect experts in particular domains to know everything in that domain. The knowledge that experts possess about their domain of expertise is determined by what they actually do in that domain. This feature of expertise is illustrated well by an experiment reported by Myles-Worsley *et al.* (1988). In this experiment, three groups of people with varying amounts of experience in the field of radiology were presented with three different types of pictures for a later recognition test: (1) Faces; (2) X-ray slides depicting body parts with no abnormalities; and, (3) X-ray slides depicting abnormalities. Three main results were observed: (1) Recognition memory for faces was uniformly high across all levels of radiological experience; (2) memory for abnormal X-ray slides increased with radiological experience and, for the most experienced radiologists, this was equivalent to memory for faces; and (3) recognition memory for normal X-ray slides actually decreased with radiological experience from above chance to a chance level. This last result is very curious—expert radiologists were the worst in terms of recognizing normal X-ray slides. Why would this be the case? Myles-Worsley *et al.* suggested that:

> Radiological experience improves memory for abnormal (slides) because it improves the likelihood of detection of the abnormal features that distinguish these (slides) from one another and from normal (slides). On the other hand, radiological experience

reduces memory for X-Ray (slides) that do not reveal pathologies because the search for particular disease-related abnormalities reduces the likelihood of detecting other, more innocuous abnormalities. Thus, expertise in a particular domain is likely to be a two-edged sword: It can bias perception toward some classes of stimuli in that domain and away from others.

(p. 557)

Therefore experts' skill is related to what they do. Expertise is not necessarily a general increase of knowledge in a particular domain.

One of us (Speelman, 1998b) has made a similar point before with respect to the common observation that experts in many domains reveal an implicit form of expertise. Implicit expertise refers to the situation where experts are able to perform certain tasks at a level unsurpassed by most people and yet they seem quite incapable of describing how they achieve their extraordinary feats. It is as if the knowledge they obviously possess that enables their superior performance is not accessible to consciousness.

As individuals master more and more knowledge in order to do a task efficiently as well as accurately, they also lose awareness of what they know. The very knowledge we wish to represent in a computer program as well as the knowledge we wish to teach others, often turns out to be knowledge that individuals are least able to talk about.

(Johnson, 1983, p. 79)

It should not be surprising that in some situations, expertise is implicit. Various models of skill acquisition, and indeed the Component theory, all point to mechanisms whereby skills may be acquired initially in an explicit form (e.g. list of instructions for how to perform a task, conscious memories for what worked in the past), but with practice become implicit (i.e. chunking leads to intermediate steps being lost to consciousness; speed of processing becomes too fast for consciousness to follow steps; eventually tasks are performed by direct retrieval of solutions or responses). Ultimately, though, expertise may be implicit because of the limited nature of transfer of training. That is, in most cases where implicit expertise has been observed, the nature of the tasks that experts are expert at do not require verbalization of the underlying knowledge and processing. As a result, the experts have never become expert at this type of performance. Thus, it is unrealistic to expect experts to be expert at all aspects of performance in a particular domain, especially being able to describe the nature of their expertise when such description is not part of their expertise.

6.4.3 Universality

An essential element of our theory that the mind is a complex system is that there are basic design constraints on the way the mind functions that reflect design constraints that exist throughout nature. As mentioned earlier, properties of complex systems have been observed in a vast range of physical phenomena, leading some (e.g. Buchanan, 2000; Halloy, 1998; Halloy and Whigham, 2004) to suggest that these properties represent laws of nature. Thus, our claim is that the mind possesses certain properties that are universal. Clearly, this claim refers to the fact that certain features of human behaviour will mimic phenomena found in other areas of nature (e.g. Zipf's law). Less obviously, perhaps, we are also suggesting that this universality applies within the discipline of Psychology. That is, those features of the mind that we have identified through work in the fields of skill acquisition and word recognition, and distilled into the five principles, should be apparent in all other areas of Psychology, if only one is to look. Unfortunately, looking with this purpose in mind is not an approach all that common in modern Psychological research.

The modal way in which modern Psychology is taught in universities is to begin with an introductory course that provides an overview of the discipline, and then follow that with a course of study that provides a more in-depth view of the introduced concepts. If one was to peruse a random sample of the textbooks that are produced for introductory courses in Psychology, one would be excused the impression that Psychology possesses a number of highly developed domains of study that are so independent of each other that each domain warrants a chapter on its own. Furthermore, the boundaries between domains are seemingly so clear to everyone, that these chapter topics appear in just about all textbooks. The strong implication of this impression of the discipline perpetuated by the producers of these introductory texts is that there is very little connecting the phenomena appearing in the various chapters of such books. This impression has been exacerbated in recent years with an innovative option provided by publishers to the adopters of their textbooks. Instructors are able to customize texts by selecting chapters from a number of books within a publisher's stable. In this way instructors can design a book to suit the needs of their course and the expertise of the teaching staff. Of course, this practice implies that Psychology is made up of a number of discrete or maybe even optional modules with seemingly little in common with each other. A student reading through one of these texts could be forgiven the question of what is common about all the domains of Psychology that warrants them being lumped together in the same field of study. A glib answer would be that they all concern the study of the human mind, but that is where the common ground apparently ends because this issue is usually only given a cursory discussion in the preface or introduction to such texts. It is our contention that the discipline of Psychology can do much better than this, that there should be some concern for how it is that the mind can give rise to all the phenomena appearing in separate chapters of an introductory Psychology text. Furthermore, we feel it is important that such considerations honour the constraint that it is a mind with one set of characteristics that gives rise to all these phenomena, not a different mind for each chapter of the book. In this section, we consider various topics in Psychology from this perspective.

Our theory of the mind as a complex system implies that the contents of the mind are a product of its interactions with the world. In particular, we claim that different types of mental structures will emerge from different types of experiences. Attempts to adapt to an environment will lead to mental processes that are shaped by that environment. The extent to which the mind is shaped by the environment will, to a large extent, be a function of the amount of practice the mind has at dealing with the environment. The manner in which the environment and practice shapes the mind, and the types of mental structures that may emerge from particular experiences, are described by the five principles of skill acquisition we have noted. Thus, we are proposing that these five principles, in describing the basic features of skill acquisition, also describe the characteristics of all behaviour acquisition.

One theme that runs through this entire book is the impact of practice on behaviour. Practice can lead to mental processes and structures that are vastly different to those that we might develop after only a little experience in a domain. And yet, the power of practice is often overlooked. Among Psychology researchers there appears to be a strong motivation to describe and theorize about mental structures and processes as they appear now, but a general reluctance to consider where they came from, and admit that practice is probably responsible. We argue that a more explicit consideration of the role of practice in the development of mental structures and processes would enable a more complete understanding of the nature of the mind, and also give rise to potential solutions to problems that are associated with the structure of the mind. We will illustrate this idea with the concept of a schema.

The idea of a schema gained popularity through Bartlett's (1932) work with memory for short stories. Bartlett was struck by the observation that his student's memories for stories were not only rife with distortions and gaps, but that these errors were similar among the group of students. Bartlett explained this observation by suggesting that each student possessed similar ideas about the content of the stories, particularly, with respect to typical events and concepts. When stories did not match the students' knowledge of how things work typically, their memories for the stories were distorted so as to match better their knowledge. Bartlett referred to this type of knowledge of the typical nature of things as a schema. A schema is now understood within Psychology to be a knowledge structure that contains information about some entity (e.g. situations, events, objects, people) that enables a person to comprehend a description about or a reference to the entity, and develop expectations about a typical sequence of events associated with the entity, or other entities that might be related. Thus, the main functions of a schema are said to be that they enable comprehension, and the development of expectations, and in addition, they influence memory. We will elaborate on these features of schemata below, but for a more complete review see Alba and Hasher (1983).

Although the functions of schemata have been illustrated in a number of areas, we will illustrate these functions with respect to research in the area of discourse comprehension. The first function mentioned above, that schemata assist with comprehension, can be illustrated with the following sentence:

The manager deposited the money in the bank.

The word 'bank' has several meanings (e.g. a financial institution, the side of a river, a turning motion of an aeroplane). A literal interpretation of each word in this sentence, then, could lead to several interpretations for the meaning of the sentence. The ambiguity of such a sentence, however, is not usually apparent to readers. A normal reading of the sentence would typically generate the interpretation that a person known as a manager put some money into a financial institution. The schema explanation for such a smooth comprehension process is that most readers possess a schema that reflects their knowledge about banks and their relationship with the depositing of money. Thus schemata can assist in resolving ambiguities. They can also enable us to fill in obvious gaps in discourse. For instance, consider the following passage:

Frank went to a restaurant. He waved over the waitress. He ordered a pasta dish and a side salad. He ate the food and then walked back to his hotel.

There are actually a lot of gaps in this passage, although most readers would not normally be aware of them. For example, although nothing is stated explicitly in this passage about what Frank did while he was eating, or about payment for the food, most readers would probably draw the inferences that Frank sat down while he was in the restaurant and that he paid his bill before he left. According to Schank and Abelson (1977), there are many situations in a person's life that are so stereotypical we have strong expectations about the sequence in which particular events occur. Schank and Abelson suggest such situations are mentally represented as special types of schemata, they refer to as scripts. Thus, each of us possesses a restaurant script that represents the typical actions and events that occur at a restaurant. These might include being seated, looking at the menu, ordering food, eating food, paying the bill, and leaving. Not only does possessing such a schema enable someone to know how to behave in that situation, it also enables them to develop expectations about how others will behave. Schank and Abelson also suggest that a script helps to fill the gaps in discourse about a stereotypical situation. Thus, when we read the description about Frank in the restaurant, even though there is no mention of payment of the bill, we can safely assume that this must have occurred. The basis for this assumption is that our knowledge of restaurants is such that if someone leaves without paying the bill, then something drastic usually occurs. In the absence of any mention of the waitress chasing Frank with the bill, we can only assume that everything is alright on the money front (i.e. events conformed to the script).

The final feature of schemata that we will mention is that they influence a person's memory. As Bartlett (1932) reported, and has been observed many times since, people's memory for discourse is not perfect. Details of the way sentences are phrased disappear quickly (Sachs, 1967). In addition, memory for the details of events is also subject to errors, and analysis of the types of errors that are made reveal the operations of schemata. First, if an event is described that violates the normal expectations represented in a schema, memory for such an event is usually good. In other words, memory appears to be accurate for things that are wildly out of the ordinary, such as Frank pulling out a gun and stating that he was not going to pay the bill (Alba and Hasher, 1983). If, however, events occur that differ only slightly from the stereotypical course of events, then such events are usually remembered poorly. Memory for such events appears to be distorted in the direction of the schema. That is, someone will remember the event as being more stereotypical than it actually was (e.g. Bower et al., 1979). Finally, events that are not mentioned as having occurred, but are consistent with the normal experience of such events, usually appear in a person's memory of the event (Friedman, 1979).

Evidence for the existence of schemata is more likely to be observed when the situations or events in question are high frequency (Alba and Hasher, 1983). In other words, someone's knowledge of something is more likely to be schematic in nature if the 'something' is experienced many times. This, of course, suggests that practice may play a role in the development of schemata. Certainly there has been some consideration of the role that practice plays in the acquisition of schemata in the area of Cognitive Psychology (e.g. Anderson, 1983a; Rumelhart and Norman, 1981; Rumelhart et al. 1986) although these considerations do not appear to have transferred to theorizing about the nature of schemata. Nonetheless, the similarities between schematic behaviour and behaviour associated with large amounts of practice are so great that it is hard to believe that they are not spoken of in the same breath. Elsewhere in this book we have described situations where practice leads to the chunking of information so that complex features of the environment (e.g. chess configurations, groups of letters) can immediately suggest an interpretation, trigger a sequence of mental processes and behaviours, and influence later memory for those features. In our view, then, it is not a great leap to argue that schemata are merely another example of the mental structures that develop through the acquisition of skills. In the case of schemata, the skills relate to learning how to interpret and interact with the world. Clearly, these are a broad set of skills, however, hints of all five principles of skill acquisition can be observed in instances of schematic behaviour (Eysenck and Keane, 1995).

The concept of a schema has been heavily influential outside of the field of Cognitive Psychology. For instance, it sits at the centre of Piaget's theory of development (Piaget, 1967), the concept of stereotypes (Carr, 2003), gender schema theory (Bem, 1993), and cognitive theories of clinical disorders (Beck, 1964). Unfortunately, the usage of the schema concept typically extends only so far as the nature of an existing schema (i.e. for Behaviour X to occur, a person must possess a schema with such and such properties), and does not include consideration to any great depth of the origin of the schema. We argue, however, that consideration of the role of practice in the development of schemata in these areas may enlighten discussions of the mechanisms underlying seemingly schematic behaviour and suggest reasons why schemata in general are so resistant to change. For example, many clinical disorders may simply reflect an automatic way of thinking that has developed through extensive practice. The cognitive-information processing framework of depression (i.e. Beck's theory) claims that information from the world is processed via schemata. It is these schemata that provide the interpretations of the world. Someone with depression has schemata that are providing negative interpretations and these interpretations in turn impact upon the person's affect. Thus, if one assumes that clinical disorders like depression result from the interpretation of the world through negatively biased schemata, understanding the development of the disorder becomes a quest for understanding the acquisition of the schemata.

Although clinical disorders may represent maladaptive modes of behaviour, their development may actually represent an attempt to adapt to a particular situation (cf. Rosenhan, 1973). Thus an abnormal situation may lead to abnormal behaviour. That is, the behaviour may seem abnormal in a normal situation, but may be considered adaptive in the context within which it was acquired. Consider, for example, the case of obsessive-compulsive disorder (OCD). People afflicted with this disorder tend to avoid certain behaviours because they are highly anxiety provoking. Often the anxiety centres on the riskiness of the behaviours. An OCD sufferer may have experienced an unfortunate consequence of a particular behaviour and so avoided repeating the behaviour. Alternatively, they may have merely imagined an unfortunate event (e.g. amputation) resulting from a particular behaviour. Continually avoiding the behaviour acts as a reinforcement to the avoidance behaviour because the unfortunate consequence is never experienced. Furthermore, failing to engage in the behaviour can also mean that there is no opportunity for disconfirming the belief that the behaviour is associated with risk. Thus, a person with OCD can be locked into a cycle of avoidant behaviour that is continually strengthened by the constant reinforcement provided by the reduction of risk, as well as the temporary reduction in anxiety that is associated with the perceived risk reduction. Similarly, sufferers of OCD can be prone to engage in ritual behaviours as a means of warding off unfortunate consequences. Again, doing so leads to temporary relief in anxiety about the likelihood of risk, as well as failing to disconfirm their hypothesis that not engaging in the ritual behaviour will result in disaster.

If it is true that clinical disorders represent a form of adaptation, then this suggests a method of treatment for such disorders. First, the nature of the relationship between the precipitating situation and the resultant behaviour needs to be determined as far as is possible. Second, a training program is necessary to reduce the efficacy of the abnormal behaviour (i.e. arrange a situation where the abnormal behaviour no longer provides the usual result) and to provide alternate modes of behaviour (i.e. provide behaviours that ensure appropriate outcomes and are more socially acceptable, and to provide the opportunity to see that an alternative behaviour does not lead to catastrophe). This, of course, is a strategy used in standard cognitive therapy (Beck, 1995). However, in our view, a major component of the acquisition of the situation–behaviour relationship is being ignored in this strategy. If abnormal behaviours result from inappropriate interpretations of the world and these result from the operation of schemata, then the offending schemata require attention. Although traditional cognitive therapy attempts to target a client's thought processes with re-training, the extent of training typically given in such therapy may be sufficient to enable 'management' of the disorder but is probably insufficient to ever provide a cure. Cognitive behaviour therapy programs typically involve weekly therapy sessions of around one hour each for anywhere from 10 to 20 weeks, and require clients to engage in 'homework' exercises between sessions. If schemata are indeed like any other mental structure acquired through practice, then the 'training' engaged in by a person with a clinical disorder as they were acquiring their schemata and developing their disorder could have involved years of hourly reinforcement of patterns of thinking and modes of behaviour. A similar amount of re-training may therefore be necessary to combat the effects of the initial training. This amount of re-training may be impractical if traditional therapeutic practices are followed, but the further refinement of virtual reality devices may make massive practice of appropriate thoughts and behaviours in a safe and non-threatening environment more realistic.

Other versions of the schema concept have been invoked in the field of Social Psychology. Stereotypes (e.g. sexual, racial) and their role in discrimination have been interpreted as schemata that represent expectations about characteristics of particular groups of people (Nesdale and Durkin, 1998). Furthermore, stereotypes have proven resistant to attempts to alter or remove them (Gringart, 2003), but none of these attempts have involved training that could match a lifetime's worth of thoughts that are reinforced by one's culture. Many such attempts appear to be aimed at developing short campaigns, courses, or programs for re-educating people. This aim ignores the fact that mental structures with the properties of a schema are acquired from years of practice and are not forgotten easily or quickly. So it may be the case that the only way to achieve a long-lasting change to a stereotype is to engage in substantial amounts of practice with an alternative stereotype. Again, the practicalities of such an approach would need to be considered. Nonetheless, such a conclusion may point to preventative measures and away from rehabilitative programs.

So what of other areas of Psychology? Could they benefit from consideration of the origin of behaviours and processes from a learning perspective along the lines of the discussion of clinical disorders? Ultimately the question to be asked in such reflections is to what extent are the behaviours, processes, and constructs that are central to a particular area of study considered to be stable and largely immune to changes in a person's environment. If some feature of a person changes in response to some environmental change, is there any evidence that the feature represents the outcome of an intermediate amount of learning such that asymptotic performance has not yet been reached and virtual 'permanence' has not been attained? If, however, the feature seems stable in the face of environmental change, could it be that the feature reflects 'over' learning, where no discernible change in behaviour is obvious with further practice, and behaviours are so entrenched as to be elicited by particular stimuli in exactly the same way every time?

In summary, we have presented the view that the mind is a complex system whereby mental structures are created by interaction with the world. In this section, we have illustrated how such a view holds some important implications for many domains in Psychology. In particular, we have suggested that there should be greater efforts to discover similarities among seemingly dissimilar domains. We feel that closer scrutiny of many behaviours may reveal the presence of the five principles of skill acquisition we have identified, and thus create the potential for developing learning accounts of psychological phenomena. We have no doubt, though, that there will be researchers who believe that their area of Psychology is immune to this kind of treatment. In our view, researchers with this belief should explain how it is that a mind that reflects universal laws of nature in the areas we have identified can also give rise to phenomena that are untouched by these laws.

We feel it is inevitable that there will be retorts from our fellow researchers that the Component Theory of Skill Acquisition does not apply for particular phenomena. We suspect many readers are already saying to themselves that, in Domain X, learning is not demonstrated, that transfer does not occur in the prescribed manner, that there are no plateaus or stages in learning, that what might apply to learning to read does not apply to learning to speak, etc. Our response would be to say that our theory is a description of the potential of the human mind. The extent to which all of the features are evident in a particular behaviour will be determined by the particular environmental challenge to which a person has adapted. All tasks differ in some respects, and in addition, each task may enable many different forms of adaptation to that task, just as there are many ways to fill an environmental niche. As a result, the types of skills that will be developed by people are bound to vary. The challenge we would like to present to our fellow psychologists is, rather than look at what is different about particular behaviours, look for what is similar, and consider whether or not the learning principles we have presented in this book can provide an explanation for why people behave in the manner that they do.

6.4.4 Psychology as a scientific discipline

The field of Psychology has traditionally had a large chip on its shoulder. Psychology is often portrayed as a soft science, certainly softer than obviously hard sciences, such as Physics and Chemistry. This view has probably emerged from the realization that the human mind is 'fuzzy'—that is, it is not as straightforward as a rock or an element—and hence any attempts to study it are going to be similarly fuzzy. As a result, over the past century researchers in Psychology have developed an arsenal of methods for conducting research with humans that are designed to take out the fuzzy element. In fact, it is probably fair to characterize Psychology as being more obsessed about the validity of research design than any other field of science. As a consequence Psychology has uncovered some 'facts' about the human mind that most would not dispute, such as the effect of serial position on recall, and the effects of reinforcement on behaviour.

Psychology accepts that human behaviour is determined by a range of factors. The research techniques used in Psychology are designed to enable examination of the effects of individual factors. To do this psychological research must somehow control the effects of all the other factors. This control can take many forms, such as eliminating the effects of other factors, equalizing their effects, and monitoring their effects. One unfortunate consequence of this method of research is that researchers begin to lose perspective. It becomes difficult to see the forest for the trees. Psychology has certainly fallen victim to this malady. Psychological journals are full of experiments on highly focussed topics, with little obvious connections between them, even in journals supposedly devoted to the same area. It is difficult to avoid the impression that Psychology is a science with as many sub-areas as there are tasks that can be developed for research participants to perform. An outsider could be forgiven for the impression that progress in Psychology proceeds in the following manner: One researcher develops a new technique for looking at a particular mental phenomenon. The new technique throws up interesting additional phenomena. Other researchers perform similar experiments with a few tweaks on the design, and before you know it, a new area has developed, and conferences are organized.

It is difficult for us to resist the impression that the science of Psychology operates according to the same principles as the complex system view of the mind. That is, Psychology is a system comprising agents (individual researchers, teams of researchers) all 'greedy' for the same resource—attention to products of their work. Research agents typically conduct empirical studies and report these in journal articles and conference presentations. When other research agents pay attention to this work in terms of accepting it for publication/presentation, referring to it in subsequent works, granting research funds, offering employment, the original research agent survives and grows, allowing the attraction of more resources in future. In this vein, it is interesting to note that citation rankings tend to a log-normal distribution (Bianconi and Barabasi, 2001; Cohen, 2002). One consequence of a system of this nature, as we have outlined at the beginning of the chapter, is that in particular environments, it can encourage differentiation. In Psychology this has become obvious in terms of the proliferation of sub-fields and task-specific paradigms and explanations that exist. By being rewarded for making one's mark by being different, everyone is trying to be different. Indeed, the very cornerstone of scientific training, the Ph.d., is usually required to represent a novel contribution to a field. As a result, few are trying to discover what is similar.

On one hand it may be unfair to characterize Psychology in this way because the same process occurs in other sciences. On the other hand, though, we feel it is time that psychological researchers begin to consider how sub-areas may in fact be related to other sub-areas. It is unlikely we will ever develop an idea of how the human mind works if we concentrate our efforts on an ever-expanding range of sub-processes. Some of the mechanisms involved in the experiments reported in one issue of Memory and Cognition or The Journal of Experimental Psychology: Learning, Memory and Cognition must be common. It is time we started trying to identify them. In the next section we provide some recommendations for how Psychology should proceed in order to be a more unified science.

6.5 **Recommendations**

6.5.1 **How the science of Psychology should be conducted**

Collecting data

Our view of the mind as a complex system has important implications for the way in which Psychology collects data about behaviour. We will discuss three such implications here relating to individual differences, the dynamic nature of behaviour, and the possibility of gaining insight into the nature of the mind by observing other complex systems.

Many research techniques used in Psychology are designed to provide tight controls on factors that affect behaviour. That is, although there is acceptance that there may be many influences on behaviour, the aim is often to remove these influences so that one or a set of target factors can be studied. Our highlighting this point should not be construed as merely another argument for greater external validity in research. Claims that traditional laboratory experiments that are highly constrained to increase internal validity are too constrained for generalizable results have certainly been made before. Our view, however, goes beyond such claims. We argue that the highly controlled laboratory context still reveals the operation of influences on behaviour that are not normally considered. In addition, these same factors certainly operate in real situations and may have substantial effects on performance. Importantly, we argue that these factors, and their interactions, must be considered in order to gain a fundamental understanding of behaviour and the limits on performance. For instance, many cognitive psychology experiments involve participants sitting in isolated booths performing de-contextualized tasks on computers. The assumption we make when we perform such experiments is that participants are concentrating solely on the task at hand. Most of us would incorporate performance criteria to ensure some minimum engagement with the task occurred. But surely, this does not rule out the possibility that participants are free to think about many other things while performing the experimental task (e.g. 'I can't wait to finish this experiment so that I can go down to the mall', 'Boy this experiment is boring—who thinks up this stuff?', 'What are the researchers interested in and what will they think of me when they see my results?', 'I wonder what my boyfriend is doing right now', 'Am I ever going to finish this degree and get a job?') and that these off-task thoughts influence their performance on the task. Furthermore, there are all sorts of factors relating to a person's background (e.g. experiences, motivations, anxieties, abilities, interests) that will no doubt influence the ability of each participant to engage with the task and perform adequately. Normally experiments are designed to ignore these individual differences—the assumption is that they represent random noise, and if we select participants carefully enough, this noise will not have a systematic influence on the results of the experiment. But does this represent a case of throwing out the baby with the bathwater?

Everyone's experiences of the world are different, if for no other reason than that there are physical differences between us all that are associated with having slightly different bodies and being in different physical spaces. Everything else about a person can potentially be influenced by, or indeed snowball from these initial physical differences. As a result, everyone's cognitive systems will develop to be slightly (or largely) different. Most of the time the same sorts of constraints will exist on the development of a person's cognitive system. For example, in learning to drive, everyone is subject to cars that operate according to similar generic principles, the same physical laws of motion, and roads that have similar laws, so driving behaviour is constrained to occur within clear limits. Given similar environmental constraints, then, it would be expected that the cognitive systems that people develop will acquire similar characteristics. Psychology's aim, then, is often to determine the nature of these systems.

The process whereby researchers attempt to determine the nature of cognitive systems involves testing many people and inducing from the resultant data general principles underlying the observed performance. But there is a complication in this induction process that certainly does not exist in the physical sciences—individual differences. Psychology certainly recognizes that these exist—the whole panoply of psychological research and statistical methods is based on the fact that people differ and somehow this needs to be controlled for or taken into account when conclusions are reached. Essentially, though, psychology attempts to gloss over the detail of individual differences so that the 'real' system can emerge from the data. But this approach seems to assume that everyone has a copy of the 'real' system in their head, but it is not accurately reflected in an individual's behaviour because of something else about them that adds noise to their data. In our view, though, the behaviour exhibited by an individual is a perfect reflection of their own real system. That is, the system that they developed through their own idiosyncratic experience with the world. Their system may well share features with other people because they are all subject to similar environmental constraints, however, no two systems will be exactly the same because no two people will share identical experiences. Hence, the attempt to discover the nature of 'real' systems is doomed to failure because no such system exists. The best we can hope for is to extract general principles about behaviour (that reflect the impact of generic constraints on the development of systems), but realize that we may never be able to fully understand an individual's behaviour on the basis of these principles, or indeed predict their behaviour except in very broad terms. There may well be scope, however, for studying individuals in depth to understand their personal system, and on the basis of this understanding make predictions about their behaviour. Of course, the pay-off for such focussed research may be debatable.

Another unfortunate result of many of the research designs utilized in Psychology is that they restrict our ability to observe the dynamic nature of most behaviour. A great deal of research in cognitive psychology involves presenting discrete stimuli (e.g. letters, words, sentences, pictures) to subjects and requiring them to make some response. It should come as no surprise that many of the theories that have emerged to explain behaviour in these situations are based on connections between stimuli and responses. Indeed the two major theories of skill acquisition we have considered throughout this book, the ACT theory and the Instance theory, explicitly claim that knowledge is comprised of mental representations of such associations. Even our own theory of agents processing stimulus information to produce some outcome retains this flavour. Real-life behaviour, however, does not have this static nature. Following sufficient practice, people are capable of performing with ease highly dynamic tasks, such as engaging in a conversation, playing the piano, watching a football game, and driving a car through a city. At present, although theorists may claim that such dynamic behaviour could be understood by breaking up each behaviour into components that represent stimulus–response associations, no one has been brave enough to attempt such an explanation. In any case, we would suggest that the effort would be wasted. Psychology has in fact been trying to understand such tasks by dividing them into more easily examinable components (e.g. the lexical decision task as a means of studying reading) but all this approach has resulted in is a static view of behaviour—lots of little theories of small aspects of behaviour with no means of combining them to understand dynamic behaviour as it occurs in the real world.

There is no doubt that studying dynamic behaviour is a difficult problem, and not something for which we can propose a quick and easy fix. For now, though, we would suggest that Psychology should at least accept the dynamic nature of most human activity and realize that a different approach to studying behaviour is necessary. Researchers should be open to considering many influences on the mental processes they study, links between apparently different areas, and potential means for taking account of all relevant influences on dynamic processes. Further, we would venture that stimuli, such as whole passages of speech, are better objects of study than words in isolation if one is trying to understand the processes underlying speech perception.

Another possible means of studying dynamic behaviour, as well as any other forms of behaviour, in order to examine underlying mental processes, is to make use of the suggestion we made above that in many situations people themselves act as agents in complex systems. Our argument is that within each person, mental agents exist at many levels of analysis. That is, the principle of 'self-similarity' operates in the mind such that agents can grow and combine to create 'super' agents at one level of analysis that could be considered particles or minor agents at a higher level of analysis (cf. Halloy, 1998). Extending this principle ever upward leads to the notion of people as agents (e.g. individuals within an organization, individual researchers within a discipline), as well as groups of people as agents (e.g. sporting teams, corporations, countries), all greedy for some resource. An example of the existence of complex system characteristics at the level of individuals is provided by the following quote:

> graduates working in the knowledge economy were expected to put in long hours and to be agile. The industry was based on teams solving problems where *the reward for getting a job done on time included being the first called to fix the next crisis*. There followed 'a permanent state of being, in effect, on call'.
>
> (O'Keefe, 2003, italics inserted).

The properties exhibited by the people in this work situation sound similar to common descriptions of frequently used skills, frequently used words, and indeed agents with large mass. Thus, the performance of individuals may be understood through analyses at many different levels. Within a group of people, individual performance could be analysed in terms of the demands placed upon each person, the group dynamics that emerge as a reflection of the resource available to the individuals, and the behaviour of the group as a whole in terms of the resource available to the group. In a similar vein, studying the development of mental processes could be approximated by observing the development of 'people' processes—if processes are all subject to the same characteristics of complex systems, then observing how teams of people are created and disbanded within an organization to solve a particular problem (e.g. producing a new product) could inform questions about how the mind develops processes for performing a new task. It may be that studying such processes at the 'people' level is more tractable than at the mental level where such processes are often hidden and have to be observed indirectly. Of course it should be realized that all situations will differ in ways that could impact on the types of systems that develop, and so only generic principles may be discerned by this method.

Theorizing

Psychology, and in particular, cognitive psychology, is dominated by an approach to research and theorizing that treats mental systems as if they are permanent features of a person's brain that were somehow magically acquired at around the time the person became an adult. On the basis of this assumption, researchers strive to determine the nature and parameters of each system. One curious aspect of this approach is that rarely do researchers consider the origins of such systems. Instead they operate as if someone has placed a system on their laboratory bench and given them the task of finding out how it works. For evidence of this claim, one only needs to examine again first year Psychology textbooks. These books all have separate chapters on Developmental Psychology, and indeed this field of Psychology operates as just another separate field within the discipline, with the occasional interaction between fields. So researchers outside of Developmental Psychology appear to be leaving the issue of the origin of the systems they study to the developmentalists. In our view, trying to understand the nature of a mental system by studying it in its current state will only reveal half of the story, and possibly a misleading one at that (see discussion of modules in Chapter 4). Given our claim that all mental systems result from the interaction of a person with the world, the nature of these interactions, and the type of adaptations that have been made in response to these experiences are essential ingredients in the origin of any system. Thus, to completely understand a mental system, there must be some consideration of its origin. After all, if learning led to the existence of a current system, then learning mechanisms may still play some role in the current operations of the system. These learning mechanisms will be overlooked if a learning origin is not considered.

We feel that one attraction of our theory is that it depicts a system that is not designed to learn language, or to read words, or to play a musical instrument. Other models of cognition typically are designed to explain some behaviour, with the explanation being along the lines of 'here's a system, and this is how it does this task'. Our theory is that the brain is a system that contains agents which have as their sole *raison d'être* a need to be used, and being used increases the chances of being used in the future. The learning of all the tasks that humans do is a remarkable side effect of the competition among agents to be used. Explanations of behaviours, then, become a matter of determining the way in which a system full of competing agents adapted to the environment to create a set of processes that enable those behaviours to occur.

Although, we are critical of theories of cognition that are highly specific to one set of behaviours, there are other theories of cognition that we feel are on the right track. For instance, the proposed unified theories of cognition, such as ACT and SOAR, are certainly explicit about learning being one of the fundamental features of the development of cognitive systems. Of course, we have already identified what we consider to be shortcomings of these other theories and why we think our own theory has advantages over them. For instance, one aspect of our theory that we feel is particularly attractive from a parsimony perspective is that it is based on the mechanisms and principles of complex systems, and these appear to be ubiquitous in nature. Other unified theories of cognition rely on mechanisms that are posited to be peculiar to the brain.

6.5.2 Theoretical paths not to follow

So far we have used our theory of the mind to propose some alternative approaches to the conduct of psychological research. We also think there are some lessons in the theory regarding the fruitfulness of certain theoretical concepts. Two such concepts are considered here. They are critical periods in development, and the innateness of mental systems.

Developmental critical periods as biologically determined

Some skills have been observed to have limits with respect to the point in a person's life at which they are more likely to be acquired. For instance, the acquisition of language skills (i.e. learning to speak and comprehend a language) and the development of absolute pitch (i.e. the ability to identify a tone's pitch) are skills that are said to be subject to a critical period of development (Hurford, 1991; Takeuchi and Hulse, 1993). That is, if a child is exposed to appropriate stimuli during a particular period in their childhood, then the chances of acquiring these skills is far greater than if exposure occurs outside of this period. Thus, it is often difficult for adults to acquire skills with a second language that even approximate the level of facility acquired with their first language. Adults also seem incapable of acquiring absolute pitch to anything like the extent exhibited by people who acquired this skill as children (Takeuchi and Hulse, 1993).

One interpretation of the existence of critical periods is that throughout childhood, neural circuits are developed that enable particular skills and this development requires interplay between the child and environmental stimuli in order to proceed. One assumption of this interpretation is that the development of these circuits ceases at a particular age of the child. Thus, the neural circuits responsible for language or pitch identification skills require particular stimuli to be available in the environment at a specific time for the circuits to develop. Some theorists go even further to suggest that the potential to develop these skills is pre-wired into our brains and thus has some genetic component (Keenan, *et al.*, 2001; Zatorre, 2003). This view suggests that there are highly specific neural circuits that are responsible for these skills that are present in the newborn brain, albeit in only a rudimentary form, that are waiting for the appropriate environmental stimuli to come along and spark the development of these circuits. Since most people acquire language skills, acquiring such skills must be a genetic potential for all people. Absolute pitch, however, is only acquired by a small number of people, and is suggested to reflect a peculiar phenotype (Keenan, *et al.*, 2001; Zatorre, 2003).

The biological explanation of critical periods implies that the brain is structured to have the potential to develop particular skills during some finite period of time. If the appropriate environmental stimuli are not experienced during this period, then the biological structure of the brain changes in such a way as to limit the potential for acquiring those skills at some later time. In our view there are several alternate explanations of critical periods that do not assume some pre-wired changes to the way the brain functions as a critical period comes to an end. For instance, an explanation that is similar to one introduced in Chapter 5 to explain age-of-acquisition data in lexical phenomena is applicable here. When a person starts to learn their first language, it comes at a time when learning to communicate with others, particularly those providing food and warmth, is extremely important. As a result, acquiring this skill is probably of greatest concern to the infant, and so most of its cognitive faculties are devoted to this task. As a person gets older, they have already mastered communication and so are probably less motivated to learn to communicate in a different language. In addition, they are more likely to be distracted by other concerns, so they would be less prepared to devote almost all their mental resources to learning a new language. Only in certain circumstances is the need sufficient to warrant so much resource expenditure. For example, Paul, the father of one of us, migrated to Australia as a 15-year-old with no English language skills. Paul's strong desire to fit in with his peers in his adopted country presumably provided him with sufficient motivation to acquire English language skills to such an extent that he ended up speaking English with no sign of an accent and spent his whole working life as an editor on a major metropolitan newspaper correcting native speakers' English.

Another alternate explanation to the biological explanation of critical periods has been suggested for the acquisition of absolute pitch. Takeuchi and Hulse (1993) report that absolute pitch is often observed to follow musical training that involves an emphasis on absolute pitch recognition and reproduction. However, if early musical training emphasizes pitch relationships between elements of music over absolute pitch values, then absolute pitch ability is rarely acquired. The implication is that once a person learns to perceive music in terms of pitch relationships rather than absolute pitch values, they are less likely to perceive tones as isolated entities and this makes it difficult to identify a tone's absolute pitch. Takeuchi and Hulse suggest then that it is possible to acquire absolute pitch only at a time before musical appreciation is focussed on pitch relationships. Once music is perceived relationally, absolute pitch is difficult, if not impossible, to acquire. This explanation of critical periods has a similar flavour to the discussion of schemata above. In both cases, learning to perceive some feature of the world in one way disrupts the ability to perceive it in a different way.

The explanations presented here as alternatives to the biological explanation of critical periods are both essentially learning explanations. In our view, an explanation that is just another application of the learning principles identified in the acquisition of many other behaviours suggests that these explanations are more parsimonious than one that involves the operation of an extra mechanism (i.e. genetic/biological).

Innateness explanations

The biological explanation of critical periods mentioned above belongs to a class of explanations in Psychology that posit some biological origin to particular human behaviours. More specifically, these explanations assume that certain behaviours are innate, and therefore have some genetic component. We question, however, the utility of such theories and hence their continued popularity. Although we are not going to attempt to disprove all such theories here, we pose the question of whether such theories are necessary. Is it not possible that those behaviours seen by some to have an inherited origin actually have an origin that stems from learning? If the mind is a complex system, and development follows the actions of 'greedy' agents, then everything about a person is practically determined by their adaptation to the world. There may well be hereditary differences about the way neurons sprout connections, and are activated, and connections wither from lack of use, but ultimately the way we end up as adults is a product of our adaptation to what we have been exposed. Common cognitive developmental milestones, then, can be reconstrued as the outcomes of humans, with brains that work according to the same principles (i.e. learning via actions of a complex system), adapting to life among similar beings, and hence societies with similar constraints, and a world with constant physical laws. Therefore, common developmental trajectories may be a reflection of logical sequences determined by the nature of a task and the limits on one's ability to acquire new skills (i.e. the need to develop simple skills to a certain extent before more complex tasks can be attempted), rather than some invariant way in which biological development must proceed. Behaviours or skills that seem to run in families (e.g. musical ability) can then be interpreted as family members growing up in similar environments.

Theories that posit innate knowledge in humans (e.g. Chomsky, 1968) and biologically determined patterns of development (Piaget, 1967) all agree that skills cannot develop without some interaction with the environment. Curiously such theories are essentially suggesting that some part of the skill is untouched by the environment (e.g. grammatical rules) but other parts are heavily influenced by the environment (e.g. the particular language someone learns). Where the line is drawn appears to us to be fairly arbitrary. Why draw any line? Why not assume that the mind is a complex system, and all the skills that it acquires are a function of its interactions with the environment? Similarities that occur between people will reflect similar environmental constraints. The existence of individual differences is also catered for as these will be related to the peculiarities of an individual's experiences. Many theories of the innate origins of behaviour claim that a particular behavioural phenomenon could not have resulted from learning because people are not exposed to enough of the right sort of learning experiences. Is it not possible, though, that as yet we do not have enough evidence about how much learning is actually occurring in the development of particular skills? It is also possible that the power of learning has been underestimated, particularly in domains such as language where acquisition of skills occurs at a time when few other domains hold the same importance. Learning under these conditions can produce outcomes that are seemingly qualitatively different to learning under laboratory conditions. For instance, some theorists (e.g. Miller, 1989) suggest that idiot savants develop their extraordinary skills because of a great deal of mental practice. Often these people possess some physical restriction on their ability to receive or produce information in one domain (e.g. vision), and possibly as a result of this disability they develop an obsession with another domain (e.g. music). Thus, although the outside world does not see the practice they engage in, their obsession may result in many thousands of trials of mental practice. This mental practice then leads to the development of extraordinary skills, the existence of which may be a complete mystery to the onlooker. There is no *prima facie* reason why positing a learning mechanism as the first assumption of the origins of behaviour is any more questionable than proposing that, in the absence of any evidence of learning being involved, there must be a genetic origin. In our view, the former is far more justifiable as a beginning assumption, especially with recognition of the learning power associated with the mind being a complex system. Once we start positing genetic origins for behaviours, the onus is on us to propose an evolutionary advantage for those behaviours.

Although our argument here may suggest the opposite, our conclusion is not that no behaviour has an innate component. Instead our suggestion is that sometimes there might be a little too much eagerness to opt for an innate origin for behaviours. That is, when no evidence can be found for a learned component to a behaviour, the default assumption is usually that the behaviour must be innate. Our challenge to researchers is that there should be greater effort to look for evidence of learning. In particular, there should be greater cognisance of the power of practice, specifically practice that may not be immediately obvious to an observer (i.e. mental practice).

One element of a person's cognitive make-up that we think may well be inherited relates to motivation. Acquiring any sort of skill usually requires a great deal of effort, especially if the tasks involved are difficult for a novice, and enormous amounts of practice are necessary to progress towards expert status. Acquiring skills in playing a musical instrument is one such example. Many people start to learn to play music during their childhood, but very few persist with the many years of practice necessary to perform at a professional level (Ericsson, et al., 1993). As Ericsson et al. have pointed out, inherent ability in being able to play an instrument rarely distinguishes those who give up on music and those who persist. Instead, the main determiner of later musical success is preparedness to practice for many hours per day for many years. What determines this preparedness to endure such practice regimens is an open question, although we feel there is some merit in Ericsson and co-workers' suggestion that this may be where biological inheritance plays a role. There are many reports in the expertise literature, and in biographies of great scientists, of an early, all-consuming interest in the particular field of endeavour in which the person later excels (e.g. Ericsson et al., 1993; Holmes, 1996; Howe, 1996). These reports suggest that there is something about the target domain that holds great intrinsic interest for the person, and this interest is sufficient to drive the person through many years of hard work at mastering the domain. Working in the domain provides enormous satisfaction for the person and so acts as a powerful reinforcer. As a result there develops a cycle of drive and reinforcement that feed upon each other to motivate higher levels of performance.

Clearly an intrinsic interest in a particular domain could reflect the reinforcement that would be received by engaging in tasks that are encouraged by family members who work in the same domain. Thus, it is common for people growing up in musical families to develop musical skills. It is also possible, though, that these family members share something in their cerebral make-up that makes music more intrinsically interesting than for someone in a different family. Furthermore, it is also possible that someone could be born with such an intrinsic interest in music but the environment into which they are born does not support this interest and so the interest does not receive the opportunity to flourish. All of these scenarios are possible, and, in our view, consistent with each other. The way that we see that they can all be consistent is to consider the brain as an organ in which a complex system can develop through interacting with the world. The brain will be limited in the ways in which it can develop by the nature of the neurons that it consists of, and the types of connections that can be established between neurons and between neural circuits and sensory and motor organs. Thus, there are physical constraints on the way that the brain can develop following conception and particularly following birth. It is surely not inconceivable that the limits that exist on a brain's development, although similar for all humans, are more similar across families, in the same way that physical features, such as eye colour, nose shape, and smile are passed on through generations. We suggest that these limits on the brain's development could determine the things in the world that are of intrinsic interest to people. That is, someone who finds music exciting as soon as they encounter it in life is someone whose brain is structured in such a way as to facilitate the development of agents that receive reinforcement readily for performing music-related operations. This ready reinforcement for engaging in such activities becomes a self-serving motivation to continue exploring the domain. Other domains that do not spark the same interest will leave a person with little intrinsic motivation to tackle tasks in those domains for long periods.

Having propounded the virtues of intrinsic motivation, there is still a lot to be said for the power of extrinsic motivation. For everyone, there will be domains that do not hold any intrinsic interest. These domains are boring and we would normally find it extremely difficult to spend the long hours necessary to develop skills in the domain. Nevertheless, there may exist sufficient extrinsic motivation for us to be driven to acquire skills in the domain. For example, consider the case of a person who is heavily motivated to becoming a medical doctor. To gain entrance into the necessary university course to achieve this goal, they must excel in a number of subjects in their high school course. These subjects could include calculus, for which the person has no intrinsic interest. Nonetheless, the drive to study medicine is so strong that this motivation could transfer to a drive to master calculus. It is arguable whether such a person has an extrinsic motivation in studying calculus (i.e. they are driven by the external rewards of grades) or they are simply able to transfer their intrinsic interest in medicine to the task of studying calculus, or indeed whether all apparently extrinsic motivations are merely means of satisfying internal drives. Regardless of which of these interpretations applies, this example illustrates that it is not always necessary to possess an intrinsic interest in a domain in order to acquire skills in that domain.

The view that our brains come with genetically related limits on development should not be construed as a suggestion that some people's brains are pre-programmed to be good at music, or mathematics, or catching fish. What is inherited, in our view, is a way of processing information, and for receiving reinforcement for doing such tasks. Thus, someone who shows early interest in music, for instance, is someone who can process musical information in a way that facilitates the later development of skills in music. But this is not to say that the person has a 'musical brain' necessarily, or that they have music in the genes. It just means that their brain is good at processing musical information. There is a subtle difference here between the two positions that can be illustrated with a simple analogy. Computers are excellent machines for performing mathematical calculations—they can certainly perform some calculations far quicker than a human brain can. This does not mean, however, that computers are calculating machines in the sense that they are designed to perform calculations. Computers are in fact designed to perform operations that are specified by the software commands programmed into the computer. These software commands tell the computer how to transform one set of on/off codes (i.e. strings of 1's and 0's) into other sets of on/off codes. Essentially, then, computers are designed to transform one set of codes into another set of codes. The codes, of course, can vary dramatically, and so too can the programs that run on the computer. In this way computers can perform a wide range of tasks, from playing music, to controlling visual animations, to enabling document editing. All the while, though, the computers are simply transforming strings of 1's and 0's into other strings. Thus it is not really appropriate to describe the computer in any of these situations as a musician, an animator, or a document editor. Similarly, someone who seems to have a musical brain is simply someone whose brain just happens to be good at processing information of a particular type. Because music constitutes information of this type, the person can process it well. There could, however, be other domains that fall within the same information type, and so the person is likely to be good at performing tasks in these domains as well. Thus, there is no need to posit theories about why musical skill should be passed on through families, and what evolutionary advantage it provides. It is sufficient to argue for why the ability to process information of a particular sort, which includes music, and possibly other domains, should be inherited.

The limits we propose that exist on brain development, and the impacts of these limits on behaviour, can be understood with respect to a geographical analogy. The course of a river is typically determined by the lay of the land— water flows in ways that are dictated by gravity and so will usually flow to and in the lowest points in any area of land. In a similar vein, urban development is usually restricted by geographical features, such as rivers, lakes, mountains, and ravines. If a city is built near a mountain, it will typically surround the bottom of the mountain rather than stretch up the mountain. In particular, major infrastructure, such as highways, railroads, and skyscrapers will be positioned at the foot of the mountain. Applying this analogy to the brain suggests a way of understanding how some knowledge could appear to be innate. Take for example, the idea that there is a grammar that is universal to all human languages, and that this grammar is built into the human brain (Chomsky, 1968). Rather than such knowledge being innate, the universal grammar may simply reflect a brain restriction that is universal. That is, the brain may be restricted in the way it can process particular types of information, of which language is one example. These restrictions may in turn reflect constraints that exist in nature, such as physical laws that relate to causation. Hence, the human brain has evolved in a way that represents an adaptation to the world and the physical laws that exist, and this has meant that the brain is limited to processing certain types of information in a particular manner. Thus the brain is wired to process information in one way, and just cannot process it in other ways. So, the existence of what appears to be a universal grammar among all the languages of the world does not mean that every person has a copy of this grammar in their head. Rather than indicating the existence of innate knowledge, it could instead indicate the existence of innate ways of processing information. Thus, whenever a culture is faced with the task of representing the world in a verbal manner, the brains of the people in that culture are restricted in the ways in which they can perform this task. Furthermore, the structure of a solution to this task does not already sit in their brain, as would be the case with an innate universal grammar. Instead, potential solutions are limited by the brain's capabilities and yet these will reflect constraints that already exist in the world. Thus, there will be a similar underlying structure in every attempt to represent the world verbally.

6.6 Conclusions

The Problem we identified with Cognitive Psychology now has a solution. The first part of this solution is the claim that learning underlies much of cognitive phenomena. The second part of the solution is the Component Theory of

Skill Acquisition. This theory explains how learning, as the adaptation of a complex system to environmental demands, leads to the development of the cognitive systems which are the typical targets of cognitive research. This solution has myriad implications for Psychology as a discipline, not least of which are the ways in which research is conducted and the types of theories considered acceptable. Our view is that Psychology has some way to go in terms of forging a path towards enlightenment about the nature of cognition, but we would like to think that we have suggested some steps in this direction.

Up until now, Psychology has been a science mainly concerned with description: describing behaviour, describing relationships between variables that affect behaviour, and ultimately describing the nature of systems that might lead to behaviour. Thus, Psychology has been striving towards providing explanations. At last, in our view, we are now at a point where we can start to speculate on a complete explanation for *why* the systems, or indeed, *the* system, is the way it is. That is, we are no longer restricted to just the 'what does the system do?' issue. We can now consider the 'why is the system like that?' question. For instance, when we wonder why someone behaves in a certain way, we might have once been satisfied with an explanation that went along the lines of 'because they have a system in their brain that has such-and-such a structure and works in such-and-such a manner'. Now, though, we are in a position to ask 'but why do they have such-and-such a system in their brain?' According to our theory, the system follows some basic laws of nature (i.e. it is a complex adaptive system) and is built with a survival instinct. The quest for survival is built into every cell. In neural tissue that manifests as a quest for information that will be useful for continued survival. Every other feature of the system, then, reflects adaptations to the environment in which the system exists. Hence, there is no need to posit a mental architecture as the starting point for an explanation of behaviour. Rather, the architecture emerges through interaction with the world, and to a large extent then, the type of interaction experienced will determine the type of architecture that develops.

References

Ackerman, P.L. (1988). Determinants of individual differences during skill acquisition: Cognitive abilities and information processing. *Journal of Experimental Psychology: General*, **117**, 288–318.

Adamic, L.A. (2000). Zipf, Power-laws, and Pareto—a ranking tutorial. (http://www.hpl.hp.com/research/idl/papers/ranking/ranking.html)

Adams, C. (2003). Passenger injuries in crashes in Western Australia, 1996–2000. Report to The Royal Automobile Club of WA (Inc), April 2003. (Summarized in *Road Patrol Magazine*, April/May 2003)

Adams, J.A. (1987). Historical review and appraisal of research on the learning, retention, and transfer of human motor skills. *Psychological Bulletin*, **101**, 41–74.

Adams, J.A. and Reynolds, B. (1954). Effect of shift in distribution of practice conditions following interpolated rest. *Journal of Experimental Psychology*, **47**, 32–36.

Adelson, B. (1981). Problem solving and the development of abstract categories in programming languages. *Memory & Cognition*, **9**, 422–433.

Adelson, B. (1984). When novices surpass experts: The difficulty of a task may increase with expertise. *Journal of Experimental Psychology: Learning, Memory and Cognition*, **10**, 483–495.

Alba, J.W. and Hasher, L. (1983). Is memory schematic? *Psychological Bulletin*, **93**(2), 203–231.

Alibali, M.W. and Goldin-Meadow, S. (1993). Gesture-speech mismatch and mechanisms of learning: What the hands reveal about a child's state of mind. *Cognitive Psychology*, **25**(4), 468–523.

Allard, F. and Burnett, N. (1985). Skill in sport. *Canadian Journal of Psychology*, **39**, 294–312.

Allard, F. and Stakes, J.L. (1991). Motor-skill experts in sports, dance, and other domains. In K.A. Ericsson and J. Smith (Eds), *Toward a theory of expertise: Prospects and limits*. New York: Cambridge University Press.

Allen, P.A., Madden, D.J., Weber, T.A., and Groth, K.E. (1993). Influence of age and processing stage on visual word recognition. *Psychology and Aging*, **8**(2), 274–282.

Altmann, C.F., Deubelius, A., and Kourtzi, Z. (2004). Shape saliency modulates contextual processing in the human lateral occipital complex. *Journal of Cognitive Neuroscience*, **16**(5), 794–804.

Anderson, J.R. (1976). *Language, memory, and thought*. Hillsdale, NJ: Erlbaum.

Anderson, J.R. (1982). Acquisition of cognitive skill. *Psychological Review*, **89**, 369–406.

Anderson, J.R. (1983a). *The architecture of cognition*. Cambridge, MA: Harvard University Press.

Anderson, J.R. (1983b). Retrieval of information from long-term memory. *Science*, **220**, 25–30.

Anderson, J.R. (1986). Category learning: Things aren't so black and white. The *Behavioral and Brain Sciences*, **9**, 651

Anderson, J.R. (1987). Skill acquisition: Compilation of weak-method problem solutions. *Psychological Review*, **94**, 192–210.

Anderson, J.R. (1989a). The analogical origins of errors in problem solving. In D. Klahr and K. Kotovsky (Eds), *Complex information processing*. Hillsdale, NJ: Erlbaum.

Anderson, J.R. (1989b). Practice, working memory, and the ACT* theory of skill acquisition: A comment on Carlson, Sullivan, and Schneider (1989). *Journal of Experimental Psychology: Learning, Memory, and Cognition*, **15**, 527–530.

Anderson, J.R. (1992). Automaticity and the ACT* theory. *American Journal of Psychology*, **105**(2), 165–180.

Anderson, J.R. (Ed.) (1993). *Rules of the mind*. Hillsdale, NJ: Erlbaum.

Anderson, J.R. and Bower, G. (1973). *Human associative memory*. Washington, DC: Winston.

Anderson, J.R. and Corbett, A.T. (1993). Tutoring of cognitive skill. In J.R. Anderson (Ed.), *Rules of the mind*. Hillsdale, NJ: Erlbaum.

Anderson, J.R. and Fincham, J.M. (1994). Acquisition of procedural skills from examples. *Journal of Experimental Psychology: Learning, Memory, and Cognition*, **22**, 259–277.

Anderson, J.R. and Lebiere, C. (Eds) (1998). *Atomic components of thought*. Mahwah, NJ: Erlbaum.

Anderson, J.R. and Reiser, B.J. (1985). The LISP tutor. *Byte*, **10**, 159–175.

Anderson, J.R. and Schooler, L.J. (1991). Reflections of the environment in memory. *Psychological Science*, **2**(6), 396–408.

Anderson, J.R. and Singley, M.K. (1993). The identical elements theory of transfer. In J.R. Anderson (Ed.), *Rules of the mind*. Hillsdale, NJ: Erlbaum.

Anderson, J.R., Kline, P.J., and Beasley, C.M. (1979). A general learning theory and its application to schema abstraction. In G.H. Bower (Ed.), *The psychology of learning and motivation*, Vol. **13**. New York: Academic Press.

Anderson, J.R., Kline, P.J., and Beasley, C.M. (1980). Complex learning processes. In R.E. Snow, P.A. Frederico, and W.E. Montague (Eds), *Aptitude, learning, and instruction*, Vol. **2**. Hillsdale, NJ: Erlbaum.

Anderson, J.R., Greeno, J.G., Kline, P.J., and Neves, D.M. (1981). Acquisition of problem-solving skill. In J.R. Anderson (Ed.), *Cognitive skills and their acquisition*. Hillsdale, NJ: Erlbaum.

Anderson, J.R., Boyle, C.F., and Reiser, B.J. (1985). Intelligent tutoring systems. *Science*, **228**, 456–462.

Anderson, J.R., Conrad, F.G., and Corbett, A.T. (1989). Skill acquisition and the LISP tutor. *Cognitive Science*, **13**, 467–505.

Anderson, J.R., Bellezza, F.S, and Boyle, C.F. (1993a). The geometry tutor and skill acquisition. In J.R. Anderson (Ed.), *Rules of the mind*. Hillsdale, NJ: Erlbaum.

Anderson, J.R., Conrad, F.G., and Corbett, A.T. (1993b). The LISP tutor and skill acquisition. In J.R. Anderson (Ed.), *Rules of the mind*. Hillsdale, NJ: Erlbaum.

Anderson, J.R., Conrad, F.G., Corbett, A.T., Fincham, J.M., Hoffman, D., and Wu, Q. (1993c). Computer programming and transfer. In J.R. Anderson (Ed.), *Rules of the mind*. Hillsdale, NJ: Erlbaum.

Anderson, J.R., Fincham, J.M., and Douglass, D. (1997). The role of examples and rules in the acquisition of a cognitive skill. *Journal of Experimental Psychology: Learning, Memory, and Cognition*, **23**(4), 932–945.

Anderson, J.R., Lebiere, C., and Lovett, M. (1998). Performance. In J.R. Anderson and C. Lebiere (Eds.), *Atomic components of thought*. Mahwah, NJ: Erlbaum.

Anderson, J.R., Fincham, J.M., and Douglass, D. (1999). Practice and retention: A unifying analysis. *Journal of Experimental Psychology: Learning, Memory and Cognition*, **25**(5), 1120–1136.

Aunola, K., Leskinen, E., Lerkkanen, M.K., and Nurmi, J.E. (2004). Developmental dynamics of math performance from preschool to grade 2. *Journal of Educational Psychology*, **96**(4), 699–713.

Baayen, R.H. and Tweedie, F.J. (1998). *Mixture models and word frequency distributions*. Paper presented at the ALLC/ACH Conference, Debrecen.

Baddeley, A. (1990). *Human memory: Thought and practice*. Hove, UK: Erlbaum, pp. 40–42.

Bainbridge, J.V., Lewandowsky, S., and Kirsner, K. (1993). Context effects in repetition priming are sense effects. *Memory & Cognition*, **21**(5), 619–626.

Barnes, C.A. (1979). Memory deficits associated with senescence: A neurophysiological and behavioral study in the rat. *Journal of Comparative Physiology*, **43**, 74–104.

Bartlett, F.C. (1932). *Remembering: A study in experimental and social psychology*. Cambridge, England: Cambridge University Press.

Bartlett, F.C. (1948). The measurement of human skill. *Occupational Psychology*, **22**, 83–91.

Baumgaertner, A. and Tompkins, C.A. (1998). Beyond frequency: Predicting auditory word recognition in normal elderly adults. *Aphasiology*, **12**(7–8), 601–617.

Bechtel, W. (2002). Decomposing the brain: A long term pursuit. *Brain and Mind*, **3**, 229–242.

Beck, A.T. (1964). Thinking and depression: II. Theory and therapy. *Archives of General Psychiatry*, **10**, 561–571.

Beck, J.S. (1995). *Cognitive therapy: Basics and beyond*. New York: The Guilford Press.

Bem, S.L. (1993). *The lenses of gender: Transforming the debate on sexual inequality*. New Haven, CT: Yale University Press.

Bianconi, G. and Barabasi, A.L. (2001). Competition and multiscaling in evolving networks. *Europhysics Letters*, **54**, 436–442.

Blessing, S. and Anderson, J.R. (1996). How people learn to skip steps. *Journal of Experimental Psychology: Learning, Memory, and Cognition*, **22**, 576–598.

Bloom, P. (2000). Overview: Controversies in language development. In P. Bloom (Ed.), *Language acquisition: Core readings*. Cambridge: MIT Press.

Bloom, P. (2002). *How children learn the meaning of words*. Cambridge, MA: MIT Press.

Bodner, G.E. and Masson, M.E.J. (1997). Masked repetition priming of words and nonwords: Evidence for a nonlexical basis for priming. *Journal of Memory and Language*, **37**(2), 268–293.

Bolger, D.J. and Schneider, W. (2002). Representation of visual word forms in fMRI habituation paradigms. Paper presented at the 43rd Annual Meeting of the Psychonomics Society, Kansas City, Missouri, Nov. 2002.

Book, W.F. (1925). *The psychology of skill*. New York: Grigg.

Bourke, P. (1993). Sierpinski gasket. http://astronomy.swin.edu.au/~pbourke/fractals/gasket/

Bower, G.H., Black, J.B., and Turner, T.J. (1979). Scripts in memory for text. *Cognitive Psychology*, **11**, 177–220.

Bradley, D. (1979). Lexical representation in derivational relation. In M. Aranoff and M. Kean (Eds), *Juncture*. Cambridge, MA: MIT Press.

Briggs, G.E. (1969). Transfer of training. In E.A. Bilodeau and I.Mc. Bilodeau (Eds), *Principles of skill acquisition*. New York: Academic Press.

Brown, H.L., Sharma, N.K., and Kirsner, K. (1984). The role of script and phonology in lexical representation. *Quarterly Journal of Experimental Psychology*, **36**A, 491–505.

Brown, T.L. and Carr, T.H. (1989). Automaticity in skill acquisition: Mechanisms for reducing interference in concurrent performance. *Journal of Experimental Psychology: Human Perception and Performance*, **15**, 686–700.

Bruer, J.T. and Greenough, W.T. (2001). The subtle science of how experience affects the brain. In D.B. Bailey Jr., J.T. Bruer, F.J. Symons, and J.W. Lichtman (Eds), *Critical thinking about critical periods*. Baltimore, MD: Paul H. Brooks Publishing Co.

Bryan, W.L. and Harter, N. (1897). Studies in the physiology and psychology of the telegraphic language. *Psychological Review*, **4**, 27–53.

Bryan, W.L. and Harter, N. (1899). Studies on the telegraphic language: The acquisition of a hierarchy of habits. *Psychological Review*, **6**, 345–375.

Brysbaert, M., Lange, M., and Wijnendaele, I.V. (2000). The effects of age-of-acquisition and frequency-of-occurrence in visual word recognition: Further evidence from the Dutch language. *European Journal of Cognitive Psychology*, **12**(1), 65–85.

Buchanan, M. (2000). *Ubiquity*. London: Pheonix Orion Books.

Buck, R. and Duffy, R.J. (1980). Nonverbal communication of affect in brain-damaged patients. *Cortex*, **16**(3), 351–362.

Byrne, B. (1984). On teaching articulatory phonetics via an orthography. *Memory & Cognition*, **12**(2), 181–189.

Byrne, B. and Carroll, M. (1989). Learning artificial orthographies: Further evidence of an acquisition procedure. *Memory & Cognition*, **17**(3), 311–317.

Cabeza, R., Burton, A.M., Kelly, S.W., and Akamatsu, S. (1997). Investigating the relation between imagery and perception: Evidence from face priming. *Quarterly Journal of Experimental Psychology: Human Experimental Psychology*, **50**A(2), 274–289.

Camerer, C.F. and Johnson, E.J. (1991). The process-performance paradox in expert judgment: How can experts know so much and predict so badly? In K.A. Ericcson and J. Smith (Eds), *Toward a general theory of expertise*. Cambridge, England: Cambridge University Press, pp. 195–217.

Campbell, J.I.D. (1987). Network-interference and mental multiplication. *Journal of Experimental Psychology: Learning, Memory, and Cognition*, **13**, 109–123.

Campione, E. and Veronis, J. (2002). *A large-scale multilingual study of silent pause duration*. www.lpl.univ-aix.fr/sp2002/pdf/campione-veronis.pdf

Cancho, R.F. and Sole, R.V. (2003). Least effort and the origins of scaling in human language. *Proceedings of the National Academy of Sciences of the United States of America*, **100**(3), 788–791.

Carlesimo, G.A., Fadda, L., Sabbadini, M., and Caltagirone, C. (1994). Visual repetition priming for words relies on access to the visual input lexicon: Evidence from a dyslexic patient. *Neuropsychologia*, **32**(9), 1089–1100.

Carlisle, J.F. and Fleming, J. (2003). Lexical processing of morphologically complex words in the elementary years. *Scientific Studies of Reading*, **7**(3), 239–253.

Carlson, R.A. (1997). *Experienced cognition*. Mahwah, NJ: Erlbaum.

Carlson, R.A. and Yaure, R.G. (1990). Practice schedules and the use of component skills in problem solving. *Journal of Experimental Psychology: Learning, Memory, and Cognition*, **16**, 484–496.

Carlson, R.A., Sullivan, M.A., and Schneider, W. (1989). Practice and working memory effects in building procedural skill. *Journal of Experimental Psychology: Learning, Memory, and Cognition*, **15**, 517–526.

Carlson, R.A., Khoo, B.H. and Elliott, R.G., II (1990a). Component practice and exposure to a problem-solving context. *Human Factors*, **32**(3), 267–286.

Carlson, R.A., Khoo, B.H., Yaure, R.G., and Schneider, W. (1990b). Acquisition of a problem-solving skill: Levels of organization and use of working memory. *Journal of Experimental Psychology: General*, **119**(2), 193–214.

Carr, S.C. (2003). *Social psychology*. Milton, Queensland: Wiley. (Chapter 7)

Case, R. (1978). Intellectual development from birth to adulthood: A neo-Piagetian approach. In R.S. Seigler (Ed.), *Children's thinking: What develops?* Hillsdale, NJ: Erlbaum.

Case, R. (1985). *Intellectual development: A systematic reinterpretation*. New York: Academic Press.

Cave, C.B. (1997). Very long-lasting priming in picture naming. *Psychological Science*, **8**(4), 322–325.

Chase, W.G. (Ed.) (1973). Visual information processing. New York: Academic Press.

Chase, W.G. and Simon, H.A. (1973). The mind's eye in chess. In W.G. Chase (Ed.), *Visual information processing*. New York: Academic Press.

Chi, M.T.H. (1978). Knowledge structure and memory development. In R.S. Siegler (Ed.), *Children's thinking: What develops?* Hillsdale, NJ: Erlbaum.

Chiu, C.-Y.P. and Schacter, D.L. (1995). Auditory priming for nonverbal information: Implicit and explicit memory for environmental sounds. *Consciousness and Cognition*, **4**(4), 440–458.

Chomsky, N. (1968). *Language and mind*. New York: Harcourt, Brace and World.

Chomsky, N. (1975). *Reflections on language*. New York: Pantheon.

Chomsky, N. (1986). *Knowledge of language: Its nature, origin and use*. New York: Praeger.

Ciccone, N., Hird, K., and Kirsner, K. (2000). Treatment efficacy: An explanation of new learning in patients with aphasia. *Asia Pacific Journal of Speech, Language and Hearing*, **5**(1), 79–84.

Clarke, D.D. and Nerlich, B. (1991). Word-waves: A computational model of lexical semantic change. *Language & Communication*, **11**(3), 227–238.

Clark, R.E. and Jones, C.E. (1962). Manual performance during cold exposure as a function of practice level and the thermal conditions of training. *Journal of Applied Psychology*, **46**, 276–280.

Clawson, D.M., King, C.L., Healy, A.F., and Ericsson, K.A. (1995). Training and retention of the classic Stroop task: Specificity of practice effects. In A.F. Healy and L.E. Bourne, Jr. (Eds), *Learning and memory of knowledge and skills: Durability and specificity*. Thousand Oaks, CA: Sage.

Cohen, D. (2002). All the world's a net. *New Scientist*, **174**, 22–29.

Cohen, J. (1994). The earth is round ($p < .05$). *American Psychologist*, **49**(12), 997–1003.

Cohen, J.D., Dunbar, K., and McClelland, J.L. (1990). On the control of automatic processes: A parallel distributed processing account of the Stroop effect. *Psychological Review*, **97**, 332–361.

Cole, P., Beauvillain, C., and Segui, J. (1989). On the representation and processing of prefixed and suffixed derived words: A differential frequency effect. *Journal of Memory and Language*, **28**(1), 1–13.

Collins, A.M. and Quillian, M.R. (1969). Retrieval time from semantic memory. *Journal of Verbal Learning and Verbal Behavior*, **8**, 240–247.

Collins, A.M. and Quillian, M.R. (1972). How to make a language user. In E. Tulving and W. Donaldson (Eds), *Organisation and memory*. New York: Academic Press.

Coltheart, M. (1978). Lexical access in simple reading tasks. In G. Underwood (Ed.), *Strategies of information processing*. London: Academic Press. pp. 151–216.

Coltheart, M. (1985). Cognitive neuropsychology and the study of reading. In M.I. Posner and O.S.M. Marlin (Eds), *Attention and performance*, Vol. **XI**. Hillsdale, NJ: Lawrence Erlbaum Associates.

Coltheart, M. (1999). Modularity and cognition. *Trends in Cognitive Science*, **3**(3), 115–120.

Coltheart, M., Curtis, B., Atkins, P., and Haller, M. (1993). Models of reading aloud: Dual-route and parallel-distributed-processing approaches. *Psychological Review*, **100**(4), 589–608.

Corbett, A.T. and Anderson, J.R. (1992). The LISP intelligent tutoring system: Research in skill acquisition. In J. Larkin, R. Chabay, and C. Scheftic (Eds), *Computer assisted instruction and intelligent tutoring systems: Establishing communication and collaboration*. Hillsdale, NJ: Lawrence Erlbaum Associates. pp. 73–110.

Cristoffanini, P.M., Kirsner, K., and Milech, D. (1986). Bilingual lexical representation: The status of Spanish-English cognates. *The Quarterly Journal of Experimental Psychology*, **38**A, 367–393.

Crossman, E.R. (1959). A theory of the acquisition of speed-skill. *Ergonomics*, **2**, 153–166.

Crovitz, H.F., Harvey, M.T., and McClanahan, S. (1981). Hidden memory: A rapid method for the study of amnesia using perceptual learning. *Cortex*, **17**, 273–278.

Crowder, R.G. (1972). *Principles of learning and memory*. Hillsdale, NJ: Erlbaum.

Cycowicz, Y.M. and Friedman, D. (1998). Effect of sound familiarity on the event-related potentials elicited by novel environmental sounds. *Brain and Cognition*, **36**(1), 30–51.

de Groot, A.M.B. and Nas, G.L.J. (1991). Lexical representation of cognates and noncognates in compound bilinguals. *Journal of Memory and Language*, **30**(1), 90–123.

De Jong, J.R. (1957). The effects of increasing skill on cycle-time and its consequences for time-standards. *Ergonomics*, **1**, 51–60.

Delaney, P.F., Reder, L.M., Staszewski, J.J., and Ritter, F.E. (1998). The strategy-specific nature of improvement: The power law applies by strategy within task. *Psychological Science*, **9**(1), 1–7.

Dennis, S. (1995). *The Sydney Morning Herald word database*. http://www2.psy.uq.edu.au/CogPsych/Noetica/OpenForumIssue4/SMH.html

Dishon-Berkovits, M. and Algom, D. (2000). The Stroop effect: It is not the robust phenomenon that you have thought it to be. *Memory & Cognition*, **28**(8), 1437–1449.

Doehring, D.G. (1976). Acquisition of rapid reading responses. *Monographs of the society for research in child development*, **41**(2), 1–53.

Downie, R., Milech, D., and Kirsner, K. (1985). Unit definition in the mental lexicon. *Australian Journal of Psychology*, **37**(2), 141–155.

Draganski, B., Gaser, C., Busch, V., Schuierer, G., May, A., and Bogdahn, U. (2004). Changes in grey matter induced by training. *Nature*, **427**(6972), 311–312.

Dumais, S.T. (1979). *Perceptual learning in automatic detection: Processes and mechanisms.* Unpublished doctoral dissertation, Indiana University.

Dunn, J.C. and Kirsner, K. (1988). Discovering functionally independent mental processes: The principle of reversed association. *Psychological Review*, **95**(1), 91–101.

Dunn, J.C. and Kirsner, K. (2003). What can we infer from double dissociations? *Cortex*, **39**(1), 1–7.

Duncan, C.P. (1958). Transfer after training with single verses multiple tasks. *Journal of Experimental Psychology*, **55**, 63–72.

Ebbinghaus, H. (1885). *Memory: A contribution to experimental psychology* (translated by H.A. Ruger and C.E. Bussenues, 1913). New York: Teachers College, Columbia University.

Eberts, R. and Schneider, W. (1986). Effects of perceptual training of sequenced line movements. *Perception & Psychophysics*, **39**, 236–224.

Eccles, J.C. (1972). Possible synaptic mechanisms subserving learning. In A.G. Karyman and J.C. Eccles (Eds), *Brain and human behaviour*. New York: Springer-Verlag.

Elio, R. (1986). Representation of similar well-learned cognitive procedures. *Cognitive Science*, **10**, 41–73.

Ellis, A.W., Young, A.W., Flude, B.M., and Hay, D.C. (1987). Repetition priming of face recognition. *Quarterly Journal of Experimental Psychology*, **42**A(3), 495–512.

Epple, D., Argote, L., and Devadas, R. (1991). Organizational learning curves: A method for investigating intra-plant transfer of knowledge acquired through learning by doing. *Organization Science*, **2**(1), 58–70.

Ericsson, K.A. and Polson, P.G. (1988). Memory for restaurant orders. In M.T.H. Chi, R. Glaser, and M.J. Farr (Eds), *The nature of expertise*. Hillsdale, NJ: Erlbaum.

Ericsson, K.A. and Staszewski, J.J. (1989). Skilled memory and expertise: Mechanisms of exceptional performance. In D. Klahr and K. Kotovsky (Eds), *Complex information processing*. Hillsdale, NJ: Erlbaum.

Ericsson, K.A., Krampe, R.T., and Tesch-Römer, C. (1993). The role of deliberate practice in the acquisition of expert performance. *Psychological Review*, **100**(3), 363–406.

Eyring, J.D., Johnson, D.S., and Francis, D.J. (1993). A cross-level units-of-analysis approach to individual differences in skill acquisition. *Journal of Applied Psychology*, **78**(5), 805–814.

Eysenck, M.W. and Keane, M.T. (1995). *Cognitive psychology: A student's handbook*, 3rd edn. Hove, East Sussex: Erlbaum. Chapter 11.

Fendrich, D.W., Healy, A.F., and Bourne, L.E., Jr. (1991). Long-term repetition effects for motoric and perceptual procedures. *Journal of Experimental Psychology: Learning, Memory, and Cognition*, **17**, 137–151.

Fendrich, D.W., Healy, A.F., and Bourne, L.E., Jr. (1993). Mental arithmetic: Training and retention of multiplication skill. In I. Chizuko (Ed.), *Cognitive psychology applied*. Hillsdale, NJ: Lawrence Erlbaum. pp. 111–113.

Fernald, A. (2000). Human maternal vocalizations to infants as biologically relevant signals: An evolutionary perspective. In P. Bloom (Ed.), *Language Acquisition*. Cambridge, MA: The MIT press.

Ferrand, L. (1996). The masked repetition priming effect dissipates when increasing the inter-stimulus interval: Evidence from word naming. *Acta Psychologica*, **91**(1), 15–25.

Ferster, C.B. and Skinner, B.F. (1957). *Schedules of reinforcement*. New York: Appleton-Century-Crofts.

Fitts, P.M. (1964). Perceptual-motor skill learning. In A.W. Melton (Ed.), *Categories of Human Learning* New York: Academic Press. pp. 243–285.

Fitts, P.M. and Posner, M.I. (1967). *Human performance*. Belmont, CA: Brooks/Cole.

Fleishman, E.A. (1972). On the relation between abilities, learning, and human performance. *American Psychologist*, **27**, 1017–1032.

Fodor, J.A. (1979). *Representations: Essays on the foundations of cognitive science*. Cambridge, MA: MIT Press.

Fodor, J.A. (1983). *The modularity of mind*. Cambridge, MA: MIT/Bradford Books.

Forbes, J. (2000). *The effects of conceptual change on the transfer of established skills*. Unpublished honour's thesis, Edith Cowan University, Joondalup, Western Australia.

Forster, K.I. (1976). Accessing the mental lexicon. In R.J. Wales and E.C.T. Walker (Eds), *New approaches to language mechanisms*. Amsterdam: North Holland. pp. 257–287.

Forster, K.I. and Davis, C. (1984). Repetition priming and frequency attenuation in lexical access. *Journal of Experimental Psychology: Learning, Memory, and Cognition*, **10**, 680–698.

Forster, K.I. and Davis, C. (1991). The density constraint on form-priming in the naming task: Interference effects from a masked prime. *Journal of Language and Memory*, **30**, 1–25.

Frensch, P.A. (1991). Transfer of composed knowledge in multistep serial task. *Journal of Experimental Psychology: Learning, Memory, and Cognition*, **17**(5), 996–1016.

Friedman, A. (1979). Framing pictures: The role of knowledge in automatized encoding and memory for gist. *Journal of Experimental Psychology: General*, **108**, 316–355.

Gallivan, J. (1987). Correlates of order of acquisition of motion verbs. *Perceptual and Motor Skills*, **64**(1), 311–318.

Gardner, M.K., Rothkopf, E.Z., Lapan, R., and Lafferty, T. (1987). The word frequency effect in lexical decision: Finding a frequency-based component. *Memory & Cognition*, **15**(1), 24–28.

Gick, M.L. and Holyoak, K.J. (1983). Schema induction and analogical transfer. *Cognitive Psychology*, **6**, 270–292.

Giesen, K. (2000). *The effect of conceptual context changes on skill transfer performance*. Unpublished honour's thesis, Edith Cowan University, Joondalup, Western Australia.

Goodglass, H. and Kaplan, E. (1972). *The assessment of aphasia and related disorders*. Philadelphia, PA: Lea & Febiger.

Goodwyn, S., Acredolo, L., and Brown, C. (2000). Impact of symbolic gesturing on early language development. *Journal of Nonverbal Behavior*, **24**, 81–103.

Gordon, P. and Alegre, M. (1999). Is there a dual system for regular inflections? *Brain and Language*, **68**(1–2), 212–217.

Gottsdanker, R., Broadbent, L., and Van Sant, C. (1963). Reaction time to single and to first signals. *Journal of Experimental Psychology*, **66**, 163–167.

Graf, P.S. and Schacter, D.L. (1985). Implicit and explicit memory for new associations in normal and amnesic subjects. *Journal of Experimental Psychology: Learning, Memory, and Cognition*, **11**, 501–518.

Greenberg, J.H. and Ruhlen, M. (1992). Linguistic origins of native Americans. *Scientific American*, **267**(5), 94–99.

Greene, J.O., Rucker, M.P., Zauss, E.S., and Harris, A.A. (1998). Communication anxiety and the acquisition of message-production skill. *Communication Education*, **47**, 337–347.

Greig, D. and Speelman, C.P. (1999). Is skill acquisition general or specific? In E. Watson, G. Halford, T. Dartnall, D. Saddy, and J. Wiles (Eds), *Perspectives on Cognitive Science: Theories, Experiments, and Foundations*, Vol. **2** Stamford, CT: Ablex.

Gringart, E. (2003). *The role of stereotypes in age discrimination in hiring: Evaluation and intervention*. Unpublished doctoral dissertation, Edith Cowan University, Joondalup, Western Australia.

Grose, E.M. and Damos, D.L. (1988). Automaticity and the transfer of mental rotation skills. *Proceedings of the Human Factors Society – 32nd Annual Meeting*.

Gurel, A. (1999). Decomposition: To what extent? The case of Turkish. *Brain and Language*, **68**(1–2), 218–224.

Haider, H. and Frensch, P.A. (2002). Why aggregated learning follows the power law of practice when individual learning does not: Comment on Rickard (1997, 1999), Delaney *et al.* (1998) and Palmeri (1999). *Journal of Experimental Psychology: Learning, Memory, and Cognition*, **28**(2), 392–406.

Halloy, S.R.P. (1998). A theoretical framework for abundance distributions in complex systems. *Complexity International*, **6**, 12.

Halloy, S.R.P. and Whigham, P.A. (2004). The lognormal as universal descriptor of unconstrained complex systems: a unifying theory for complexity. *Proceedings of the 7th Asia–Pacific Complex Systems Conference*, Cairns Convention Centre, Cairns, QLD, Australia (pp. 309–320).

Hammond, G. (1996). The objections to null hypothesis testing as a means of analysing psychological data. *Australian Journal of Psychology*, **48**(2), 104–106.

Harrington, A. (1987). *Medicine, mind and the double brain: Study in nineteenth-century thought*. Princeton, NJ: Princeton University Press.

Healy, A.F., Clawson, D.M., McNamara, D.S., Marmie, W.R., Schneider, V.I., Rickard, T.C., Crutcher, R.J., King, C.L., Ericsson, K.A., and Bourne, L.E. Jr. (1993). The long-term retention of knowledge and skills. *The Psychology of Learning and Motivation*, **30**, 135–164.

Heathcote, A.S., Brown, S., and Mewhort, D.J.K. (2000). The power law repealed: The case for an exponential law of practice. *Psychonomic Bulletin & Review*, **7**(2), 185–207.

Herman, L.M. and Kantowitz, B.H. (1970). The psychological refractory period effect: Only half the double stimulation story? *Psychological Bulletin*, **73**, 74–88.

Hertzog, C., Cooper, B.P., and Fisk, A.D. (1996). Aging and individual differences in the development of skilled memory search performance. *Psychology and Aging*, **11**(3), 497–520.

Hillstrom, A.P. and Logan, G.D. (1998). Decomposing visual search: evidence of multiple item-specific skills. *Journal of Experimental Psychology: Learning, Memory, and Cognition*, **24**(5), 1385–1398.

Hirst, W., Spelke, E.S., Reaves, C.C., Caharack, G., and Neisser, U. (1980). Dividing attention without alternation or automaticity. *Journal of Experimental Psychology: General*, **109**, 98–117.

Holmes, F.L. (1996). Expert performance and the history of science. In K.A. Ericsson (Ed.), *The road to excellence: The acquisition of expert performance in the arts and sciences, sports, and games*. Mahwah, NJ: Erlbaum.

Holyoak, K.J. (1985). The pragmatics of analogical transfer. *The Psychology of Learning and Motivation*, **19**, 59–87.

Howe, M.J.A. (1996). The childhoods and early lives of geniuses: Combining psychological and biographical evidence. In K.A. Ericsson (Ed.), *The road to excellence: The acquisition of expert performance in the arts and sciences, sports, and games*. Mahwah, NJ: Erlbaum.

Hubel, D.H. and Wiesel, T.N. (1962). Receptive fields, binocular interaction, and functional architecture in the cat's visual cortex. *Journal of Physiology*, **160**, 106–154.

Humphreys, G.W. and Riddoch, M.J. (1987). Routes to object constancy: implications from neurological impairments of object constancy. *Quarterly Journal of Experimental Psychology*, **36**A, 385–415.

Hunter, W.S. (1929). Learning: II. Experimental studies of learning. In C. Murchison (Ed.), *The foundations of experimental psychology*. Worcester, MA: Clark University Press.

Hurford, J. (1991). The evolution of the critical period for language acquisition. *Cognition*, **40**(3), 159–201.

Hyönä, J., Vainio, S., and Laine, M. (2002). A morphological effect obtains for isolated words but not for words in sentence context. *European Journal of Cognitive Psychology*, **14**, 417–433.

Iverson, J.M. and Thelen, E. (1999). Hand, mouth, and brain: The dynamic emergence of speech and gesture. *Journal of Consciousness Studies*, **6**, 19–40.

Jacoby, L.L. (1983). Remembering the data: Analyzing interactive processes in reading. *Journal of Verbal Learning and Verbal Behavior*, **22**, 485–508.

Jaffe, J. and Feldstein, S. (1970). *Rhythms of dialogue*. New York: Academic Press.

Jastrzembski, J.E. (1981). Multiple meanings, frequency of occurrence, and the lexicon. *Cognitive Psychology*, **13**, 278–305.

Jelsma, O., van Merrienboer, J.J.G., and Bijlstra, J.P. (1990). The ADAPT design model: Towards instructional control of transfer. *Instructional Science*, **19**, 89–120.

Jemel, B., George, N., Chaby, L., Fiori, N., and Renault, B. (1999). Differential processing of part-to-whole and part-to-part face priming: An ERP study. *Neuroreport: For Rapid Communication of Neuroscience Research*, **10**(5), 1069–1075.

Johnson, P.E. (1983). What kind of expert should a system be? *The Journal of Medicine and Philosophy*, **8**, 77–97.

Johnson-Laird, P.N. (1983). *Mental models*. Cambridge, MA: Cambridge University Press.

Johnston, R.A., Barry, C., and Williams, C. (1996). Incomplete faces don't show the whole picture: Repetition priming from jumbled faces. *Quarterly Journal of Experimental Psychology: Human Experimental Psychology*, **49**A(3), 596–615.

Josephs, R.A., Silvera, D.H., and Giesler, R.B. (1996). The learning curve as a metacognitive tool. *Journal of Experimental Psychology: Learning, Memory, and Cognition*, **22**, 510–524.

Joyce, C.A., Paller, K.A., Schwartz, T.J., and Kutas, M. (1999). An electrophysiological analysis of modality-specific aspects of word repetition. *Psychophysiology*, **36**(5), 655–665.

Juffs, A. (1996). *Learnability and the lexicon*. Amsterdam: John Benjamins.

Just, M.A. and Carpenter, P.A. (1980). A theory of reading: From eye fixation to comprehension. *Psychological Review*, **87**, 329–354.

Kail, R. (1988). Developmental functions for speeds of cognitive processes. *Journal of Experimental Child Psychology*, **45**, 339–364.

Kail, R. and Park, Y. (1990). Impact of practice on speed of mental rotation. *Journal of Experimental Child Psychology*, **49**, 227–244.

Karmiloff-Smith, A. (1979). Micro- and macrodevelopmental changes in language acquisition and other representational systems. *Cognitive Science*, **3**(2), 91–117.

Karmiloff-Smith, A. (1992). *Beyond modularity—a developmental perspective on cognitive science*. Cambridge, MA: MIT Press.

Kasparov, G. (1985). *Learn chess*. London: Redwood Books.

Keenan, J.P., Thanaraj, V., Halpern, A.R., and Schlaug, G. (2001). Absolute pitch and planum temporale. *Neuroimage*, **14**(6), 1402–1408.

Kessler, C. and Anderson, J.R. (1986). Learning flow of control: Recursive and iterative procedures. *Human Computer Interaction*, **2**, 135–166.

Kieras, D.E. and Bovair, S. (1986). The acquisition of procedures from text: A production-system analysis of transfer of training. *Journal of Memory and Language*, **25**, 507–524.

Kirby, S. (2001). Spontaneous evolution of linguistic structure: An iterated learning model of the emergence of regularity and irregularity. *IEEE Transactions on Evolutionary Computation*, **5**(2), 102–110.

Kirby, S. and Hurford, J. (2002). The emergence of linguistic structure: An overview of the iterated learning model. In A. Cangelosi and D. Parisi (Eds), *Simulating the evolution of language*, London: Springer-Verlag. Chapter 6, pp. 121–148.

Kirsner, K. and Dunn, J.C. (1985). The perceptual record: A common factor in repetition priming and attribute retention. In M.I. Posner and O.S.M. Marin (Eds), *Mechanisms of Attention: and Performance XI*. Hillsdale, N.J.: Lawrence Erlbaum.

Kirsner, K. and Smith, M.C. (1974). Modality effects in word identification. *Memory and Cognition*, **2**, 637–640.

Kirsner, K. and Speelman, C.P. (1993). Is lexical processing just an "ACT"? In A.F. Collins, S.E. Gathercole, M.A. Conway, and P.E. Morris (Eds), *Theories of memory*. Hove, UK: Erlbaum.

Kirsner, K. and Speelman, C. (1996). Skill acquisition and repetition priming: One principle, many processes. *Journal of Experimental Psychology: Learning, Memory, and Cognition*, **22**(3), 563–575.

Kirsner, K., Brown, H.L., Abrol, S., Chaddha, A., and Sharma, N.K. (1980). Bilingualism and lexical representation. *Quarterly Journal of Experimental Psychology*, **32**, 565–574.

Kirsner, K., Milech, D., and Standen, P. (1983). Common and modality-specific processes in the mental lexicon. *Memory & Cognition*, **11**(6), 621–630.

Kirsner, K., Smith, M.C., Lockhart, R.S., King, M.-L., and Jain, M. (1984). The bilingual lexicon: Language-specific effects in an integrated network. *Journal of Verbal Learning and Verbal Behavior*, **23**, 519–539.

Kirsner, K., Dunn, J.C., Kinoshita, S., Standen, P., and Hasslacher, T. (1993). Repetition priming effects in English, Kanji and the Kanas: One principle, many processes. In J.-T. Huang and O.J.L. Tzeng (Eds), *Advances in the study of Chinese language processing*, Vol. 1. Department of Psychology, National Taiwan University, Taipei.

Kirsner, K., Dunn, J., Hird, K., Parkin, T., and Clark, C. (2002). *Time for a pause . . . .* Paper presented at the ninth Australian International Conference on Speech Science, Melbourne.

Kirsner, K., Dunn, J.C., and Standen, P. (1989). Domain-specific resources in word recognition. In S. Lewandowsky, J.C. Dunn, and K. Kirsner (Eds), *Implicit memory: Theoretical issues*. Hillsdale, NJ: Erlbaum. pp. 99–122.

Klapp, S.T., Boches, C.A., Trabert, M.L., and Logan, G.D. (1991). Automatizing alphabet arithmetic: II. Are there practice effects after automaticity is achieved? *Journal of Experimental Psychology: Learning, Memory, and Cognition*, **17**(2), 196–209.

Kolers, P.A. (1976). Reading a year later. *Journal of Experimental Psychology: Human Learning and Memory*, **2**, 554–565.

Kolers, P.A. (1979a). A pattern analyzing basis of recognition. In L.S. Cermak and F.I.M. Craik (Eds), *Levels of processing in human memory*. Hillsdale, NJ: Erlbaum.

Kolers, P.A. (1979b). Reading and knowing. *Canadian Journal of Psychology*, **33**(2), 106–117.

Kornai, A. (1999). Zipf's law outside the middle range. *Proceedings of the Sixth Meeting on Mathematics of Language*. University of Central Florida, Orlando. pp. 347–356.

Kramer, A.F., Strayer, D.L., and Buckley, J. (1990). Development and transfer of automatic processing. *Journal of Experimental Psychology: Human Perception and Performance*, **16**(3), 505–522.

Kruskal, J.I., Dyer, I., and Black, P. (1971). The vocabulary method for reconstructing family trees: Innovations and large scale applications. In F.R. Hodson, D.G. Kendall, and P. Tautu (Eds), *Mathematics in the archaeological and historical sciences*. Edinburgh: Edinburgh University Press.

Kucera, H. and Francis, W.N. (1967). *Computational analysis of present-day American English*. Providence, RI: Brown University Press.

Laird, J.E., Newell, A., and Rosenbloom, P.S. (1987). Soar: An architecture for general intelligence. *Artificial Intelligence*, **33**, 1–64.

Lalor, E. and Kirsner, K. (2000). Cross-lingual transfer effects between English and Italian cognates and non-cognates. *International Journal of Bilingualism*, **4**(3), 385–398.

Larkin, J.H. (1983). The role of problem representation in physics. In D. Gentner and A.L. Stevens (Eds), *Mental models*. Hillsdale, NJ: Erlbaum.

Lassaline, M.E. and Logan, G.D. (1993). Memory-based automaticity in the discrimination of visual numerosity. *Journal of Experimental Psychology: Learning, Memory, and Cognition*, **19**(3), 561–581.

Latham-Radocy, W.B. and Radocy, R.E. (1996). Basic physical and psychoacoustical processes. In D.A. Hodges (Ed.), *Handbook of Music Psychology*. San Antonio, TX: IMR Press.

Lee, T.D. and Genovese, E.D. (1988). Distribution of practice in motor skill acquisition: Learning and performance effects reconsidered. *Research Quarterly for Exercise and Sport*, **59**, 277–287.

Lee, T.D. and Genovese, E.D. (1989). Distribution of practice in motor skill acquisition: Different effects for discrete and continuous tasks. *Research Quarterly for Exercise and Sport*, **60**, 59–65.

Lee, T.D. and Magill, R.A. (1983). The locus of contextual interference in motor-skill acquisition. *Journal of Experimental Psychology: Learning, Memory, and Cognition*, **9**, 730–746.

Lesgold, A., Glaser, R., Rubinson, H., Klopfer, D., Feltovich, P., and Wang, Y. (1988). Expertise in a complex skill: Distinguishing x-ray pictures. In M.T.H. Chi, R. Glaser, and M.J. Farr (Eds), *The nature of expertise*. Hillsdale, NJ: Erlbaum.

Levy, B.A. (1983). Proofreading familiar text: Constraints on visual processing. *Memory & Cognition*, **11**, 1–12.

Levy, B.A. and Kirsner, K. (1990). Re-processing text: Indirect measures of word and message level processes. *Journal of Experimental Psychology: Learning, Memory, & Cognition*, **15**, 407–417.

Levy, F.K. (1965). Adaptation in the production process. *Management Science*, **11**(6), B136–B154.

Levy, Y. (1996). Modularity of language reconsidered. *Brain and Language*, **55**, 240–263.

Li, R.W. and Levi, D.M. (2002). *Mechanisms of perceptual learning for vernier acuity*. Paper presented at the Fall Vision Meeting, San Francisco, CA, USA.

Lintern, G., Roscoe, S.N., and Sivier, J. (1990). Display principles, control dynamics, and environmental factors in pilot performance and transfer of training. *Human Factors*, **32**, 299–317.

Logan, G.D. (1988). Toward an instance theory of automatization. *Psychological Review*, **95**, 492–527.

Logan, G.D. (1990). Repetition priming and automaticity: Common underlying mechanisms. *Cognitive Psychology*, **22**, 1–35.

Logan, G.D. (1992). Attention and preattention in theories of automaticity. *American Journal of Psychology*, **105**(2), 317–339.

Logan, G.D. and Etherton, J.L. (1994). What is learned during automatization? The role of attention in constructing an instance. *Journal of Experimental Psychology: Learning, Memory, and Cognition*, **20**(5), 1022–1050.

Logan, G.D. and Klapp, S.T. (1991). Automatizing alphabet arithmetic: I. Is extended practice necessary to produce automaticity? *Journal of Experimental Psychology: Learning, Memory, and Cognition*, **17**, 179–195.

Logan, G.D., Taylor, S.E., and Etherton, J.L. (1996). Attention in the acquisition and expression of automaticity. *Journal of experimental Psychology: Learning, Memory and Cognition*, **22**(3), 620–638.

Luchins, A.S. (1942). Mechanization in problem solving. *Psychological Monographs*, **54**, 248.

Luscombe, N.M., Qian, J., Zhang, Z., Johnson, T., and Gerstein, M. (2002). The dominance of the population by a selected few: Power-law behaviour applies to a wide variety of genomic properties. *Genome Biology*, **3**(8), research0040.1–0040.7.

MacKay, D.G. (1981). The problem of rehearsal or mental practice. *Journal of Motor Behavior*, **13**, 274–285.

MacKay, D.G. (1982). The problems of flexibility, fluency and speed-accuracy trade-off in skilled behavior. *Psychological Review*, **89**, 483–506.

MacKay, D.G. and Bowman, R.W. (1969). On producing the meaning in sentences. *American Journal of Psychology*, **82**, 23–39.

MacLeod, C. (1992). The Stroop task: The "gold standard" of attentional measures. *Journal of Experimental Psychology: General*, **121**(1), 12–14.

MacLeod, C.M. and Dunbar, K. (1988). Training and stroop-like interference: Evidence for a continuum of automaticity. *Journal of Experimental Psychology: Learning, Memory, and Cognition*, **14**, 126–135.

Masson, M.E.J. (1986). Identification of typographically transformed words: Instance-based skill acquisition. *Journal of Experimental Psychology: Learning, Memory, and Cognition*, **12**, 479–488.

Mayes, A.R., Gooding, P.A., and van Eijk, R. (1997). A new theoretical framework for explicit and implicit Memory. *PSYCHE*, **3**(2), http://psyche.cs.monash.edu.au/v2/psyche-3-02-mayes.html

McClelland, J.L. and Rumelhart, D.E. (Eds), *Parallel distributed processing: Explorations in the microstructure of cognition*(Vol. 2). Cambridge, MA: MIT Press/Bradford Books.

McGeoch, J.A. (1931). The acquisition of skill. *Psychological Review*, **28**, 413–466.

McGeoch, J.A. (1942). *The psychology of human learning*. New York: Longmans, Green.

McGeoch, J.A. and Irion, A.L. (1952). *The psychology of human learning*, 2nd edn. New York: Longmans, Green.

McKeithen, K.B., Reitman, J.S., Reuter, H.H., and Hirtle, S.C. (1981). Knowledge organization and skill differences in computer programmers. *Cognitive Psychology*, **13**, 307–325.

McKendree, J. and Anderson, J.R. (1987). Effect of practice on knowledge and use of basic LISP. In J.M Carroll (Ed.), *Interfacing thought: Cognitive aspects of human-computer interaction*. Cambridge, MA: MIT Press.

McNeill, D. and Duncan, S. (2000). Growth points in thinking-for-speaking. In D. McNeill (Ed.), *Language and gesture*. Cambridge: Cambridge University Press.

McNeil, M.R., Odell, K., and Tseng, C.-H. (1991). Toward the integration of resource allocation into a general theory of aphasia. In T.E. Prescott (Ed.), *Clinical aphasiology*. Austin: Pro-Ed.

Meunier, F. and Segui, J. (1999). Frequency effects in auditory word recognition: The case of suffixed words. *Journal of Memory and Language*, **41**(3), 327–344.

Midford, R. and Kirsner, K. (2005). Implicit and explicit learning in aged and young adults. *Aging, Neuropsychology and Cognition*, **12**(4).

Mieklejohn, A. (1908). Is mental training a myth? *Education Review*, **37**, 126–141.

Miller, G.A. (1956). The magic number seven, plus or minus two: Some limits on our capacity for processing information. *Psychological Review*, **63**, 81–93.

Miller, K.F. and Paredes, D.R. (1990). Starting to add worse: Effects of learning to multiply on children's addition. *Cognition*, **37**, 213–242.

Miller, L.K. (1989). *Musical savants: Exceptional skill in the mentally retarded*. Hillsdale, NJ: Erlbaum.

Minsky, M. (1975). A framework for the representation of knowledge. In P. Winston (Ed.), *The psychology of computer vision*. New York: McGraw Hill.

Morrison, C.M. and Ellis, A.W. (1995). Roles of word frequency and age of acquisition in word naming and lexical decision. *Journal of Experimental Psychology: Learning, Memory and Cognition*, **21**, 116–133.

Morrison, C.M. and Ellis, A.W. (2000). Real age of acquisition effects in word naming and lexical decision. *British Journal of Psychology*, **91**(2), 167–180.

Morton, J. (1969). Interaction of information in word recognition. *Psychological Review*, **76**, 165–178.

Morton, J. and Patterson, K. (1980). A new attempt at an interpretation or an attempt at a new interpretation. In M. Coltheart, K.E. Patterson, and J.C. Marshall (Eds), *Deep Dyslexia*. London: Routledge & Kegan Paul.

Muller, B. (1999). Use specificity of cognitive skills: Evidence for production rules. *Journal of Experimental Psychology: Learning, Memory, and Cognition*, **25**(1), 191–207.

Munro, D. (1992). Process vs structure and levels of analysis in psychology: Towards integration rather than reduction of theories. *Theory & Psychology*, **2**(1), 109–127.

Murray, L.L., Holland, A.L., and Beeson, P.M. (1997). Auditory processing in individuals with mild aphasia: A study of resource allocation. *Journal of Speech, Language and Hearing Research*, **40**, 792–808.

Myles-Worsley, M., Johnston, W.A., and Simons, M.A. (1988). The influence of expertise on x-ray image processing. *Journal of Experimental Psychology: Learning, Memory, and Cognition*, **14**(3), 553–557.

Myung, I.J., Kim, C., and Pitt, M.A. (2000). Toward an explanation of the power law artifact: Insights from response surface analysis. *Memory & Cognition*, **28**(5), 832–840.

Nation, I.S.P. (1990). *Teaching and Learning Vocabulary*. Boston, MA: Heinle & Heinle.

Nesdale, D. and Durkin, K. (1998). Stereotypes and attitudes: Implicit and explicit processes. In K. Kirsner, C.P. Speelman, M. Maybery, A. O'Brien-Malone, M. Anderson, and C. MacLeod (Eds), *Implicit and explicit mental processing*, Hillsdale, NJ: Erlbaum.

Neves, D.M. and Anderson, J.R. (1981). Knowledge compilation: Mechanisms for the automatization of cognitive skills. In J.R. Anderson (Ed.), *Cognitive skills and their acquisition*. Hillsdale, NJ: Erlbaum.

Newcombe, F. and Young, A.W. (1989). Prosopagnosia and object agnosia without overt recognition. *Neuropsychologia*, **27**, 179–191.

Newell, A. (1973). You can't play 20 questions with nature and win: Projective comments on the papers of this symposium. In W.G. Chase (Ed.), *Visual information processing*. New York: Academic Press Inc. pp. 283–310.

Newell, A. (1989). Putting it all together. In D. Klahr and K. Kotovsky (Eds), *Complex information processing*. Hillsdale, NJ: Erlbaum.

Newell, A. (1990). *Unified theories of cognition*. Cambridge, MA: Harvard University Press.

Newell, A. (1992). Preface to the theme issue on dynamical approaches to motor skill acquisition. *Journal of Motor Behavior*, **24**, 2.

Newell, A. and Rosenbloom, P.S. (1981). Mechanisms of skills acquisition and the law of practice. In J.R. Anderson (Ed.), *Cognitive skills and their acquisition*. Hillsdale, NJ: Erlbaum.

Newell, A. and Simon, H.A. (1972). *Human problem solving*. Englewood Cliffs, NJ: Prentice-Hall.

Ohlsson, S. (1992). The learning curve for writing books: Evidence from Professor Asimov. *Psychological Science*, **3**(6), 380–382.

O'Keefe, B. (2003). Cancel HECS, and give female graduates a fecund chance. *The Australian*, **27** August, 19.

Oldfield, R.C. (1966). Things, words and the brain. *Quarterly Journal of Experimental Psychology*, **18**, 340–353.

Orata, P.T. (1928). *The theory of identical elements*. Coloumbus: Ohio State University Press.

Osgood, C.E. (1949). The similarity paradox in human learning: A resolution. *Psychological Review*, **56**, 132–143.

Palmeri, T.J. (1997). Exemplar similarity and the development of automaticity. *Journal of Experimental Psychology: Learning, Memory, and Cognition*, **23**(2), 324–354.

Pashler, H. and Baylis, G. (1991). Procedural learning: 1. Locus of practice effects in speeded choice tasks. *Journal of Experimental Psychology: Learning, Memory, and Cognition*, **17**, 20–32.

Patel, V.L. and Groen, G.J. (1991). The general and specific nature of medical expertise: A critical look. In A. Ericsson and J. Smith (Eds), *Toward a general theory of expertise: Prospects and limits*. New York, NY: Cambridge Unversity Press.

Pear, T.H. (1948). Professor Bartlett on skill. *Occupational Psychology*, **22**, 92–93.

Pennington, N., Nicolich, R., and Rahm, J. (1995). Transfer of training between cognitive subskills: Is knowledge use specific? *Cognitive Psychology*, **28**(2), 175–224.

Piaget, J. (1953). *The origins of intelligence in the child*. London: Routledge & Kegan Paul.

Piaget, J. (1967). *The child's conception of the world*. Totowa, NJ: Littlefield, Adams.

Pinker, S. (1989). *Learnability and cognition: The acquisition of argument structure*. Cambridge, MA: MIT Press.

Pirolli, P.L. and Anderson, J.R. (1985a). The role of learning from examples in the acquisition of recursive programming skills. *Canadian Journal of Psychology*, **39**, 240–272.

Pirolli, P.L. and Anderson, J.R. (1985b). The role of practice in fact retrieval. *Journal of Experimental Psychology: Learning, Memory, and Cognition*, **11**, 136–153.

Plotkin, H. (1993). *Darwin machines and the nature of knowledge*. Cambridge, MA: Harvard University Press.

Port, R.F. and Leary, A. (2002). Speech timing in linguistics. *Indiana University Linguistics Club Working Papers, 09A*.

Posner, M.I. and Snyder, C.R.R. (1975). Attention and cognitive control. In R.L. Solso (Ed.), *Information processing and cognition: The Loyola symposium*. Hillsdale, NJ: Erlbaum. pp. 55–85.

Powers, D.M.W. (1998) Applications and explanations of Zipf's Law. In *New methods in language processing and computational natural language learning*, ACL, pp. 152–160, http://www.uia.ac.be/conll98/pdf/151160po.pdf

Proctor, R.W. and Dutta, A. (1995a). *Skill acquisition and human performance*. London: Sage Publications.

Proctor, R.W. and Dutta, A. (1995b). Acquisition and transfer of response selection skill. In A.F. Healy and L.E. Bourne, Jr. (Eds), *Learning and memory of knowledge and skills: Durability and specificity*. Thousand Oaks, CA: Sage.

Proctor, R.W. and Healy, A.F. (1995). Acquisition and retention of skilled letter detection. In A.F. Healy and L.E. Bourne, Jr. (Eds), *Learning and memory of knowledge and skills: Durability and specificity*. Thousand Oaks, CA: Sage.

Pulvermuller, F. and Schumann, J. (1994). Neurobiological mechanisms of language acquisition. *Language Learning*, **44**, 681–734.

Pylkkanen, L., Feintuch, S., Hopkins, E., and Marantz, A. (2004). Neural correlates of the effects of morphological family frequency and family size: an MEG study. *Cognition*, **91**(3), B35–B45.

Rabinowitz, M. and Goldberg, N. (1995). Evaluating the structure-process hypothesis. In F.E. Weinert and W. Schneider (Eds), *Memory performance and competencies: Issues in growth and development*. Hillsdale, NJ: Erlbaum. pp. 225–242.

Rasmussen, J. (1983). Skills, rules, and knowledge: Signals, signs, and symbols, and other distinctions in human performance models. *IEEE Transactions on Systems, Man, and Cybernetics, SMC-13*, 257–266.

Rasmussen, J. (1986). *Information processing and human-machine interaction: An approach to cognitive engineering*. Amsterdam: North-Holland.

Rastle, K. and Coltheart, M. (1999). Lexical and nonlexical phonological priming in reading aloud. *Journal of Experimental Psychology: Human Perception and Performance*, **25**(2), 461–481.

Ratcliff, R. (1989). Parallel-processing mechanisms and processing of organized information in human memory. In G. Hinton and J. Anderson (Eds), *Parallel models of associative memory. The cognitive science series: Technical monographs and edited collections* Hillsdale, NJ: Erlbaum. pp. 309–327.

Rayner, K. (1998). Eye movements in reading and information processing: 20 years of research. *Psychological Bulletin*, **124**(3), 372–422.

Reber, A.S. (1967). Implicit learning of artificial grammars. *Journal of Verbal Learning and Verbal Behavior*, **6**, 855–863.

Renault, B., Signoret, J.L., Debruille, B., and Breton, F. *et al.* (1989). Brain potentials reveal covert facial recognition in prosopagnosia. *Neuropsychologia*, **27**(7), 905–912.

Rueckl, J.G. (1995). Letter-level effects in repetition priming. *American Journal of Psychology*, **108**(2), 213–234.

Rickard, T.C. (1997). Bending the power law: A CMPL theory of strategy shifts and the automatization of cognitive skills. *Journal of Experimental Psychology: General*, **126**(3), 288–311.

Rickard, T.C. (1999). A CMPL alternative account of practice effects in numerosity judgement tasks. *Journal of Experimental Psychology: Learning, Memory, and Cognition*, **25**(2), 532–542.

Rickard, T.C. and Bourne, L.E., Jr. (1996). Some tests of an identical elements model of basic arithmetic skills. *Journal of Experimental Psychology: Learning, Memory and Cognition*, **22**, 1281–1295.

Rickard, T.C., Healy, A.F., and Bourne, L.E., Jr. (1994). On the cognitive structure of basic arithmetic skills: Operation, order, and symbol transfer effects. *Journal of Experimental Psychology: Learning, Memory, and Cognition*, **20**(5), 1139–1153.

Robertson, C. and Kirsner, K. (2000). Indirect memory measures in spontaneous discourse in normal and amnesic subjects. *Language and Cognitive Processes*, **15**(2), 203–222.

Roediger, H.L. and Blaxton, T.A. (1987). Effects of varying modality, surface features, and retention interval on priming in word-fragment completion. *Memory & Cognition*, **15**(5), 379–388.

Roediger, H.L., III (1990). Implicit memory: Retention without remembering. *American Psychologist*, **45**(9), 1043–1056.

Rosenbloom, P.S. and Newell, A. (1987). An integrated computational model of stimulus-response compatibility and practice. In G.H. Bower (Ed.), *The psychology of learning and motivation* Vol.21, San Diego, CA: Academic Press. pp. 1–520.

Rosenbloom, P.S., Newell, A., and Laird, J.E. (1991). Toward the knowledge level in Soar: The role of the architecture in the use of knowledge. In K. VanLehn (Ed.), *Architectures for intelligence: The Twenty-second Carnegie Mellon Symposium on Cognition*. Hillsdale, NJ: Erlbaum, pp. 75–111.

Rosenhan, D.L. (1973). On being sane in insane places. *Science*, **179**, 250–258.

Rumelhart, D.E. and McClelland, J.L. (Eds.) (1986). *Parallel distributed processing: Explorations in the microstructure of cognition*, Vol. **1**. Cambridge, MA: MIT Press/Bradford Books.

Rumelhart, D.E. and Norman, D.A. (1981). Analogical processes in learning. In J.R. Anderson (Ed.), *Cognitive skills and their acquisition*. Hillsdale, NJ: Erlbaum.

Rumelhart, D.E., Smolensky, P., McClelland, J.L., and Hinton, G.E. (1986). Schemata and sequential thought processes in PDP models. In J.L. McClelland, D.E. Rumelhart, & The PDP Research Group (Eds), *Parallel distributed processing: Vol 2. Psychological and biological models*. Cambridge, MA: MIT Press.

Sachs, J.S. (1967). Recognition memory for syntactic and semantic aspects of connected discourse. *Perception & Psychophysics*, **2**, 437–442.

Salthouse, T.A. (1989). Aging and skilled performance. In A.M. Colley and J.R. Beech (Eds), *Acquisition and performance of cognitive skills*. Chichester: Wiley. pp. 247–264.

Salthouse, T.A. and Somberg, B.L. (1982). Skilled performance: Effects of adult age and experience on elementary processes. *Journal of Experimental Psychology: General*, **111**, 176–207.

Schacter, D.L. (1987). Implicit memory: History and current status. *Journal of Experimental Psychology: Language, Memory, & Cognition*, **13**(3), 501–518.

Schank, R.C. and Abelson, R. (1977). *Scripts, plans, goals, and understanding*. Hillsdale, NJ: Erlbaum.

Schneider, W. and Fisk, A.D. (1984). Automatic category search and its transfer. *Journal of Experimental Psychology: Learning, Memory, and Cognition*, **10**(1), 1–15.

Schneider, W. and Shiffrin, R.M. (1977). Controlled and automatic human information processing: I. Detection, search, and attention. *Psychological Review*, **84**, 1–66.

Schneider, W., Dumais, S.T., and Shiffrin, R.M. (1984). Automatic and control processing and attention. In R. Parasuraman and D.R. Davies (Eds), *Varieties of attention*. New York: Academic Press.

Schreuder, R. and Baayen, R.H. (1997). How complex simple words can be. *Journal of Memory and Language*, **37**(1), 118–139.

Searle, A.D. and Gody, C.S. (1945). Productivity changes in selected wartime shipbuilding programs. *Monthly Labor Review*, **61**, 1132–1149.

Searle, J.R. (2002). *Consciousness and language*. Cambridge: Cambridge University Press.

Shallice, T. (1988). *From neuropsychology to mental structure*. Cambridge, MA: Cambridge University Press.

Shea, J.B. and Morgan, R.L. (1979). Contextual interference effects on the acquisition, retention, and transfer of a motor skill. *Journal of Experimental Psychology: Human Learning and Memory*, **5**, 179–187.

Shepard, R. (1987). Toward a universal law of generalization for psychological science. *Science*, **237**(4820), 1317–1323.

Shiffrin, R.M. and Schneider, W. (1977). Controlled and automatic human information processing: II. Perceptual learning, automatic attending, and a general theory. *Psychological Review*, **84**, 127–190.

Siegler, R.S. (1987). The perils of averaging data over strategies: An example from children's addition. *Journal of Experimental Psychology: General*, **116**(3), 250–264.

Siegler, R.S. and Jenkins, E. (1989). *How children discover new strategies*. Hillsdale, NJ: Erlbaum.

Singley, M.K. and Anderson, J.R. (1985). The transfer of text-editing skill. *International Journal of Man-Machine Studies*, **22**, 403–423.

Singley, M.K. and Anderson, J.R. (1989). *The transfer of cognitive skill*. Cambridge, MA: Harvard University Press.

Smith, E.R. and Lerner, M. (1986). Development of automatism of social judgments. *Journal of Personality and Social Psychology*, **50**(2), 246–259.

Smith, K.V. and Sussman, H. (1969). Cybernetic theory and analysis of motor learning and memory. In E.A. Bilodeau and I.Mc. Bilodeau (Eds), *Principles of skill acquisition*. New York: Academic Press.

Snoddy, G.S. (1926). Learning and stability. *Journal of Applied Psychology*, **10**, 1–36.

Snyder, F.W. and Pronko, H.H. (1952). *Vision with spatial inversion*. Wichita, KS: University of Whichita Press.

Spears, W.D. (1983). *Processes of skill acquisition: A foundation for the design and use of training equipment* (navtraequipcen 78-CO113-4). Orlando FL: Naval Training Equipment Center.

Speelman, C.P. (1991). *Skill acquisition: Estimating the contributions of old skills to performance on new tasks*. Unpublished doctoral dissertation, University of Western Australia, Nedlands, Australia.

Speelman, C.P. (1995). The shape of learning functions during transfer. In P. Slezak, T. Caelli, and R. Clark (Eds), *Perspectives on Cognitive Science: Theories, Experiments & Foundations* Norwood, NJ: Ablex. pp. 79–102.

Speelman, C.P. (1998a). Implicit processes in discourse processing. In K. Kirsner, C.P. Speelman, M. Maybery, A. O'Brien-Malone, M. Anderson, and C. MacLeod (Eds), *Implicit and explicit mental processing*. Hillsdale, NJ: Erlbaum.

Speelman, C.P. (1998b). Implicit expertise: Do we expect too much from our experts? In K. Kirsner, C.P. Speelman, M. Maybery, A. O'Brien-Malone, M. Anderson, and C. MacLeod (Eds), *Implicit and explicit mental processing*. Hillsdale, NJ: Erlbaum.

Speelman, C.P. and Kirsner, K. (1993). New goals for HCI training: How to mix old and new skills in the trainee. *International Journal of Human-Computer Interaction*, **5**(1), 41–69.

Speelman, C.P. and Kirsner, K. (1997). The specificity of skill acquisition and transfer. *Australian Journal of Psychology*, **49**(2), 91–100.

Speelman, C.P. and Kirsner, K. (2001). Predicting transfer from training performance. *Acta Psychologica*, **108**, 247–281.

Speelman, C., Simpson, T., and Kirsner, K. (2002). The unbearable lightness of repetition priming. *Acta Psychologica*, **111**(2), 205–242.

Sproat, R. and Shih, C.A. (1996). Corpus-based analysis of Mandarin nominal root compound. *Journal of East Asian Linguistics*, **5**, 49–71.

Stanners, R.F., Neiser, J.J., Hernon, W.P., and Hall, R. (1979). Memory representation for morphologically related words. *Journal of Verbal Learning and Verbal Behavior*, **18**, 399–412.

Staszewski, J.J. (1988). Skilled memory and expert mental calculation. In M.T.H. Chi, R. Glaser, and M.J. Farr (Eds), *The nature of expertise*. Hillsdale, NJ: Erlbaum.

Stroop, J.R. (1935). Studies of interference in serial verbal reactions. *Journal of Experimental Psychology*, **18**, 643–662.

Stumpfl, V. and Kirsner, K. (1986). Context effects in word recognition: A single dissociation. *Bulletin of the Psychonomic Society*, **24**, 175–178.

Sumargi, A. (2001). *Development of young children's communicative behaviours*. Unpublished Master of Psychology (Applied Development) thesis, University of Western Australia, Nedlands, Australia.

Tainturier, M.-J., Tremblay, M., and Lecours, A.R. (1989). Aging and the word frequency effect: A lexical decision investigation. *Neuropsychologia*, **27**(9), 1197–1203.

Tainturier, M.-J., Tremblay, M., and Lecours, A.R. (1992). Educational level and the word frequency effect: A lexical decision investigation. *Brain and Language*, **43**(5), 460–474.

Takeuchi, A.H. and Hulse, S.H. (1993). Absolute pitch. *Psychological Bulletin*, **113**(2), 345–361.

Tamaoka, K., Kirsner, K., Yanase, Y., Miyaoka, Y., and Kawakami, M. (2002). A web-accessible database of characteristics of the 1,945 basic Japanese Kanji. *Behavior Research Methods, Instruments & Computers*, **34**(2), 260–275.

Teuber, H.L. (1955). Physiological psychology. *Annual Review of Psychology*, **6**, 267–296.

Thelen, E. (1988). Dynamical approaches to the development of behavior. In A.S. Kelso, A. Mandell, and M. Shlesinger (Eds), *Dynamic patterns in complex systems*. Singapore: World Scientific.

Thelen, E., Kelso, J.A., and Fogel, A. (1987). Self-organizing systems and infant motor development. *Developmental Review*, **7**, 39–65.

Thomas, R.C. (1998). *Long term human-computer interaction: An exploratory perspective.* London: Springer-Verlag.

Thorndike, E.L. (1906). *Principles of teaching.* New York: A.G. Seiler.

Thorndike, E.L. and Woodworth, R.S. (1901). The influence of improvement in one mental function upon the efficiency of other functions. *Psychological Review*, **8**, 247–261.

Thorndike, E.L. and Lorge, I. (1944). *The Teacher's Word Book of 30,000 Words.* New York: Teachers College, Columbia University.

Treisman, A., Vieira, A., and Hayes, A. (1992). Automaticity and preattentive processing. *American Journal of Psychology*, **105**, 341–362.

Tulving, E. (1983). *Elements of episodic memory.* Oxford: Clarendon Press.

Turner, J.E., Valentine, T., and Ellis, A.W. (1998). Contrasting effects of age of acquisition and word frequency on auditory and visual lexical decision. *Memory & Cognition*, **26**(6), 1282–1291.

Vallar, G. (1999). The methodological foundations of neuropsychology. In G. Denes and L. Pizzamiglio (Eds), *Handbook of clinical and experimental neuropsychology*. Hove, UK: Psychology Press.

van Gelder, T. (1998). The dynamical hypothesis in Cognitive Science. *Behavioural and Brain Sciences*, **21**, 615–665.

Waksler, R. (1999). Cross-linguistic evidence for morphological representation in the mental lexicon. *Brain & Language*, **68**(1–2), 68–74.

Weiss, Y., Edelman, S., and Fahle, M. (1993). Models of perceptual learning in vernier hyperacuity. *Neural Computation* **5**, 695–718.

Welford, A.T. (1968). *Fundamentals of skill.* London: Methuen.

Wenger, C.G. (1999). Advantages gained by combining qualitative and quantitative data in a longitudinal study. *Journal of Aging Studies*, **13**(4), 369–376.

Whittlesea, B.W.A. and Brooks, L.R. (1988). Critical influence of particular experiences in the perception of letters, words, and phrases. *Memory & Cognition*, **16**, 387–399.

Wilkinson, L. and Task Force on Statistical Inference. (1999). Statistical methods in psychology journals: Guidelines and explanation. *American Psychologist*, **54**(8), 594–604.

Willingham, D.B. and Preuss, L. (1995). The death of implicit memory. *Psyche*, **2**(15).

Willshaw, D. (1989). Holography, associative memory, and inductive generalization. In G.E. Hinton and J.A. Anderson (Eds), *Parallel models of associative memory*. Hillsdale, NJ: Erlbaum.

Winnick, W.A. and Daniel, S.A. (1970). Two kinds of response priming in tachistoscopic recognition. *Journal of Experimental Psychology*, **84**, 74–81.

Winter, D. (1982). *The first of the few: Fighter pilots of the first world war*. London: Penguin.

Woltz, D.J. (1988). An investigation of the role of working memory in procedural skill acquisition. *Journal of Experimental Psychology: General*, **117**, 319–331.

Woltz, D.J., Bell, B.G., Kyllonen, P.C., and Gardner, M.K. (1996). Memory for order of operations in the acquisition and transfer of sequential cognitive skills. *Journal of Experimental Psychology, Memory, and Cognition*, **22**(2), 438–457.

Zatorre, R.J. (2003). Absolute pitch: A model for understanding the influence of genes and development on neural and cognitive function. *Nature Neuroscience*, **6**(7), 692–695.

Index